THE MIGRANT CANON IN

TWENTY-FIRST-CENTURY FRANCE

The Migrant Canon in Twenty-First-Century

France | OANA SABO

UNIVERSITY OF NEBRASKA PRESS | LINCOLN AND LONDON

Publication of this volume was assisted by
the Virginia Faulkner Fund, established in
memory of Virginia Faulkner, editor in chief
of the University of Nebraska Press.

Library of Congress Cataloging-in-Publication Data
Names: Sabo, Oana, author.
Title: The migrant canon in twenty-
first-century France / Oana Sabo.
Description: Lincoln: University of Nebraska Press,
2018. | Includes bibliographical references and index.
Identifiers: LCCN 2017042872
ISBN 9781496204943 (cloth: alk. paper)
ISBN 9781496205605 (epub)
ISBN 9781496205612 (mobi)
ISBN 9781496205629 (pdf)
Subjects: LCSH: French literature—21st century—
History and criticism. | Emigration and immigration
in literature. | Literature and globalization—France.
| Globalization in literature. | Multiculturalism in
literature. | Migrations of nations in literature.
Classification: LCC PQ317 .S23 2018
DDC 840.9/0092—dc23
LC record available at
https://lccn.loc.gov/2017042872

Set in Lyon by E. Cuddy.
Designed by N. Putens.

For my mother

and in memory of my father

CONTENTS

Acknowledgments
ix

INTRODUCTION
The French Literary Field in the New Millennium
1

1. PRODUCTION
Publishing Houses and Their Marketing Practices
33

2. RECEPTION
Online Readers in the Global Literary Marketplace
65

3. CONSECRATION
The Prix littéraire de la Porte Dorée and Its
Migrant Archive
97

4. CANONIZATION
Dany Laferrière at the Académie française
127

CONCLUSION
French Migrant Literature in a Global Context
161

Notes
167

References
187

Index
195

ACKNOWLEDGMENTS

I am extremely grateful for all the support I have received over the years in completing this project. My first thanks go to Roberto Ignacio Díaz for sowing the seeds of *The Migrant Canon* and providing much-needed guidance from beginning to end. I am deeply indebted to Natania Meeker, whose rigorous feedback has inspired me to be a better writer. I also thank Karen Pinkus for her incisive questions and comments on earlier drafts. I am grateful to Viet Thanh Nguyen for steering me toward questions of value, which have become central concerns in the book. I would like to thank Rebecca Walkowitz for her generous feedback at a crucial stage. My gratitude also goes to Warren Motte for his support of this project and to Charles Forsdick for stimulating conversations. I give my thanks to Alicia Christensen at the University of Nebraska Press for her enthusiastic support of this project and her always helpful editorial work. I also thank the anonymous readers who provided very useful commentary on my manuscript.

At Tulane University I was fortunate to receive generous grants from the School of Liberal Arts and the Newcomb College Institute to conduct research at the Bibliothèque nationale de France and the Musée national de l'histoire de l'immigration in Paris, as well as the Bibliothèque et Archives nationales du Québec in Montréal in 2013. I am grateful to Carole Haber and Sally Kenney for their support. I also thank the School of Liberal Arts and the Office of the Provost for a Book Subvention Grant and for travel grants that allowed me to present my work at the 2015 MLA conference in Canada and the 2016 MLA International Symposium in Germany. Tulane University granted me a junior leave that allowed me to complete this book.

My work has benefited greatly from the feedback of colleagues, students, and friends. I thank Jean-Godefroy Bidima for stimulating intellectual exchanges. I am grateful to Felicia McCarren, Marilyn Miller, Michael Syrimis, Edwige Tamalet Talbayev, and Teresa Villa-Ignacio for their advice, encouragement, and feedback on my writing. Thanks also to Elizabeth Poe for her generous mentorship. I would like to thank Linda Carroll, Fayçal Falaky, Thomas Klingler, Vaheed Ramazani, and Jeanny Keck for their advice and encouragement. My sincere appreciation also goes to Toby Wikström for his camaraderie and solidarity throughout. I would also like to acknowledge the graduate students in my seminar on migrant and transnational literature whose questions challenged my own. Within my larger academic community I am indebted to Subha Xavier for a fruitful conversation about migrant texts and to James Penner for his valuable professional advice. My warm thanks to Catalina Botez, Monica Cure, Roxana Galusca, Ramona Mielusel, and Gratiana Pol. This book would not have been possible without their intellectual generosity and unflagging support.

Finally I would like to thank friends and family for their personal support over the years. I give special thanks to Hajni Kohn, Johanna Ramirez, Annette Sojic, and Ioana Urma for their friendship. I am immensely thankful to my mother, Maria Sabo, who has been my staunchest supporter. John Charles has been my best reader. For his affection and encouragement as I was completing this book, I am forever grateful.

INTRODUCTION

The French Literary Field
in the New Millennium

In October 2009 Éditions Libre Expression launched *Ru*, the debut novel of Kim Thúy that recounted the story of a young Vietnamese immigrant in Québec. Its slim chapters, consisting of one or two paragraphs each and together comprising just 140 pages, could hardly qualify it as a conventional novel. But *Ru* took the Québécois literary establishment by storm and propelled its author to global fame, winning a host of national and international literary prizes.[1] Its sales totaled more than 120,000 French-language copies in Canada and abroad, and it was translated into more than twenty languages. The novel was issued in paperback, digital, and audio formats, adapted to film, and included on school syllabi. Thúy's biography was no less surprising. A former seamstress, interpreter, lawyer, and restaurateur, she wrote *Ru* for her own pleasure, without any intention of becoming famous. When an acquaintance secretly submitted her manuscript to Libre Expression, the publisher applauded the work, even though it was written in one long sentence. Libre Expression took Thúy's raw text, broke it up into chapters, and marketed it as a novel. Québécois critics, unaware of the editorial intervention, praised *Ru* for being the first novel in French by a Vietnamese Québécois author and for renewing the migrant genre through its unique formal aesthetics.

In Québec *Ru* fit within an already well established tradition of migrant writing and was perceived as filling a gap in literary representations of Vietnamese immigration. In France, where Vietnamese authors are less of a novelty, it owed its meteoric success to its publisher and the media. As the journalist Louis-Bernard Robitaille explains, Thúy's French editor, Liana Levi—emboldened by an Italian publishing agent, who had already sold the translation rights in Italy, Spain, Germany, and Sweden—decided on a print run of ten thousand copies (a rare achievement for a debut novel).[2] Levi also ensured a full-page laudatory review in *Libération* on January 3, 2010, two days before the book's official launch. The *Libération* article was immediately followed by reviews in *Télérama, Le Nouvel Observateur, Elle, Les Échos, Marianne, L'Express*, and *Le Figaro Magazine*, among others, and Thúy was invited to speak on France Inter public radio and to appear on France 5's widely watched television show *La Grande Librairie*. In no time *Ru* occupied twenty-fourth place on *Livres Hebdo*'s Top 50 list of best-selling novels during the week of January 11–17, 2010, and it remained on *Livres Hebdo*'s best-seller lists for another twelve weeks, while also being a finalist for several French literary prizes. *Ru*'s transformation into an iconic Québécois migrant novel and French best seller reveals the great influence—today more than ever—of publishers, booksellers, journalists, translators, prize juries, teachers, and readers on the literary and commercial value of migrant novels. Clearly the making of *Ru* into a commodity and of Thúy into a celebrity would not have been possible without various agents of the literary, editorial, and journalistic fields. Such mediating processes highlight not only the recent cachet of migration narratives in the Global North but also new mechanisms of literary consecration in the twenty-first century. Both are phenomena the present book sets out to examine in fresh detail.

The Migrant Canon in Twenty-First-Century France is the story of the canonization of "migrant literature," a once-marginal genre that originated in France and Québec in the 1980s and has become an integral part of criticism and publishing today. Taking metropolitan France as its focus, the book examines literary texts, authors, and agents that have emerged since 2000 on the French cultural scene. Authors of migrant novels (Delphine Coulin, Mathias Énard, Michaël Ferrier, Laurent Gaudé, Gauz, Milan Kundera, Dany Laferrière, Henri Lopes, Andreï Makine, Marie Redonnet, Éric-Emmanuel Schmitt, and Alice Zeniter) as well as their consecrating authorities (publishing houses and their prestigious series, online reviewers, the Prix littéraire de la Porte Dorée, and the Académie française) come together in a single frame of analysis. Combining close readings with sociological analysis, *The Migrant Canon* reveals that a profitable market for migrant fiction informs and sustains literary production in contemporary France. The book reconstructs this niche market by tracing changes in the literary field since 2000: the appearance of an intermediary marketplace consisting of small and independent presses whose editors position migrant novels for both symbolic and commercial success, the rise of digital audiences that review migrant novels and thus participate in value-making processes, the creation of a new literary prize for the migrant genre, and the opening of national institutions to migrant authors.

The Migrant Canon argues that French migrant literature is best understood as a commodity that occupies a middle ground in today's cultural industries: it mediates between literary and economic forms of value, academic and mass readerships, and national and global literary markets. The study aims to naturalize migration in definitions of contemporary French literature by revealing the mechanisms through which institutional and reading practices legitimize migrant literature as a distinctive and conspicuous genre amid the plethora of genres. It contributes to contemporary literature, migration studies, and literary sociology by reading French migrant literature in light of recent political, economic, and cultural changes and studying very recent literary texts and institutions that have not yet been the subject of significant critical study.

Migrant texts offer a privileged vantage point from which to ask questions about the role of migration in French literary history and the impact of global capitalism on contemporary literary productions. Who writes migrant texts and for whom? How do cultural institutions mediate the symbolic and commercial value of these works, and to what effect? Each chapter gets at the heart of these value-making processes, disclosing the frictions between authorial agency, narrative strategies, institutions' ideological agendas, and the tastes and desires of readers. The chapters are organized according to concepts related to literary legitimation (the distinct yet overlapping processes of production, reception, consecration, and canonization) and legitimating mechanisms (institutional, editorial, and reading practices).

Because this study investigates how institutional and economic forces legitimize migrant texts, its text selections aim to illustrate broader trends. It is therefore less concerned with the distinctive traits of individual works, while remaining nonetheless sensitive to their features and effects. To show that migrant texts' consecration is intimately connected to their promotion, the first chapter examines several novels that garnered success due to their publishers' marketing techniques. The second chapter juxtaposes two elite novels with their online reviews to show that migrant texts' aesthetic ambitions are not incompatible with their popular consumption. Chapter 3 focuses on the laureates of the Prix littéraire de la Porte Dorée, not because of their alleged literary value but to analyze the institutional mechanisms of their consecration. In the final chapter a discussion of three novels by Dany Laferrière helps to interpret the author's ambivalent attitude vis-à-vis his induction into the Académie française.

Together the chapters offer a complex portrait of a contemporary French literary field in transition, with migration putting pressure on existing structures. They also reveal the discursive and material conditions by which we produce and consume migrant literature in a global age, creating canons in the process. *The Migrant Canon* makes no claim that these texts hold enduring canonical status; the value of works over time will be determined by future generations. Nor does it argue that literary texts addressing the topic of migration form a separate or alternative canon to the French one. Instead the book shows how the processes of bestowing value on migrant novels establish them as constitutive of contemporary French literature.

Migrant literature in French is a category that comprises several genres. Poems include, among others, Jamal Khairi's *Patrie-cide: Poèmes transférés de l'arabe marocain* (2011), Josué Guébo's *Songe à Lampedusa* (2014), and Jean-Paul Inisan's *Étranger est l'Éternel: Chants et poèmes pour migrants et autres mal-aimés de ce monde* (2015). Authors have also narrated the migrant experience in plays—Sonia Ristic's *Migrants* (2013), Laurent Gaudé's *Daral Shaga* (2014), and Matéi Visniec's *Migraaaants* (2016)— and short stories—Léonora Miano's *"Afropean Soul" et autres nouvelles* (2008) and the multiauthor anthology *Bienvenue! 34 auteurs pour les réfugiés* (2015). Migration is also a prevalent theme in comic books (Alfred et al.'s *Paroles sans papiers* [2007], Charles Masson's *Droit du sol* [2009], Jérôme Piot and Sébastien Vassant's *Frères d'ombre* [2013], and Mana Neyestani's *Petit manuel du parfait réfugié politique* [2015]), as well as children's and young adult literature (Sandra Poirot Cherif's *L'Oiseau de Mona* [2008], Vincent Karle's *Un clandestin aux Paradis* [2009], and Maryline Desbiolles's *Lampedusa* [2012]). Debates on migration in the French public sphere have triggered politically engaged responses from authors such as Nicole Caligaris and Éric Pessan, who spearheaded a literary project that resulted in the publication of literary correspondence among numerous authors: *Il me sera difficile de venir te voir: Correspondances littéraires sur les conséquences de la politique française d'immigration* (2008). Testimonials such as La Cimade's *Votre voisin n'a pas de papiers: Paroles d'étrangers* (2006), Omar Ba's *Soif d'Europe: Témoignage d'un clandestin* (2008), Wali Mohammadi's *De Kaboul à Calais* (2009), and Mehdi Sayed and Virginie Lydie's *Ma vie de clandestin en France: 17 ans d'errance dans la France d'en dessous* (2011) also highlight migration as a sociopolitical and economic phenomenon that stems from inequality.[3]

Yet none of these genres enjoy the wide popularity of migrant novels. A heteroglossic genre, in the Bakhtinian sense, the novel accommodates multiple perspectives, appeals to varied audiences, and can simultaneously inform, instruct, and entertain. Novels moreover do not merely tell a story; they often theorize the process of its writing. Many contemporary novels display self-reflexivity, musing on their conditions of production and reception, parodying the publishing industry, or critiquing the commodification of literature. Deeply embedded in their cultural and economic context, they address current events and shed light on contemporary societies in specifically literary ways. It is not surprising that novels that tackle clandestine Mediterranean crossings or the terrorist attacks on the *Charlie Hebdo* staff make it to best-seller lists, as they lure readers with real-life issues, responding to their desire to understand the world in which they live.[4]

A lucrative genre, novels feature prominently on *Le Figaro*, *Lire*, and *Livres Hebdo* best-seller lists. *Livres Hebdo*, for instance, issues a weekly list of the 50 best-selling novels and another of the 15 best-selling paperback novels, respectively, as well as a monthly list of the 25 best-selling novels for young adults. Such commercial success is, in part, also due to the French literary prizes they attract. A case in point, Atiq Rahimi's *Syngué sabour: Pierre de patience*, initially published in a 15,000-copy print run, has sold 337,000 copies after winning the 2008 Prix Goncourt.[5] Major literary prizes often go to novels published during *la rentrée littéraire d'automne* (France's peak publishing season, from August to the beginning of November) and *la rentrée d'hiver* (from the beginning of January to the end of March). During the 2013 winter publishing season alone, 558 novels were published, 347 of which were French and 221 foreign.[6] These publishing events and the literary awards that novels garner undoubtedly contribute to the genre's promotion, as does the Prix littéraire de la Porte Dorée, which rewards primarily novels, even though in recent years it has gone to literary texts that disrupt traditional novelistic boundaries. The 2016 Porte Dorée winner, Doan Bui's *Le Silence de mon père*, was not a conventional novel but an archival investigation of the immigrant history of the author's family. It was nevertheless labeled as fiction, which upholds Jean-Yves Tadié and Blanche Cerquiglini's (2012) argument that "[i]n today's editorial landscape, everything is a novel. A dominant genre, the novel appropriates other narrative genres" from stories to history books to autobiographies (427).

While this study focuses on the novel, it acknowledges that contemporary migrant texts extend beyond its generic confines.

"FRENCH" MIGRANT LITERATURE

Although migrant literature is a global literary genre not restricted to the French literary and linguistic tradition, it holds particular sway in current French literary criticism and in the French institutional authorities founded since the early 2000s.[7] Québec, where the term "migrant literature" was first coined to designate the genre, is hardly alone as a key publishing center for migrant writing. A great number of recent French-language migrant novels are also published in France, by presses both large and small. The genre's popularity is due not only to its marketability but also to the infrastructure of the French publishing industry. The concentration of houses, distribution networks, and literary prizes in Paris continues to uphold the French capital as a major site of literary legitimation. Véronique Porra (2008) acknowledges the power imbalances between Paris and other French-speaking cities such as Montréal and Bruxelles. While these are publishing centers in relation to their own peripheries, they are also "satellites" or peripheries in relation to the Parisian center (51). For this reason perhaps some migrant authors (Québec-based Ying Chen, Dany Laferrière, and Kim Thúy, as well as Switzerland-based Agota Kristof) also publish—simultaneously or with a brief delay—in France, because literary consecration by the Parisian center continues to enhance the authors' symbolic capital in their respective adoptive countries.

Migrant texts have also generated sustained interest among French critics, journalists, and readers, especially in response to new European political realities, such as economic migration and the ongoing "migrant crisis" in Europe.[8] What is more, newly established cultural institutions have shown great interest in the sociopolitical phenomenon of migration and its literary representations. The founding of the Cité nationale de l'histoire de l'immigration in 2007 and of the Prix littéraire de la Porte Dorée for migrant literature in 2010 attests to migration's centrality in French culture today. Laferrière's and Makine's inductions into the Académie française in 2013 and 2016, respectively, only add to the genre's cachet.

In recent years French literary prizes have frequently celebrated migrant authors. In 2006 the Goncourt, the Femina, the Renaudot, the Grand Prix du roman de l'Académie française, and the Goncourt des lycéens all went to authors from the francophone periphery. The windfall drew the attention of forty-four French and francophone authors, who collaborated on a literary manifesto that *Le Monde* published on March 16, 2007. This manifesto, "Pour une 'littérature-monde' en français," declared the end of the center-periphery model and the advent of a French literature open to the world. It described the "francophone" (i.e., non-French) category for postcolonial and migrant authors to be obsolete and called for a rethinking of French literary texts in light of alternative global centers. The manifesto represented a significant step in highlighting the reception of non-French authors and the field's cultural openness toward global frameworks, and it demanded new readings that reenvision the French literary canon.[9] *The Migrant Canon* aims to answer the manifesto's call frontally, by attempting to account for the transnational dimensions of contemporary French literature specifically via the migrant genre.

Against the grain of rigid categories *The Migrant Canon* takes on a heterogeneous corpus of authors: French and migrant, elite and popular, consecrated and emergent, postcolonial and nonfrancophone. What unites these writers above all are the mechanisms of their literary consecration. All have published their fictional works in France, though these works circulate globally and have won literary prizes in France and abroad. Their works are at once national and transnational, moving "between—and not *in-between*" literary fields (Xavier 2016, 18). The mechanisms of literary reception common in the 1980s and 1990s were based on the paradigm of *l'entre-deux* (in-betweenness) (Sibony 1991), according to which texts transition from the literature of migrant authors' homeland to that of their hostland. In contrast the migrant texts of the new millennium show that symbolic capital is not solely bound to Paris, even when France remains central to their literary legitimation. Some authors, for instance, seek literary legitimation in other publishing sites in addition to Paris. They thus relativize France's central position in the world republic of letters without displacing the center altogether. Their questioning of hegemonic models notwithstanding, the fact remains that the migrant literary texts examined here are the product of the French publishing industry. The afterlives of these novels may involve new editions designed for multiple readerships (i.e., global circulation), but they are novels initially published in a national context that target a national readership.

Scholars of francophone and anglophone literature have noted the cultural and linguistic hegemony of metropolitan centers, which are privileged sites of production, distribution, and reception (Ahmad 1992; Huggan 2001; Porra 2008). Studies on works by migrant authors in locales of the metropole routinely underscore how a peripheral consciousness can often shape their literary strategies. Graham Huggan's (2001) notion of "strategic exoticism" refers to the simultaneously complicit and resistant strategies of postcolonial (anglophone) authors who position themselves ambivalently vis-à-vis the center's ideological and aesthetic norms. In Huggan's view such authors deliberately market their exotic marginality for audiences of the metropole, while critiquing mainstream institutional values for fetishizing difference (xi). In this framework these peripheral writers successfully manipulate their racial, ethnic, gendered, or cultural identities in exchange for symbolic capital. However, in Pascale Casanova's (2007) model of world literary space, authors from the peripheries enter the (French) center primarily as national authors (40). Their nationality and literary position in their native literary tradition are indelible stamps that inflect their strategies (of assimilation or rebellion) and their reception in their host country (179). Both Huggan and Casanova address the circumstances of authors who move from the periphery to the center, and they stress the importance of migrant writers' national and ethnic identity to mediations of value by the metropole.

The Migrant Canon shares these scholars' prevailing focus on a particular metropolitan form of consecration: from postcolonial writer to French author. It diverges from such studies, however, by deemphasizing issues of authorial identification with French identity and therefore the binary of center and periphery. Some of the authors are French, whether they live in France or abroad. Their ethnic background and active participation in French literary circles from abroad belie Casanova's model of the

French center integrating its margins. And the migrant authors examined have been integrated over time into the French literary establishment. The question of belonging to the French literary tradition is, for them, settled. This study considers them French authors not by virtue of being born, or residing, in France but by virtue of having published their works with French presses. Book and print culture (the consecration and dissemination of works by institutional and reading practices) is here the criterion of literary inclusion. The obsolescence of binary models (center and postcolonial periphery, national and world literature) for reading migrant literature requires the implementation of different frameworks, namely those derived from literary sociology and the history of the book. A focus on institutional and reading practices, and on the variety of cultural actors involved in book promotion, establishes the widespread interest in migrant literature among French and francophone publics. In other words it is by examining the French literary field in the twenty-first century that one can highlight the multiple processes that have resulted in the recent canonization of migrant literature.

A MAINSTREAM GENRE

Migrant novels are an integral part of the French literary mainstream. They appear on best-seller lists, win literary prizes, and are discussed on radio and television shows. A look at *Livres Hebdo*'s Top 20 best-seller list attests to the fact that migrant novels conform to the tastes and expectations of large readerships. The periodical's Top 20 list mixes literary genres and includes the most popular mass-market fiction (by Marc Levy, Guillaume Musso, and Michel Bussi), comic books (by Pénélope Bagieu, Stéphane Colman, Deon Meyer), and literary fiction (by David Foenkinos, Anna Gavalda, Amélie Nothomb, and Éric-Emmanuel Schmitt). *Livres Hebdo* also publishes a weekly list of the fifty best-selling novels, and it regularly features migrant texts.

Several migrant novels have reached the *Livres Hebdo* list. Romain Puértolas's *L'Extraordinaire voyage du fakir qui était resté coincé dans une armoire Ikéa* has had the most success. It was included—in its original edition as well as paperback—among *Livres Hebdo*'s Top 20 best sellers for more than twelve weeks in 2013 and 2014.[10] Éric-Emmanuel Schmitt's *Ulysse from Bagdad* also appeared on *Livres Hebdo*'s Top 20 list (for one week in 2008) and Top 50 list—the original version for eight weeks in 2008 and six weeks in 2009, and the paperback for nine weeks in 2010. Other migrant novels that were both critically acclaimed and commercially successful were Négar Djavadi's *Désorientale* (twenty-two weeks a best seller in 2016), Magyd Cherfi's *Ma part de Gaulois* (eighteen weeks on *Livres Hebdo*'s Top 50 list in 2016), Gauz's *Debout-payé* (sixteen weeks in 2014–15), Valérie Zenatti's *Jacob, Jacob* (eight weeks in 2015), Mathias Énard's *Rue des voleurs* and Maylis de Kerangal's *À ce stade de la nuit* (seven weeks in 2012 and 2015, respectively), Andreï Makine's *La Vie d'un homme inconnu* and Saphia Azzeddine's *La Mecque-Phuket* (five weeks in 2009 and 2010, respectively), Faïza Guène's *Un homme, ça ne pleure pas* (four weeks in 2010), and Tahar Ben Jelloun's *Partir* (two weeks in 2006). Fatou Diome's *Le Ventre de l'Atlantique* reached the Top 20 list for one week in 2004 and Milan Kundera's *L'Ignorance* for one week in 2005, as did Chahdortt Djavann's *Comment peut-on être français?* and Laurent Gaudé's *Eldorado* in 2006, and Nahal Tajadod's *Elle joue* and Olivier Adam's *À l'abri de rien* in 2007 and 2008, respectively. Although the number of migrant novels may appear small in relation to the hundreds of novels published annually in France, the notable success of a few migrant novels that top best-seller lists underscores migrant narratives' critical and market appeal.

French migrant novels routinely are entered in national and international literary prize competitions. They have been finalists or winners in competitions ranging from the "prestigious" to the popular, which demonstrates their ability to navigate the boundary between aesthetics and commerce. Migrant novels have been shortlisted for major literary prizes: the Prix Goncourt (Magoudi's *Un sujet français* in 2011, Énard's *Rue des voleurs* 2012, Cherfi's *Ma part de Gaulois* 2016), Prix Goncourt du premier roman (David Boratav's *Murmures à Beyoğlu* 2009), Goncourt des lycéens (*Ma part de Gaulois* 2016), Renaudot (Alain Blottière's *Le Tombeau de Tommy* 2009, Shumona Sinha's *Assommons les pauvres!* 2011, Laura Alcoba's *Le Bleu des abeilles* 2013), Médicis (Adam's *À l'abri de rien* 2007, *Le Tombeau de Tommy* 2009, *Jacob, Jacob* 2014), Femina (*Le Bleu des abeilles* 2013), and Grand Prix du roman de l'Académie française (*Rue des voleurs* 2013, Tran Huy's *Voyageur malgré lui* 2014). In 2009 Laferrière's *L'Énigme du retour* won the Prix Médicis. Migrant novels also earned lesser-known awards such as the Prix Eugène-Dabit du roman populiste (*À l'abri de rien* 2007; *Assommons les pauvres!* 2011), Prix Valery-Larbaud (*Assommons les pauvres!* 2012), and Prix du Style (*Désorientale* 2016), as well as prizes that encourage new talents: the Prix SGDL André Dubreuil du premier roman (Yassaman Montazami's *Le Meilleur des Jours* 2012) and Prix Landerneau des Espaces culturels E. Leclerc (Kéthévane Davrichewy's *La Mer noire* 2010, Delphine Coulin's *Samba pour la France* 2011).

Given their coverage in the media, some novels won literary prizes whose juries include television, radio, and literary magazine audiences: the Prix Roman France Télévisions (*À l'abri de rien* 2007), Prix du Roman-News (*Rue des voleurs* 2013), and Prix du Livre Inter (*Jacob, Jacob* 2015), while *Voyageur malgré lui* was on the 2014 Prix Interallié shortlist. However, migrant novels especially garner the enthusiasm of juries composed of common readers, booksellers, and book club members, which underscores these texts' popular acclaim. For example, they won the Prix du Roman *Version Femina*-Virgin Megastore (*La Mer noire* 2010), Prix des lecteurs de l'Escale du livre (*Voyageur malgré lui* 2015), Prix des Libraires en Seine (*Jacob, Jacob* 2015—a prize for which Gauz's *Debout-payé* was also shortlisted), and Prix du Roman métis des lycéens (*Samba pour la France* 2016). Novels were also shortlisted for the Prix du roman Fnac (*Le Tombeau de Tommy* 2009, Fatou Diome's *Celles qui attendent* 2011, Hubert Haddad's *Opium Poppy* 2011, Gaëlle Josse's *Le Dernier Guardien d'Ellis Island* 2014, *Debout-payé* 2014, *Jacob, Jacob* 2014, Pascal Manoukian's *Les Échoués* 2015), Le Prix des Libraires (Stéphanie Janicot's *Dans la tête de Shéhérazade* 2008, *Murmures à Beyoğlu* 2009, *Celles qui attendent* 2011, *Opium Poppy* 2011, *Le Bleu des abeilles* 2013, Isabelle Condou's *Un pays qui n'a pas de port* 2013, *Le Dernier Guardien d'Ellis Island* 2014, *Voyageur malgré lui* 2014), the Prix des lecteurs Gallimard (Velibor Čolić's *Manuel d'exil* 2016), Prix RTL-Lire (*Samba pour la France* 2011, Guène's *Un homme, ça ne pleure pas* 2014, Davrichewy's *L'Autre Joseph* 2016), Prix Wepler (*Murmures à Beyoğlu* 2009), Prix Orange du Livre, given by *Lecteurs*'s online book club (*Un homme, ça ne pleure pas*

2014), and Prix "Des racines et des mots," awarded to a novel about exile (Fouad Laroui's *Les Tribulations du dernier Sijilmassi* 2015, Éliane Serdan's *La Ville haute* 2016).

French migrant novels also appeared in international prize competitions: *Celles qui attendent* won the 2011 Prix des cinq continents, established by the Organisation internationale de la Francophonie, and the 2015 Prix de littérature de l'Union Européenne went to *Le Dernier Guardien d'Ellis Island*, in addition to eleven other winners. In 2016 *Les Échoués* won the Belgian Prix Première and the Bourse de la Découverte (awarded by Fondation Prince Pierre de Monaco). A few prizes have rewarded novels that display openness to other cultures and peoples, such as the Prix du Cercle de l'Union Interallié (*Opium Poppy* 2012), Prix Liste Goncourt/Le Choix de l'Orient (*Rue des voleurs* 2013), Prix Littérature-monde (Carole Zalberg's *Feu pour feu* 2014), and Prix Méditerranée (*Jacob, Jacob* 2015). These awards in particular show that French migrant literature circulates beyond the francophone world and is connected to global phenomena.

Most of the above-mentioned novels received positive coverage in the written press and audiovisual media. In addition, Zeniter's *Jusque dans nos bras* (2010), Tajadod's *Elle joue* (2012), Delmaire's *Georgia* (2013), Zadig Hamroune's *Le Pain de l'exil* (2015), and Wagner's *Effacer sa trace* (2016) were discussed on radio stations France Inter, France Culture, France Info, and RFI, while the above-mentioned novels, as well as Sylvie Gracia's *Une parenthèse espagnole* (2009) and Azzeddine's *La Mecque-Phuket* (2011), were mentioned on TF1, France 2, France 3, France 5, and Canal Plus television channels. Laudatory reviews also appeared in the literary sections of French newspapers and magazines such as *Le Monde, Le Figaro littéraire, Libération, Le Nouvel Observateur, L'Obs, Le Point, Télérama, Lire, L'Express, Le Matricule des Anges, Hommes et Migrations, Livres Hebdo*, and *Elle*.

The French market for migrant literature includes not only works written in French but also translations. Translations from English include Philip Caputo's *Clandestin* (Le Cherche Midi, 2012), Brian Chikwava's *Harare Nord* (Zoé, 2011), Jeffrey Eugenides's *Middlesex* (Seuil, 2004), Chang-rae Lee's *Langue natale* (L'Olivier, 2003), Chimamanda Ngozi Adichie's *Americanah* (Gallimard, 2016), Farah Nuruddin's *Exils* (Le Serpent à Plumes, 2010), and

Julie Otsuka's *Certaines n'avaient jamais vu la mer* (Phébus, 2004), among others. Migrant works have also been translated from Finnish (Pajtim Statovci's *Mon chat Yugoslavia* [Denoël, 2016]), German (Anna Seghers's *Transit* [Le Livre de Poche, 2004]), Hungarian (Sándor Márai's *Les Étrangers* [Albin Michel, 2012]), Italian (Enaiatollah Akbari and Fabio Geda's *Dans la mer il y a des crocodiles* [Liana Levi, 2011] and Margaret Mazzantini's *La Mer, le Matin* [10 × 18, 2014]), as well as Russian (in Estonia) (Andreï Ivanov's *Le Voyage de Hanumân* [Le Tripode, 2016]), Spanish (Guillermo Rosales's *Mon ange* [Actes Sud, 2004] and Diana Guelar, Beatriz Ruiz, and Vera Jarach's *Les Enfants de l'exil* [Intervalles, 2012]), and Turkish (Nedim Gürsel's *L'Ange rouge* [Points, 2016]). Translation is a means of expanding the boundaries of the French literary canon and, in the case of migrant texts, of legitimating the genre. But what does it mean to consecrate or canonize French-language migrant texts?

MIGRANT LITERATURE AND THE FRENCH CANON

To speak of canonicity in France is to speak of the multiple institutional practices by which value is attached to literary works. These practices range from book marketing, distribution, and press reviews to literary prizes and inclusion on course syllabi. Pierre Bourdieu's sociology of culture provides useful concepts to analyze such mechanisms of consecration. His theory of "fields," which he developed in relation to late nineteenth- and early twentieth-century French culture, adheres to the production and reception of contemporary French literature as well. Bourdieu (1993) defines the literary field as a dynamic and hierarchical cultural space with its own laws, "social agents," and power relations (30). It is "a *field of struggles*" (30, original emphasis) in which various agents—authors, publishers, critics, prize juries, and so forth—compete for "symbolic capital," that is, recognition, prestige, or the authority to designate value (75). For Bourdieu no single agent or practice determines the value of a work, since the work is "a *manifestation* of the field as a whole" (37, original emphasis). As he sees it, the value of a work does not derive from its intrinsic (symbolic, economic, or other) properties but rather the "(collective) belief" in it as a work of art (35). *The Migrant Canon* highlights the ways in which the French literary field mediates the value of migrant texts. However, it avoids deterministic explanations through analysis of the literary texts themselves and their authors' "creative agency" (Xavier 2016, 15). Closer attention to the literary and economic strategies that market-savvy authors employ in their texts can build upon Bourdieu's sociological model in productive ways.

Bourdieu's concept of the field is a malleable notion that accounts for the historical evolution of genres and the role of agents in canon formation. It therefore enables the positioning of migrant literature of the last two decades within a broader network of producers, consumers, and legitimating agencies. The field, according to Bourdieu, is a dynamic space in which genres enter into and out of fashion, and changes in agents' positions—such as the promotion of unknown agents through consecration or the appearance of new ones—have restructuring effects. In the case of migrant literature the creation of a new literary prize (the Prix littéraire de la Porte Dorée) and the publication of a dictionary of migrant authors (Mathis-Moser and Mertz-Baumgartner's [2012] *Passages et ancrages en France: Dictionnaire des écrivains migrants de langue française [1981–2011]*) can be seen as "position-takings," or consecrating acts that have pushed the migrant genre into the mainstream (Bourdieu 1993, 62).

The field is also a hierarchical space in which agents, endowed with different forms of capital, hold unequal positions and therefore consecrate works according to different notions of value. Bourdieu (1993) delineates three competing principles of legitimation: an autonomous form of recognition, granted by elite producers in the "self-sufficient world of 'art for art's sake'"; a "bourgeois" form reflecting the taste of the dominant class; and "popular" consecration bestowed by mass audiences (51). This neat compartmentalization of consecrating practices must be taken critically, given that the notions of "art for art's sake" and "bourgeois" taste are largely irrelevant to today's cultural industries. However, the principle that there are competing forms of evaluation abides. In the contemporary literary field the educational system represents an elite form of consecration; the works it validates usually connote ideas of timeless value. To be included in secondary-school and university curricula, and especially on the *agréga-tion* examination list—a rare achievement for contemporary works—is to obtain the status of a classic. In contrast a literary prize, be it prestigious or popular, conflates symbolic and economic value by recognizing a work's perceived literary prestige as well as its profitable sales. The mass media invests in a book's popular and immediate success largely via book reviews in major newspapers, best-seller lists in literary magazines, and author interviews on television and radio.

Each of these agencies has a different vision of literature, legitimating a work according to the position it occupies in the field, as well as its own material or symbolic interests. The agencies' criteria vary between elite (works that endure over time), popular (texts that appeal to majority tastes), and commercial (works that perform well in the marketplace). In this sense migrant novels—and the institutional forces behind them—offer competing visions of the canon. Most often, though, different forms of capital converge on the middle ground occupied by migrant texts. Consider Gauz's *Debout-payé*, which won literary prizes, landed on best-seller lists, and was frequently reviewed in the media. Or consider Dany Laferrière, who was inducted into the prestigious Académie française but only after his literary works were sanctioned by popular or commercial authorities.

Adapting Bourdieu's (1993) model to the present case requires us to revise his conception of the literary marketplace, which he divides into the subfields of "restricted" and "large-scale" production—in other words, into an elite market that produces aesthetically valuable works and a mass market that produces the commercially viable ones (53). Seeing a literary work as either "a symbolic object" (112) or a "commodity" (113) is anachronistic in the present-day context of cultural commodification. Bourdieu (1996) himself later qualified his theory about the dual nature of the marketplace, suggesting that the line separating high and low is "now threatening to disappear, since the logic of commercial production tends more and more to assert itself over avant-garde production (notably, in the case of literature, through the constraints of the book market)" (345). The categories of "elite" and "mass" are not necessarily obsolete but rather conflated in the increasingly commercial structure of the literary field.

Contemporary migrant texts exemplify an "intermediary" conception of literature because they deploy strategies that fall between the elite and the popular, the symbolic and the commercial. However, this intermediary position should not be conflated with the "middlebrow" category. The literary middlebrow, as Beth Driscoll (2014) has convincingly argued, is "the space in contemporary culture that is neither elite nor popular" (8–9), where "literary and commercial practices are dynamically interrelated" (13). According to Driscoll, middlebrow texts, practices, and institutions are "middle class, reverential towards elite culture, entrepreneurial, mediated, feminized, emotional, recreational and earnest" (6). It would be more accurate to posit that migrant texts participate in middlebrow practices such as critics' book reviews and best-seller lists in the media, as well as Amazon customer reviews and reading challenges on digital forums. Yet, unlike middlebrow texts, migrant texts—at least in France—also partake of elite culture, without revering it. They are mediated by academic institutions (the Académie française) and literary prizes (the Prix littéraire de la Porte Dorée) that do not glorify celebrity authors but promote lesser known ones. Migrant novels today are commodities endowed with aesthetic, political, and ethical value, and they are written and packaged with niche audiences in mind. They may appeal to cultured readers through formal experimentation and to common readers through readability, while they also cater to both male and female audiences. Widely accessible, they push readers to understand migration through the lens of human rights, shared national histories, and transnational communities. The undeniable political content of migrant novels is also marketable to a liberal readership skeptical of French nationalism and xenophobia. The political field has markedly shaped the content, form, and marketability of recent migrant texts. In twenty-first-century France nationalist and xenophobic political discourses, which put forward an idea of French society as ethnically homogeneous, politically powerful, and culturally relevant, are more prevalent than ever. In 2005 in the wake of the *banlieue* riots Interior Minister Nicolas Sarkozy stigmatized North African minorities. During the 2007 presidential campaign he promised to revive republican ideals as a response to France's increasing ethnic, religious, and cultural diversity. As president, Sarkozy established the Ministère de l'immigration, de l'intégration, de l'identité nationale et du codéveloppement, whose leader, Éric Besson, moved to expel illegal immigrants from France. In 2009 Besson also launched the national identity debate to clarify what "Frenchness" meant in the twenty-first century and to urge immigrants to embrace a monolithic view of French identity. The national identity debate, which distinguished between French people (born in France of French parents) and French citizens of foreign origin (Thomas 2014, 454), solidified the latter category, rendering immigrants as Other to the nation-state and therefore unassimilable. According to Dominic Thomas (2014), the construction of otherness, especially in relation to the country's postcolonial immigrants, carries colonial resonances in French political discourse (451). It encourages visions of immigration as a threat to a French identity "whose foundations and *grandeur* were bolstered by the colonial imaginary and expansionist drive" (453).

Whereas political discourses, frequently echoed by the anti-immigration Front National, lament the alleged crisis of French values, cultural projects such as the creation of the Cité nationale de l'histoire de l'immigration in 2006 attempt to come to terms with France's colonial past. Contemporary migrant novels also tackle current debates in French politics and can be read as counternarratives to "the reluctance to address colonial history, [. . .] the refusal to embrace diversity and new modes of coexistence, and [. . .] the persistence of age-old references to former achievements" of French society (Thomas 2014, 454). *The Migrant Canon* mines the tensions between the nationalism of French political institutions and the cosmopolitanism of cultural institutions and migrant texts. While some migrant novels raise issues of colonial history, others pose questions about intercultural dialogue and human rights. Migrant literature is a zeitgeist genre indissociable from the political, cultural, and economic context of its production.

ACADEMIC RECEPTION

Scholars of French and francophone literature have approached literary immigration from a wide range of perspectives. In the majority of these studies migrant authors' ethnic origin and postcolonial ties to France appear to be the major criterion structuring the scope of their research and ensuing arguments.[11] Postcolonial authorship and its institutional and media reception are critical to understanding the work of Lopes and Laferrière, since French institutional and reading practices distinguish along racial and ethnic lines, alongside other factors such as gender, age, nationality, education, or religion. For example, one cannot overlook the significance that Lopes's Congolese origin has for his novel's publication in Éditions Gallimard's Continents noirs series. Nor can one discount the fact that, upon induction into the Académie française, Laferrière was viewed as Haitian, Caribbean, or francophone—that is, connected to France's colonial history. It is important to remember, however, that the postcolonial framework is only one approach among many for the study of French migrant literature.

Take, for instance, Tijana Miletić's (2008) *European Literary Immigration into the French Language: Readings of Gary, Kristof, Kundera, and Semprun*, which examines nonfrancophone European authors of the second half of the twentieth century. Miletić observes that the choice of French and, implicitly, adherence to French cultural values, assures migrant authors' favorable reception by the French literary establishment. Véronique Porra (2011) develops this idea further in *Langue française, langue d'adoption: Une littérature "invitée" entre création, stratégies et contraintes (1946-2000)*. Her book gathers an understudied corpus of migrant writers originating in eastern Europe, Latin America, and East Asia who pass more smoothly into French institutional structures than their postcolonial counterparts on account of their use of the French language and concomitant praise of its "genius." Porra furthermore usefully supplements the textual approach adopted by previous studies with a sociological analysis of the conditions of literary production and institutional reception. Both Miletić and Porra map out new areas of investigation within migrant literature, bringing up important and previously neglected questions—about the relationships between France and countries that are not former French colonies—relevant to discussions of migrant authors' place in the French canon.

The Migrant Canon draws on Miletić's and Porra's ideas about how authorial strategies affect literary reception, while aligning with recent studies of migrant literature that privilege generic features. Simona Pruteanu's

(2013) *L'Écriture migrante en France et au Québec (1985–2006): Une analyse comparative* innovatively describes migrant literature as a genre with recurrent thematic and stylistic traits. In a similar vein Subha Xavier's (2016) *The Migrant Text: Making and Marketing a Global French Literature* theorizes migrant literature as a mode of writing decoupled from authorial identity and therefore applicable to migrant texts from other literary and linguistic traditions. It is a global genre, as Xavier sees it, not because it rejects the nation-state (after all, migrant texts are a product of national publishing industries) but because it circulates between national literary spaces, not simply from one national space to another. Drawing on Xavier's theory, which places migrant texts at the intersection of poetics, politics, and economics, *The Migrant Canon* goes further, by identifying migrant works produced by French authors and discussing them in the context of migration studies. It argues that, although global capitalism informs the production of the migrant genre, the particularities of national literary fields shape the value constructions of migrant texts.

The Migrant Canon reconstructs the workings of the French literary field in the new millennium. Full coverage of the genre would of course be impossible given the sheer volume of migrant texts, the diversity of cultural agents, and a literary field in constant transition. Instead the book tells the story of the sudden emergence and transformation of a literary genre that has quickly come into prominence due to recent geopolitical changes and the current sociopolitical climate fueling interest in migration. It defines the sociohistorical conditions that allowed a marginal genre to occupy a mainstream position in the French literary field, new migrant themes and forms, and the mechanisms of literary legitimation that have led to migrant texts' critical and commercial acclaim. While popular in the 1980s and 1990s, the tropes of hybrid identities, cultural in-betweenness, and postcolonial resistance now fall by the wayside. Migrant novels in the new millennium tell different stories of migration. They examine above all the economic and political factors that underpin migration and turn millions of people into refugees and asylum seekers. Migrant literature since 2000 then is symptomatic of the phenomena of intensified globalization and recent mass migrations. The timeliness of immigration as a topic no doubt increases the texts' marketing appeal for publishers, journalists, and literary critics. Even nonmigrant authors have entered the genre, writing with urgency about the most pressing issues of the day.

MIGRANT LITERATURE IN THE 1980S AND 1990S

Although migration is an age-old phenomenon, most critics agree the early 1980s mark the start of the institutionalization of migrant literature as a literary genre and analytical category in France and Québec. Whether known as *écriture migrante* (migrant writing), as in Québec, or *les littératures des immigrations* (literatures of immigration), as in France, migrant texts from the 1980s through the first decade of the new millennium have addressed issues of displacement and return, hybrid identities, assimilation, and xenophobia. Migrant texts gained recognition in France and Québec at a time when multicultural policies, postmodern trends, postcolonial studies, and the institutionalization of cultural otherness were at their height in the Western academy (Brennan 1997; Spivak 1999; Huggan 2001). The recuperation of migrant and minority subjects, as well as the celebration of the tropes of hybrid and fragmented identities, became central themes in academic research.

In Québec the celebration of migrant writing and the debates it fostered are best understood with respect to the province's status as a francophone nation in a predominantly anglophone federation. Given l'Assemblée nationale du Québec's defense and promotion of the French language as a marker of its cultural identity, migrant authors' choice to write in French contributed to their favorable reception. Yet the degree to which these texts "belonged" to Québécois literature was unclear. Critics issued a series of classifications that underscored migrant writers' foreign origins and belated arrival: "allophones" (speakers whose native language is neither French nor English); "néo-Québécois" (new Quebeckers), in contrast to "Québécois de souche" (old-stock Quebeckers); and "les étrangers du dedans" (internal foreigners) (Moisan and Hildebrand 2001, 10). Such labels reflect Québécois society's ambivalent stance regarding its immigrant members. Yet, as Québécois literature became autonomous from French literary models in the wake of the Quiet Revolution of the 1960s, it was better equipped to absorb contributions from cultural minorities (Dumontet 2014, 89). The pull of nationalism and the counterweight of multiculturalism framed migrant literature's entrance into the Québécois literary canon in the last two decades of the twentieth century.

Identity politics of the 1980s was at the core of migrant authors' self-positioning and the Québécois reception of their texts. Migrant writers entered the Québécois literary field from the margins and vocally asserted their right to be there. Rich literary output aside, they owed their success to the editorial and literary networks that increased their visibility in the Québécois literary establishment, which in turn offered them a forum to promote immigrant cultures, their own works, and those of other migrant writers. In the late 1970s and 1980s Haitian and Italian migrant writers founded publishing houses, such as Guernica, Humanitas, Nouvelle-Optique, and Mémoire d'encrier, and literary magazines, such as *Dérives, Moebius, Spirale,* and *Vice Versa*. The category of migrant literature as well as the genre quickly passed into the mainstream, as Québécois critics debated, promoted, and disseminated migratory concepts and migrant texts through conferences, academic works, anthologies, and dictionaries. By the turn of the twenty-first century studies such as Clément Moisan and Renate Hildebrand's (2001) *Ces étrangers du dedans: Une histoire de l'écriture migrante au Québec (1937-1997)*, Daniel Chartier's (2003) *Dictionnaire des écrivains émigrés au Québec 1800-1999*, Simon Harel's (2005) *Les Passages obligés de l'écriture migrante*, and the chapter "L'écriture migrante" in Michel Biron et al.'s (2007) *Histoire de la littérature québécoise* confirmed the place of migrant writing in Québec's academic institutions and cultural field. Migrant literature, once on the margins, was now mainstream.[12]

In France the canonical status of migrant texts is properly viewed in relation to exclusionary ideas of national identity. From the 1970s to the 1990s the issue of how to integrate immigrant populations, especially those from Muslim cultures, held center stage in the successive governments of Valéry Giscard d'Estaing (1974-81), François Mitterrand (1981-95), and Jacques Chirac (1995-2007). A confusing ebb and flow of immigration laws—legislation that restricted immigration, encouraged foreigners' return to their native countries, or extended legal rights to clandestine immigrants—signals France's ongoing unease with ethnic and especially religious diversity. Debates about the Frenchness or, in contrast, the otherness of migrant authors also extended to the literary field. The surge in migrant texts in the 1980s and 1990s by ethnically diverse authors confronted literary institutions with fresh questions about classification. Is Vassilis Alexakis Greek or French? Is Lebanese-born Amin Maalouf French or francophone? Can Linda Lê be considered French Vietnamese even though she rejects all literary labels? To capture the specificity of these writings, new categories based on ethnic, generational, and linguistic criteria emerged. These taxonomies, however intended, further marginalized authors of immigrant background, even those who were born in France, adopted the French language, and became French citizens.

In the 1980s the phenomenon of "Beur" fiction—the literary works of second-generation North African immigrants—captivated French publishers, critics, and readers through their depiction of banlieue life, intergenerational tensions, and cultural identity quests. L'Harmattan, Le Seuil, Belfond, and Denoël, among other publishing houses, successfully marketed Beur novels for their documentary value, consistent with media stereotypes, and cast Beur authors as native informants. Whereas on the one hand consecration meant literary visibility for authors such as Azouz Begag, Mehdi Charef, and Farida Belghoul, on the other it separated their writing from the French mainstream. Works that deviated from prescribed Beur themes stood fewer chances of publication or commercial success.[13] Critics further defined this corpus as different from dominant French literature by considering it "an emerging literary space" (Bonn 1995, 11).

As interest in Beur literature dwindled in the 1990s and as Beur authors themselves abandoned the genre, another body of writing captured the spotlight: the works of authors from Sub-Saharan Africa. Although writing from the French capital, these authors differed from their vanguard African predecessors in 1920s and 1930s Paris. Innovatively they asserted a literary voice neither wholly African nor wholly French. Nathalie Etoké, Alain Mabanckou, Simon Njami, Daniel Biyaoula, and Calixthe Beyala, among others, produced "a distinct type of literature" that decentered the African and French literary canons (Cazenave 2003, 5). Despite these attempts to move beyond the role their predecessors played as native informants, the French public continued to demand representations according to stereotype. "Ethnic literature" remained the signature of migrant genre publishing by Présence Africaine, Éditions Karthala, Le Serpent à Plumes, the Espace de la parole series from Publisud, and the Encres noires series from L'Harmattan. The publication and reception of Beur and African diasporic texts underline residual imperialist perceptions of France's postcolonial subjects, which now also apply to migrant writers from countries that were not former colonies.

The mid-1990s saw the French media and literary institutions consecrate yet another set of migrant authors, originating this time from southern and eastern Europe, Latin America, and East Asia. Migrant authors from these regions—Jorge Semprún, Milan Kundera, Hector Bianciotti, François Cheng, and Dai Sijie are among the most well known of this group—enjoyed a mostly favorable reception. They were published by major presses, won prestigious prizes, and appeared on top-rated television shows such as Bernard Pivot's *Apostrophes* and *Bouillon de culture*. Their popularity was due in part to strategies of assimilation: they adopted the French language, embedded references to canonical French literature in their work, and promoted France as a land of hospitality, Paris as the world's cultural capital, and French as a "universal" (clear and invariable) language. These "allophone writers of French expression," as Porra (2011, 14) calls them, consciously used French to enhance their positive reception and assure an easier assimilation than that of earlier postcolonial authors. The migrant trajectories emphasized by writers of the 1980s and 1990s, however, are no longer a fruitful point of debate. What, then, does migrant literature look like after identity politics?

THE 2000S: MIGRANT LITERATURE GOES MAINSTREAM

Recent geopolitical upheavals in North Africa and the Middle East have made mass media representations of politically and economically driven migration ubiquitous. Contemporary novels accordingly abound in precarious figures: refugees, asylum seekers, *sans-papiers*, migrant workers, stowaways, sex workers, and victims of forced labor. Some established migrant themes continue into the 2000s: assimilation through the embrace of the French language (Chahdortt Djavann's *Comment peut-on être français?* [2006]), integration as viewed by young protagonists (Laura Alcoba's *Le Bleu des abeilles* [2013]), and fraught social and cultural integration, especially in the banlieues (Khadi Hane's *Des fourmis dans la bouche* [2011], Kidi Bebey's *Mon royaume pour une guitare* [2016], and Magyd Cherfi's *Ma part de Gaulois* [2016]). Narratives of return to the homeland also abound: Toni Cartano's *Milonga* (2004), Brina Svit's *Un cœur de trop* (2006), Fawaz Hussain's *En direction du vent* (2010), Boualem Sansal's *Rue Darwin* (2011), Amin Maalouf's *Les Désorientés* (2012), Alain Mabanckou's *Lumières de Pointe-Noire* (2013), Andrea Salajova's *Eastern* (2015), and René Depestre's *Popa Singer* (2016).

Despite the persistence of such themes, in many recent novels we are far from the representation of cosmopolitan elites and their cultural preoccupations (identity, bilingualism, urban explorations, and the acquisition of the French language), which appeared in 1990s novels by Vassilis Alexakis, Hector Bianciotti, Nancy Huston, and Eduardo Manet, to name but a few. Instead the theme of illegal immigration runs through many texts by French and migrant authors alike. Eliette Abécassis's *Clandestin* (2003), Wilfried N'Sondé's *Le Silence des esprits* (2010), and Julien Delmaire's *Georgia* (2013) all center on the love story between a sans-papiers and a French woman, both equally broken and in search of salvation. The figure of the western European woman who empathizes with a clandestine immigrant and attempts to save him recurs in Olivier Adam's *À l'abri de rien* (2007), Alice Zeniter's *Jusque dans nos bras* (2010), and Isabelle Condou's *Un pays qui n'avait pas de port* (2013). These novels address the themes of self-sacrifice, contract marriages (for nationality papers), and circumventions of the law in the name of humanitarian principles. A political message is conveyed: the need for tolerant attitudes toward undocumented immigrants as an alternative to Europe's anti-immigration policies and policing of borders.

Many novels focus on the Mediterranean region. The sea crossing between Africa and Europe is the subject of Youssef Amghar's *Il était parti dans la nuit* (2004), Rachid El Hamri's *Le Néant bleu* (2005), Marie Redonnet's *Diego* (2005), Boualem Sansal's *Harraga* (2005), Tahar Ben

Jelloun's *Partir* (2006), Mathias Énard's *Rue des voleurs* (2012), and Anne-Marie Carthé's *Azaan* (2016). All of these narratives feature migrant protagonists who undergo trials to reach Europe, usually at high cost. No setting has acquired more literary currency than the Italian isle of Lampedusa, which has occupied the front pages since the early 2000s. Many works have chosen the island as either a main setting or a stop in the migrants' passage to Europe. In Laurent Gaudé's *Eldorado* (2006), Éric-Emmanuel Schmitt's *Ulysse from Bagdad* (2008), Fabienne Kanor's *Faire l'aventure* (2014), Maylis de Kerangal's *À ce stade de la nuit* (2015), and Pascal Manoukian's *Les Échoués* (2015), images of the old continent as both "Eldorado" and "Fortress Europe" alternate. Fatou Diome's *Le Ventre de l'Atlantique* (2005) and *Celles qui attendent* (2011) narrate the sea crossings of Senegalese migrants from the perspectives of the wives and mothers who await their return.

Detention centers, the final destination of many of those making the crossing, also feature prominently. Delphine Coulin's *Samba pour la France* (2011), Hubert Haddad's *Opium Poppy* (2011), Shumona Sinha's *Assommons les pauvres!* (2011), and Carole Zalberg's *Feu pour feu* (2014) offer a hitherto unseen image of Paris: the offices for the stateless, refugees, and asylum seekers. Gauz's *Debout-payé* (2014), Sylvain Pattieu's *Beauté parade* (2016), and Hugo Boris's *Police* (2016) depict the French capital from the viewpoint of undocumented immigrants. Paola Pigani's *Venus d'ailleurs* (2015), Velibor Čolić's *Manuel d'exil: Comment réussir son exil en trente-cinq leçons* (2016), and Gaspard Koening's *Kidnapping* (2016) explore the difficulties of intra-European migration from eastern Europe and the Balkans.

The family saga is another migrant subgenre that expounds on the themes of the migrants' identity and place in France, which novels of the 1980s and 1990s also addressed. Questions of memory and filiation, previously raised by Patrick Modiano, Pierre Michon, Jean Rouaud, and others, are now revisited in light of migration. Migrant protagonists' stories have begun to surface within the broader migrant trajectory of family members. Kim Thúy's *Ru* (2010), Nahal Tajadod's *Elle joue* (2012), Yassaman Montazami's *Le Meilleur des Jours* (2012), Alexandre Civico's *La*

Terre sous les ongles (2015), and Malika Wagner's *Effacer sa trace* (2016) retrace migrants' cultural origins and memories of home. Others delve into family secrets, archival documents, and native countries' history but innovate the migrant genre through historical research (Ali Magoudi's *Un sujet français* [2011], Doan Bui's *Le Silence de mon père* [2016]), road-trip motifs (Ahmed Kalouaz's *Une étoile aux cheveux noirs* [2012]), and trauma narratives (Brigitte Paulino-Neto's *Dès que tu meurs, appelle-moi* [2010], Fabienne Swiatly's *Unité de vie* [2012]).

A subset of family sagas reconstructs the migrant trajectories of their protagonists (usually parents, grandparents, and relatives who have lived through several political regimes). This subset focuses less on French assimilation than on the imbrication of private history and official history, as well as personal and collective memory. Examples of stories that foreground individual lives against the backdrop of turbulent twentieth-century history are Vanessa Schneider's *Tâche de ne pas devenir folle* (2009), Kéthévane Davrichewy's *La Mer noire* (2010) and *L'Autre Joseph* (2016), Sophie Schultze's *Allée 7, rangée 38* (2011), Carole Zalberg's *À défaut d'Amérique* (2012), Katrina Kalda's *Arithmétique des dieux* (2013), Sylvie Weil's *Le Hareng et le Saxophone* (2013), Ahmed Kalouaz's *Les Solitudes se ressemblent* (2014), Guy Scarpetta's *Guido* (2014), Minh Tran Huy's *Voyageur malgré lui* (2014), Valérie Zenatti's *Jacob, Jacob* (2014), Michèle Sarde's *Revenir du silence* (2016), and Geneviève Brisac's *Vie de ma voisine* (2017). Finally, there are novels that explore family legacies, intergenerational conflicts, and cross-cultural values: Abdelkader Djemaï's *Le Nez sur la vitre* (2004), Carlos Batista's *Poulailler* (2005), Stéphanie Janicot's *Dans la tête de Shéhérazade* (2008), Saphia Azzeddine's *La Mecque-Phuket* (2011), Jeanne Benameur's *Ça t'apprendra à vivre* (2012), Faïza Guène's *Un homme, ça ne pleure pas* (2014), Karima Berger's *Mekhtouba* (2016), and Maryam Madjidi's *Marx et la poupée* (2017).

One major development of post-2000 migrant literature is the emergence of French authors who write about migration for a variety of reasons. In addition to those already mentioned, authors and migrant novels include Alain Blottière's *Le Tombeau de Tommy* (2009), Franck Pavloff's *Le Grand Exil* (2009), Pierre Conesa's *Zone de choc* (2011), Frédéric Ciriez's *Mélo*

(2013), and Gaëlle Josse's *Le Dernier Guardien d'Ellis Island* (2014).[14] Some are drawn to the migrant genre because of their own migrant—albeit cosmopolitan—experience (Énard, Ferrier, Prudhomme). Others find inspiration in the works of migrant authors (Ferrier cites Laferrière admiringly in *Sympathie pour le fantôme*). Some fictional narratives humanize migrants, who are otherwise routinely vilified in French political discourse. Antoine Audouard's *L'Arabe* (2009), for instance, is a novelistic response to a xenophobic remark the author had overheard. Zeniter's *Jusque dans nos bras* intervenes frontally in the French debate on national identity. Condou's *Un pays qui n'avait pas de port* was based on a piece of news the author heard about the mistreatment of clandestine immigrants, which incited her to plumb the darkest parts of the human psyche. Abécassis wrote *Clandestin* because she thought it urgent to speak about the state of immigration today. Although not politically engaged, de Kerangal's *À ce stade de la nuit* muses on the sensationalist media coverage of drowned bodies near Lampedusa. Coulin based *Samba pour la France* on her experience of working for La Cimade, an organization that defends migrants' rights. Gaudé's *Eldorado* likewise draws on his 2013 visit to a Syrian refugee camp in Kurdistan. These French authors adopt the voice of migrant writers and the dispossessed without, however, aiming at exotic effects.

Whether deeply aestheticized, overtly politicized, or both, these accounts of contemporary migration seek by and large to raise awareness of the personal costs and social consequences of the immigration crisis. These novels open new windows onto the sociopolitical and demographic changes that French society has recently undergone, as well as the historical roots of recent migrations to France. This appeal to the French literary establishment speaks to French anxieties about its growing immigrant population and declining role in the European Union and the world at large.

This book's investigation of this emerging corpus, while hardly exhaustive, nevertheless illustrates its most salient trends and themes. Chapter 1 explores how the French publishing industry creates demand for migrant novels by emphasizing their material aspects. It outlines the changes that have affected publishing houses in the past few decades, such as the rise in title production, the prevalence of mass-market fiction, and the shift in publishers' function from editing to marketing. Consecration has changed in light of these commercial realities, as the role of publishers in defining and promoting migrant texts will show. Editorial decisions are discernible in the publishing of a book in a particular series, the packaging of migrant novels, and the suggestion of new taxonomies for migrant literature. The first series of case studies considered looks at how the migrant genre is constructed in the marketplace. Format, dust jackets, cover design, blurbs, and reviews come into the analysis of Marie Redonnet's *Diego* (2005), Laurent Gaudé's *Eldorado* (2006), and Delphine Coulin's *Samba pour la France* (2011), which address clandestine immigration. These novels' paratexts highlight at once their literariness, social engagement, and commercial appeal, thus positioning migrant literature as a genre that bridges symbolic, social, and economic forms of capital. A second series of case studies, consisting of three success stories, explores alternative editorial strategies. For instance, the Continents noirs series commodified Henri Lopes's authorial identity, marketing *Une enfant de Poto-Poto* (2012) as a francophone novel through its book design and promotional text, despite the author's resistance to the label. Also examined is Éric-Emmanuel Schmitt's *Ulysse from Bagdad* (2008), which garnered critical and commercial success over time. In May 2016 it was repackaged through the addition of the "writer's diary," which reframes the novel in light of the current "migrant crisis" in Europe. Finally, marketing strategies played a large part in making Gauz's debut novel *Debout-payé* (2014) a best seller. Placing these works in the context of the "desacralization" of literature, this chapter establishes the centrality of marketing to the construction of value. The French publishing industry, it argues, identifies migrant novels as a lucrative genre, in which consecration is synonymous with promotion and houses work in tandem with media to influence reception in ways that depart from traditional procedures of canonization.

Chapter 2 treats an underexplored group of agents of the literary field who have newfound authority as cultural standard bearers: online reviewers who debate, promote, and validate migrant texts via book review websites. Drawing on reception theory, online audience studies, and discourse analysis, the chapter argues that online forms of value-making position migrant literary texts as commodities that bridge professional and popular modes of reception, while attaining national and global readerships. Online reviews have much to say about contemporary digital audiences (which consist of both academic and nonacademic readers) and the role they play in the promotion of migrant literature. In their dual role as consumers and critics online reviewers approach migrant texts in the context of the marketplace (where they purchase and review books), as well as in the context of culture (where they build communities of shared tastes). Technological shifts in the French literary field in the early 2000s—the establishment of Amazon.fr (a subsidiary of Amazon.com), French-language reading forums (Babelio, Critiques Libres, SensCritique), and readers' choice awards (the Prix des Lecteurs/Lectrices de Critiques Libres)—help to explain the emergence of these agents of consecration. The chapter also examines online criticism of two novels by "elite" authors, Milan Kundera's *L'Ignorance* (2003) and Andreï Makine's *La Vie d'un homme inconnu* (2009), to demonstrate the ways in which the heterogeneous practice of online reviewing brings together valuations of aesthetics, authorial biography, politics, and commercial appeal. In the view from online, migrant novels are commodities that should both challenge and entertain.

Chapter 3 explores the Prix littéraire de la Porte Dorée (the Golden Door Literary Prize), an award created in 2010 under the auspices of the Musée national de l'histoire de l'immigration to showcase immigration as constitutive of French history. It uncovers the Porte Dorée's unique mechanisms of consecration among French literary prizes: it creates an archive of contemporary migrant novels; promotes major and minor authors, as well as medium and small presses; and democratizes literary judgment by allowing common readers to participate in jury deliberations. Drawing on James English's and Sylvie Ducas's theorizations of literary prizes as conflating symbolic and economic value, the chapter shows how the Porte Dorée mediates between several types of capital (cultural, economic, social, and political) by legitimizing, popularizing, and politicizing migrant novels. Taking three out of the eight winners to date, it argues that Alice Zeniter's *Jusque dans nos bras* (2010), Michaël Ferrier's *Sympathie pour le fantôme* (2010), and Mathias Énard's *Rue des voleurs* (2012) advocate an ethics of recognition of France's connections with its overseas territories through the themes of shared nationality, memory, and history. Yet the Porte Dorée appropriates these novels' political agendas by sanctioning novels written in French that are published by Parisian presses and conform to the museum's celebratory agenda. Through marketing strategies, the prize encourages collective and comparative readings under the umbrella category of migrant literature, thus shaping the terms in which the texts are read. While the Porte Dorée prize is an instrument of cultural and linguistic hegemony, these novels are examples of commodities endowed with ethical and political value.

Issues of French hegemony also inform the final chapter, which interprets the 2013 election of Dany Laferrière to the Académie française as both the sign of the institution's openness to difference and an act of token multiculturalism that enlists non-French authors in the promotion of the national language. Laferrière's case is singular because he refuses to be instrumentalized for political or linguistic causes, thus bypassing the académie's traditional election criteria (French nationality, French location, and francophilia). As the chapter demonstrates, Laferrière joined the académie on his own terms, as a writer who blurs the boundary between the national and the global. He did so not as a Haitian, Québécois, or francophone author, as the various media suggested, but by simultaneously belonging to and transcending several literary traditions. The author's migrant literary trajectory and current self-positioning can be seen in three of his semi-autobiographical novels. *Comment faire l'amour avec un Nègre sans se fatiguer* (1985) stresses the staging of literary consecration, *Je suis un écrivain japonais* (2008) highlights the constructedness of literary identity, while *L'Énigme du retour* (2009) suggests the notion of interconnected consciousness as a flexible alternative to national identity. These concepts inform the present readings of his two acceptance speeches, on May 26 and 28, 2015, in which Laferrière attempts to reroute French prestige to Haiti and Québec and stage his movement across literary fields. The case of Laferrière is an example of both opportunism and opportunity, as he both accepts the symbolic capital the académie bestows on him (specifically, timeless value and inclusion in the prestigious French patrimony) and invites the conservative institution to redefine itself in relation to other geographical and literary spaces. The merit of his three novels is that they recast the notion of literary identity in light of new categories (the human, the subnational), challenging critics to find new frameworks to investigate recent migrant texts.

A NOTE ON TRANSLATIONS

When available, and for the sake of fluency, English editions are quoted. Unless otherwise noted, all other translations of text from novels and secondary sources are by the author.

1

PRODUCTION

Publishing Houses and Their
Marketing Practices

Consecration, Benoît Denis (2010) explains, is "an act that bestows sanctity." In literary terms it refers to "the action of devoting a text or an author to the sanctity of the literary," that is, of "attributing aesthetic value to them" (para. 12). How does the notion of "transubstantiation," as Denis calls it, or "transformation (from the material to the spiritual, from the economic to the symbolic, from the profane to the sacred)," endure in our present age of cultural commodification (para. 6)? The religious metaphor appears to have lost its relevance in today's processes of literary canonization, which are increasingly carried out by "profane" agents: journalists, average readers, and juries of mass media prizes. The material aspects of books moreover are crucial promotional tools for publishers, who regard books not only as symbolic goods but also as commodities. Although not a new phenomenon, the "desacralization" of literature is an accomplished fact: the cultural reach of literature has diminished, while the once-esteemed author is now considered a mere professional (Ducas 2013, 7). By the 1980s the commercial strategies involved in book promotion and the media's construction of star authors had "altered the symbolic capital of writers" and their works (197). In contemporary acts of consecration, the profane and the sacred, as well as the economic and the symbolic, are no longer binary opposites. Analysis of the marketing of migrant literature reveals the extent to which material aspects overlooked in traditional definitions of consecration—dust jackets, cover design, blurbs, and reviews—now bring about symbolic recognition. Focusing on the French publishing industry and in particular the editorial decisions behind the packaging of books, this chapter establishes the centrality of marketing to migrant novels and to the construction of their value.

In France as elsewhere the publishing industry has experienced profound changes in recent decades due to the impact of globalization and increased commodification of the marketplace. While these changes can be traced to the second half of the nineteenth century, they accelerated exponentially at the turn of the twenty-first (Squires 2009, 2; Rouet 2007, 14). Principal among them are the conglomeration of publishing companies, the rise of title production, the prevalence of mass-market fiction (especially paperbacks and best sellers), and the shift in publishers' function from editing to marketing. The Paris-based multinational conglomerates Lagardère-Hachette and Vivendi-Havas/VUP are the two main groups that dominate the French publishing field through their book distribution system (in large bookstores, specialized points of sale, and supermarkets) (Rouet 2007, 61). They represent formidable competition for medium-sized, small, and independent houses that operate outside their networks. Nonetheless, as Bertrand Legendre and Corinne Abensour (2007) have shown, there exists in France an alternative network of publishers on the margins of multinational conglomerates that are also sources of cultural legitimacy for literary fiction. There are, for instance, smaller presses that join medium-sized groups (Gallimard, Flammarion, Le Seuil, and Albin Michel) to access more efficient publishing and distribution. Smaller houses generally find it difficult to remain economically viable and achieve visibility if they avoid the mediatization of their books and promote long sellers rather than best sellers (Legendre and Abensour 2007, 16). The size of a publishing house, its affiliations to a larger group, and its embrace of the market logic greatly affect the visibility of its products in the marketplace and its capacity to capture the attention of critics, journalists, and prize juries.

The rapid increase in title production, evident since the 1950s, is another significant new feature of the book industry. Overproduction has had important side effects. Books have shorter shelf lives in bookstores, while authors are pressured to supply the market with new texts at regular intervals and, if possible, to time their publication to coincide with the *rentrée littéraire*. In turn publishers issue new releases and republications of out-of-print books, sometimes in expanded editions to enhance their commercial appeal. The market logic that drives literary production has altered the mechanisms of literary promotion and legitimation, contributing further to the commodification of literature. The development of large-scale distribution of mass-market fiction and the imperatives of commercial success no doubt prevail (Rouet 2007, 160–61).

This commercial logic can be brought into relief by comparing the different print runs for mass-market fiction (romance novels, thrillers, science fiction) and literary fiction (including migrant novels). Books by popular authors, which target mass audiences, are issued in large numbers: Amélie Nothomb's *Le Crime du comte Neville* had a 180,000-copy print run and Anna Gavalda's *Billie* had a print run of 300,000 copies.[1] In contrast the print runs of migrant novels, which appeal to mass readers as well as educated audiences, often range between 2,000 and 9,000 copies: Puértolas's *L'Extraordinaire Voyage* was issued in 2,222 copies, Zalberg's *Feu pour feu* in 4,500 copies, Montazami's *Le Meilleur des Jours* in 6,500 copies, and Davrichewy's *L'Autre Joseph* in 8,500 copies.[2] Only later, through literary prizes or exceptional commercial success, can publishers increase print runs for literary fiction. For example, Kamel Daoud's (nonmigrant novel) *Meursault, contre-enquête* (2014) was initially printed in a 3,000-copy run. After being shortlisted for the Goncourt and the Renaudot and winning the Prix François-Mauriac and the Prix des cinq continents de la francophonie, Actes Sud had reprinted up to 50,000 copies by November 2014.[3]

The *livre de poche* (literally, "pocket book" format, or paperback) series, created in the second half of the twentieth century by Gallimard, Flammarion, Le Seuil, and Albin Michel, is an example of editorial adaptation to the marketplace. In 1953 La Librairie générale française, a subsidiary of Hachette, launched Le Livre de poche, a paperback series (Le Livre de poche is now an imprint of Hachette-Livre and Albin Michel). Le Seuil followed suit with its Points series in 1970 and Gallimard with Folio in 1972. Publishing houses specializing exclusively in paperbacks also appeared. Flammarion created the paperback imprint J'ai lu in 1958, while Presses de la Cité founded Presses Pocket in 1962 (now known as Pocket) and Éditions Points in 2006. The success of the paperback format in France is due to its low price, attractive covers, and wide availability in bookstores, points of sale, supermarkets, and on the Internet. A book subsequently republished in paperback by and large sells extremely well, enough to reach mass readerships. Consider, for example, David Foenkinos's *La Délicatesse*, published by Gallimard in August 2009 and priced at €16.25. The paperback edition, issued by Folio in January 2011 at €6.20, had sold 778,700 copies by the end of 2011.[4] The price difference also explains the popularity of paperbacks, which in 2011 represented the majority of the books featured on *Livres Hebdo*'s Top 50 list of best sellers.[5]

More important, paperbacks democratize reading by making literary works of aesthetic or long-term value, such as classics and literary fiction, more available than before. By disseminating "good" literature for a mass readership, and thus conflating symbolic and economic capital, paperbacks acquire "a popular legitimacy" deriving from traditional cultural recognition (Ducas 2013, 94). Migrant novels issued in paperback illustrate well this intermediary positioning between popular and academic forms of consecration.[6] Paperbacks are also a major ground for competitions among publishers and are ideal for implementing new advertising techniques.[7] Through marketing and large-scale distribution, paperbacks, more so than original editions, consecrate authors and works.

The best seller also holds a special place in the contemporary literary marketplace. Certain works make it onto best-seller lists through strategic marketing and intense mediatization. With each year's abundant literary production, publishing houses resort to standard advertising (e.g., simply placing a work in bookstores), except for a few works marked for strategic advertising and potential commercial success (Rouet 2007, 180).[8] Best sellers are commonly thought to be closer, in a Bourdieusian sense, to the economic pole of cultural production. However, there exists a type of fiction positioned for double achievement that combines aesthetic merit and financial gain. Marie-Pierre Pouly (2016) calls such a book "a literary bestseller," that is, "a two-sided cultural product that aims at long-term consecration based on autonomous literary criteria and short-term commercial success thanks to wide-ranging marketing strategies" (20). Migrant novels fall into this category. Their narrative strategies, as well as their editors' advertising techniques, enable them to reach a double audience. The fact that canonized authors of migrant novels (e.g., Tahar Ben Jelloun, Milan Kundera) stand on this list alongside commercially popular ones (e.g., Romain Puértolas, Éric-Emmanuel Schmitt) reflects the conflation of these values. As Laura Miller (2000) explains, best-seller lists at best indicate literary tastes in a given historical moment, rather than aesthetic value, and should therefore be understood as "powerful marketing tools" (286). After making the best-seller list, books in France are routinely packaged with a strip advertising their best-seller status. The list, then, is an index of the production of belief in the value of literary works.

Finally, market pressures have affected the editorial field. As Claire Squires (2009) states, "[t]he switch from an editorial emphasis to a sales and marketing one has [. . .] arguably elevated the principle of commerce above that of culture" (47). The commercialization of contemporary writing has altered the traditional function of editors, turning them into book promoters. This process, however, dates to the turn of the twentieth century with the transformation of family businesses into large publishing groups (Ducas 2013, 17). Editors now compete through the creation of unique brands or distinctive series, as well as through book reviews and advertising space in bookstores and points of sale (Rouet 2007, 20). In a celebrity culture books are marketed by the author (especially if young, mediagenic, and ethnically different) and entered in literary prize competitions. Press catalogs moreover serve as promotional tools, offering information about authors' prizes and excerpts from laudatory reviews. The aggressive insertion of publicity into the launching of books and their authors, claims Sylvie Ducas (2013), has important consequences for editors' target readership (23). In recent decades editors have appealed less and less to elite readers and increasingly to mass audiences. Smaller presses succeed in expanding their readership through the unexpected commercial success of a few books. The editor Sylvie Gracia explains that Le Rouergue's La brune series was able to transition from the image of "a serious series that sells little" to one that reaches wider audiences when Claudie Gallay's *Les Déferlantes* and Marie-Sabine Roger's *La Tête en friche* sold three hundred thousand and seventy thousand copies, respectively.[9] An expanded mass audience, a hierarchical publishing industry, competitions between small presses and large publishing groups, paperback series, and best-seller lists: these are the contexts for the publishing of contemporary migrant literature in France.

Who publishes migrant fiction in France? Publishers of migrant novels include old, well established houses (Gallimard, Albin Michel, Flammarion, Plon), medium-sized houses (Actes Sud), and a few small and independent presses founded at the end of the twentieth century (Liana Levi, Sabine Wespieser, L'Olivier, L'Iconoclaste). Éditions de l'Olivier, founded in 1991, specializes in French literature as well as foreign translations and publishes approximately thirty-five new titles annually. Its cosmopolitan and borderless vision of literature shapes its packaging strategies. L'Olivier refuses to distinguish between French and foreign literature, or fiction and nonfiction; no generic markers appear on its dust jackets. L'Olivier recently published migrant novels by French authors Olivier Adam and Antoine Audouard and by Indian-born Shumona Sinha. However, the only clues to the migrant genre that appear on their covers are the words "refugees," "asylum seekers," and "migrants," which are incorporated into plot synopses. The press renders migrant texts a natural part of French literature without relegating them to a special group or to the peripheral category of francophone literature.

Éditions L'Iconoclaste, founded in 1995, is another home for migrant texts. A highly selective press, it conceives of the publisher primarily as an editor rather than a book promoter. It publishes only a handful of books a year but devotes great care to their content and material aspects. L'Iconoclaste evinces, as its promotional material states, "a taste for books that are refined, yet accessible to all," attempting to reconcile a view of book culture as simultaneously upmarket and popular. A publisher of renowned migrant authors such as Nancy Huston, François Cheng, and Atiq Rahimi, L'Iconoclaste achieved visibility on the migrant literary market when Doan Bui's *Le Silence de mon père* won the Prix littéraire de la Porte Dorée in 2016. Despite its claim to publish works "outside of the laws of marketing," L'Iconoclaste escapes neither the commodified context of today's literary publishing nor prize juries' valorization of fashionable genres.[10]

Migrant literature is in vogue. Several presses have not surprisingly created series centered on francophone and migrant themes. For instance, Éditions du Rouergue's La brune series, created in 1998 by Sylvie Gracia (herself an author of migrant fiction), publishes novels by Ahmed Kalouaz and Samira Sedira. And Gallimard's Continents noirs series, running since 2000, focuses on francophone African authors. In 2013 Le Seuil published the Raconter la vie book series, directed by Pierre Rosanvallon and comprising testimonials by immigrants who feel marginalized in France and who use the series as a forum for inserting their personal stories into French history. The books, issued in hard copy and digital editions, are organized around thematic clusters. One subseries, Histoire de migrants, for instance, includes autobiographical and testimonial narratives such as Dedie Sabwe Masumboko's *J'ai peu d'espoir*, Adeline R.'s *Je porte un nom d'exil*, and *Quand nous sommes arrivés en France*, written by high school students of migrant origin. Éditions Autrement created the Français d'ailleurs series for children ages nine to thirteen, which presents the history of immigration to France from the viewpoint of an immigrant child. Each book, authored by Valentine Goby and richly illustrated, addresses a particular period of French history: *Anouche ou la fin de l'errance: De l'Arménie à la valée du Rhone* (2010), *Antonio ou la résistance: De l'Espagne à la région toulousaine* (2011), or *Thiên An ou la grande traversée: Du Vietnam à Paris XIIIe* (2014), for example.

Far from offering a complete portrait of the newest publishing houses for migrant literature, these examples signal the existence of a marketplace of small and medium-sized presses that approach the production of migrant literature in different ways. Whereas some presses regard migrant texts as a natural outgrowth of the French literary tradition, others embrace them for their value as an exotic supplement to their permanent collections. Still other presses attempt to treat literary works as artifacts, as if they were immune to commercial forces. However, no text exists outside the marketplace. Editorial decisions shape the reception of migrant novels in important ways.

THE MIGRANT GENRE IN THE MARKETPLACE

When defining the genre of migrant literature, scholars tend to focus on the poetics of migrant texts, tracing shared themes and hybrid styles, as well as the texts' global circulation and uneasy fit within a single literary and linguistic tradition. Yet literary taxonomies are no doubt influenced by publishers and their marketing departments, which carefully package the novels, positioning them in relation to genre conventions, similar works by other authors, and niche audiences. The cover, the title, the author's name, and the back-cover blurbs—what Gérard Genette (1997) calls the "paratext" (2)—all signal a text's conformity to, or departure from, a given genre. Material aspects such as these and the marketing techniques around them create and reinforce generic parameters. Marketing has obvious practical implications, as taxonomies are necessary for placing a book in the appropriate section of a bookstore. But it also constructs value by highlighting a text's literariness or its commercial orientation. Preliminary clues offered by the paratext guide readers either to engage in reading or to browse further and look at another book. As Genette argues, "[m]ore than a boundary or a sealed border, the paratext is, rather, a *threshold*, or—a word Borges used a propos of a preface—a 'vestibule' that offers the world at large the possibility of either stepping inside or turning back" (1–2, original emphasis). Genette further divides the paratext into the "peritext," which includes paratextual elements within the book (the title, the preface, chapter titles, etc.), and the "epitext," which consists of elements located outside the book (interviews, conversations, diaries, and rough drafts) (5). An interface between the text and the reader, the paratext allows publishers to single out books and genres in a crowded market. Close attention to the materiality of migrant texts, then, is one way of stressing their status as commodities, even in the case of novels that would have traditionally appealed to audiences for their aesthetic value. The novel itself is today a highly commodified genre, as it always has been.

In *Genres in Discourse* Tzvetan Todorov (1990) locates genres on a historical continuum: they always emerge in reaction to previous genres and operate within society's ideological frameworks. As he states, "[i]t is because genres exist as an institution that they function as 'horizons of expectation' for readers and as 'models of writing' for authors" (18). In defining genre as an institution, Todorov underscores its ability to mediate between texts and contexts, to weave ties among authors, readers, and other agents of the cultural field, and to emphasize social norms and values as models to be reckoned with. Generic conventions, institutionally constructed and sanctioned, structure readers' reactions to texts and authors' strategies of writing—in agreement with or in opposition to dominant genres. As far as migrant literature goes, generic labels such as "migrant writer" or "migrant novel" exert their agency in the literary field, placing authors in rigid positions they then find difficult to transcend. Many authors have reacted to categorizations they considered restrictive of their creative freedom. Vassilis Alexakis, for instance, contested literary critics' reductive labels in the opening chapter of his semiautobiographical *Paris-Athènes* (1989) before moving on to the narrative. In her latest works Ying Chen has deliberately dissociated herself from the migrant genre and its readerly expectations. This was a reaction to critics' reception of *Les Lettres chinoises* (1993), a novel that brought her great critical acclaim but also slotted her into the "migrant writer" position. In contrast authors such as Éric-Emmanuel Schmitt and Julien Delmaire have intervened in the migrant genre by respecting its privileged intertexts (*The Odyssey* in *Ulysse from Bagdad*) and thematic tropes (illegal immigration in *Georgia*), respectively.

While literary critics follow generic taxonomies, labels such as "migrant novel" rarely appear on book covers. Categorizations of genre in the publishing industry are suggested by paratextual elements such as the title, cover illustration, plot summary, and review excerpts. Whereas Todorov points out the ties between genres and prevailing social structures, Claire Squires (2009), drawing on the field of publishing studies, defines genre as "the literary taxonomies that develop through marketing" (14). She stresses that genre, as a marketing concept, has both commercial and aesthetic implications. Categories of genre not only position and sell books in the marketplace but also create cultural meanings by relating books to the social contexts that valorize one novelistic type over another. Squires's definition of marketing is broad, and it covers activities including editorial strategies, book media reception, best-seller lists, and literary prize competitions. The following analysis will focus on just one of these marketing aspects, namely "the decisions publishers make in terms of the presentation of books to the marketplace, in terms of formats, cover designs and blurbs, and imprint" (2). It combines close attention to the marketing of novels' "migrant" aspects with an examination of how migrant texts dialogue with ideological contexts, in line with Todorov's argument.

Marie Redonnet's *Diego* (2005), Laurent Gaudé's *Eldorado* (2006), and Delphine Coulin's *Samba pour la France* (2011) tackle the theme of illegal immigration. Although issued by different presses and divergent in style and perspective, the novels display similar packaging strategies that emphasize the role of the plot synopsis in defining their relevance to the migrant genre. A comparison between these different texts reveals how paratextual strategies lead to new taxonomies and, in this case, to the formation of a subgenre of migrant literature that we may call illegal, clandestine, or even *sans-papiers* literature.[11] The book jackets of all three reveal how paratextual strategies position migrant literature as a genre that narrativizes the experience of migration, begetting in the process particular authorial strategies, readerly responses, and appeals to niche audiences. Individually and collectively these cases demonstrate how material features underscore at once the symbolic and commercial value of migrant novels and place them in relation to existing models of writing or conceptions of literature.

Marie Redonnet's *Diego* was published by Éditions de Minuit, a prestigious house that was founded in 1941 during the German occupation and published books clandestinely until the liberation of Paris in 1944. Known for the literary quality of its texts, it boasts a rich catalog of works by renowned authors such as Georges Bataille, Maurice Blanchot, Samuel Beckett, Alain Robbe-Grillet, Nathalie Sarraute, and Marguerite Duras, as well as works by contemporary experimental novelists such as Marie NDiaye and Éric Chevillard. White, unadorned covers are an unmistakable signature of this elite publishing house. The paratext is reduced to the bare minimum. Commercial information is absent from the back cover, which simply includes an excerpt from the novel. The book lets the text speak for itself. Yet, looking further, one discovers that the paratext intersects with the novelistic text in subtle ways.

Diego's back-cover blurb reads, "I am no longer in prison, I left Tamza and I have just arrived in France. But anxiety never leaves me. I tell myself: 'I am a free man.' I know this is not true. I arrived in France without a visa. I'm an illegal immigrant [*un clandestin*]. I didn't go through Customs. I don't reside legally on French soil. I'm free as long as the police don't ask for my identity papers. I can't live normally in France. I must live here like an illegal immigrant." This is the anguished voice of Diego Aki, who struggles to forget his traumatized past as a resistance fighter in Africa and to make a new life in France from the margins. Writing is central to Diego's survival. He attempts to heal by writing a film script that narrates his experiences as an illegal immigrant in France, but by means of a fictional double named Samir. It is only by fictionalizing his life that he can give voice to his traumatic experiences. *Diego* is thus a meditation on the restorative capacities of fiction—an overriding theme that the cover blurb intentionally omits. The plot synopsis gives away very little, in fact, almost freezing Diego in a liminal state, caught between being physically present in France and socially invisible, and between a desire to enjoy his newfound freedom and a need to avoid detection.

It is precisely this scarcity of plot-related details that underlines the novel's style. Diego voices his thoughts in simple, straightforward, and abrupt sentences that give readers pause. The repetition of the word *clandestin* inscribes the novel into the sans-papiers subgenre, prefiguring the themes of otherness, marginality, and inhospitality and shaping readers' "horizon of expectations" (Jauss 1982, 79). As Warren Motte (2008) notes, "more than anything else, that word *clandestin*, as Redonnet deploys it, designates the stranger, the foreigner, the 'other' who is characterized by his or her radical difference with regard to the social majority.... Diego the *clandestin* provides Redonnet with an acute lens through which to view French society, and to interrogate its norms from the outside in, as it were" (46). The back cover's poignant voice and its outsider's gaze on French society are the only clues that unfamiliar readers might get about Redonnet's perspective on clandestine immigration. As Motte points out, the novel is in fact a critique of the racism of French society, which appears to have lost its status as a safe haven for immigrants and refugees. Redonnet's and, in turn, Diego's interrogations of French attitudes on immigration set the novel on a new path of social engagement, which departs from the apolitical content of the author's previous works.

While *Diego* offers a moving story about illegal immigration, it is not a militant text, as some migrant novels are. Nor does it sensationalize the plight of clandestine immigrants, which is a frequent approach in migrant literature. The novel's avoidance of sentimentality might in part explain why it has achieved little critical and commercial success. Except for the positive reviews in *L'Humanité* and *L'Express* shortly after its publication in October 2015, *Diego* is absent from literary prize competitions and best-seller lists and has not been reissued in paperback. Generic markers position the novel as a migrant narrative that should appeal to general audiences. The blurb's foregrounding of Redonnet's deceptively simple style, via Diego's voice, as well as the novel's publication with a less market-oriented press, nevertheless suggests that *Diego* is endowed with primarily aesthetic value and, in light of its new commitment to the social world, political value. A commodity nonetheless, *Diego* is a novel packaged in the "great books" tradition that raises questions of social and political responsibility and of the capacities and limits of writing to confront it.

Gaudé's *Eldorado* was published by Éditions J'ai lu, a press that issues books, especially new releases, in paperback. The pocket-book format suggests a pitch to mass readership; it is worth noting the great variety of genre fiction in J'ai lu's catalog: science fiction, fantasy, detective, and romance novels, among other genres. The front-cover illustration for *Eldorado* features a small boat idly floating on the sea, carrying a few men and a woman who holds an umbrella to shield herself from the sun. The author's name, in purple, and the title, in red, are printed on a pink background that obscures the line separating the sky from the sea. The title, image, and colors present a tranquil representation of migration that runs counter to the message of the back cover. There, in an excerpt from the middle of the novel, the inner voice of a Sudanese character states that "[n]o border allows you to pass calmly. They all wound."

A plot summary located below the excerpt describes the setting and piques reader interest. It connects the border-crossing narrative to the socioeconomic contexts of recent migrations familiar to readers. Its first sentence depicts the harsh realities of the immigrants' journeys: "To flee poverty and reach 'Eldorado,' emigrants risk their lives on make-shift boats . . . before being ruthlessly pushed back by coastguards, when they haven't already fallen prey to unscrupulous smugglers." The next sentences focus on the novel's hero, Capt. Salvatore Piracci, who, as a patrol guard between Lampedusa and Catania, confronts a never-ending ethical dilemma: "Captain Piracci is among those who crisscross the sea to look for illegal immigrants [*clandestins*], sometimes saving them from drowning. But is death worse than a broken dream? By hearing a young woman's survival story, Salvatore lets compassion and humanity win over his certainties." The plot summary meets two objectives. Through terms such as "smugglers," "coastguards," and "illegal immigrants," it anchors the story in a contemporary setting, indicating a new type of migrant literature that draws on global sociopolitical phenomena and media coverage of the Mediterranean. Yet the novel goes beyond the media accounts that treat immigrants as mere statistics to explore the consciousness of an individual who comes to understand the migrant experience up close. The plot summary underscores the humanist dimension of *Eldorado*, which, though inspired by real events, explores the interiority of a character through its fictional narrative. Captain Piracci experiences a change of heart, the synopsis informs us, turning from merciless pursuer to noble savior.

The story of *Eldorado* promises insurmountable obstacles, ethical choices, and inner change—the very ingredients foregrounded in *L'Express*'s review excerpt of the novel, also featured on the back: "Voyage of initiation, sacrifice, revenge, redemption: the novelist, known for his dry lyricism, uses the themes of Greek tragedy with epic force." The review abstract and its positioning at the center of the back cover reinforce *Eldorado*'s "dramatic" elements. Implicitly the excerpt alludes to *The Odyssey*, Homer's epic that prefigures the promise and pitfalls of contemporary exile at sea. As the review suggests, *Eldorado* adapts a literary classic for the present day. To further *Eldorado*'s appeal to literary-minded readers, the paratext includes Gaudé's biographical information, printed in gold, covering his career as a playwright and novelist and his literary awards, the Goncourt and the Goncourt des lycéens among them. Through the pocket-book format and adventure-driven synopsis, J'ai lu promises an accessible and entertaining read, as well as a thought-provoking contribution to the long history of European travel literature.[12]

Coulin's *Samba pour la France* was first published in 2011 in Éditions du Seuil's prestigious Cadre rouge series (home to renowned authors such as Édouard Glissant, Elie Wiesel, Tahar Ben Jelloun, and Lydie Salvayre) and reprinted in 2014 in paperback by Éditions Points. The reprint edition preserves Le Seuil's front cover image: a close-up of the face of a black man looking anxiously over his shoulder. A red slip serves as a promotional tool, informing readers that the book inspired Éric Toledano and Olivier Nakache's film adaptation, *Samba*. The plot synopsis on the back cover sets the scene in a simple, exhortative tone: "Run, Samba, run! Thus spoke Uncle Lamouna in the village when they were flying a kite. Samba is no longer in Mali, but in Paris. He loves France, he struggled to get here, and worked hard. But France no longer wants him: without a residence permit, he can't stay. Run, Samba, to escape the police, poverty, bitterness. . . . If you want to survive, run, Samba, run!" Samba, who has lived in France for ten years, seeks to legalize his status but is then arrested and faces deportation from a center for clandestine immigrants. The blurb frames the sans-papiers novel as a love (between an illegal immigrant and his host country) gone wrong. The acquired patriotism of illegal immigrants and the limits of French hospitality clash in violent confrontation. A back-cover excerpt from the novel reinforces this idea: "In vain he told himself that France didn't want him; it didn't stop him from wanting it. On the contrary."

Love for the French language and culture is a recurrent trope in migrant literature, one that migrant authors use to position themselves within the French literary field. Coulin, however, is French and shifts attention from elite to illegal immigrants. Her aim is not to curry favor with French literary critics but to undercut the ideology of French cultural prestige and, by extension, its ties to the nation's intransigent laws and inhospitality toward those seeking integration. Coulin herself has engaged in asylum seekers' causes in Paris. In *Samba pour la France*, she gives voice to marginalized immigrants like the ones she has interviewed. It is no accident that the book cover places Coulin's picture alongside the novel excerpt to suggest the imbrication of political engagement and fiction writing. The novel itself illustrates the authorial position of "speaking for" the Other. Yet it does so in nondocumentary fashion and without appropriating the illegal immigrants' voice (the novel uses a detached third-person narration). To enhance *Samba*'s cultural legitimacy, the author's picture and biography are followed by review excerpts from *Le Monde* and *Télérama*. The first review excerpt, "[a] great book," is broad-brush. The second review is more explicit: "[a] politically engaged novel [*un roman engagé*], poetic and vindictive." In *Le Monde*'s full review, however, Fabienne Dumontet depicts the character Samba as a contemporary version of Homer's Odysseus and Alfred Jarry's Ubu because his odyssey refers not only to his voyage from Africa but also to the labyrinthine corridors of institutional power he has to traverse once in France.[13] The book design, in contrast, emphasizes only the political aspect of the novel, presumably to target a mass readership interested more in the topic of illegal immigration than in the intertextual elements of Coulin's work. Paratextual elements such as cover blurbs, more than reviews in literary magazines, shape readers' tastes and horizons of expectations.

Migrant novels such as those of Redonnet, Gaudé, and Coulin walk the fine line between two seemingly contradictory tendencies: one that values social engagement and another that insists on the literariness of texts. But the combination of social and symbolic capital is an ideal recipe for commercial success. Marginality is lucrative, and publishers use paratextual strategies that exploit both content and form. The next three case studies reveal how migrant texts are made to stand out through additional marketing practices: series development, new packaging techniques, and the inclusion of "writers' journals." Henri Lopes's *Une enfant de Poto-Poto*, Gauz's *Debout-payé*, and Éric-Emmanuel Schmitt's *Ulysse from Bagdad* represent three critically and commercially successful migrant texts. Yet their marketing histories follow different paths.

MARKETING IDENTITY: *UNE ENFANT DE POTO-POTO*

The representation of African countries' French colonial legacy is an oft-explored topic in francophone literature. One example is Henri Lopes's *Une enfant de Poto-Poto*, published in 2012, which examines hybrid identities, the attachment to origins, the global travels of the cultural elite, and the critique of a literary industry that exoticizes nonmetropolitan authors. Lopes's originality, however, is his shifting the issue of postcolonial identity to its literary reception in Europe and North America. His protagonists are writers acutely aware of the implications of writing about Africa in French for a French-language audience—a *mise en abyme* of Lopes's situation as a migrant writer in France. The author both produces francophone African fiction and reflects on the processes of its reception overseas. It is no wonder then that *Une enfant de Poto-Poto* was published in Éditions Gallimard's Continents noirs series and won the 2012 Prix littéraire de la Porte Dorée. It reflects the very mechanisms of valuation favored by these institutional agents and their overriding interest in fictional representations of a racially and linguistically diverse France.

The Continents noirs series has issued works by African and African diasporic writers since 2000. Gallimard's promotional text describes it as an "identitarian" series that examines its authors' triple identity: local, universal, singular.[14] The series' book design underscores issues of origins; each jacket features a handful of laterite, or native red soil, against a pale-yellow background. The ethnic-identitarian series thus markets Lopes as a francophone author, despite his residing in France and publishing his previous novels in Paris. The francophone label is important for his reception since francophone literature is a marketable product. Indeed various literary series (Le Seuil's Cadre rouge or Actes Sud's Afriques) and specialized presses (Dapper, Karthala, Le Serpent à Plumes, L'Harmattan, and Présence Africaine) that focus on African literature have emerged in France in the 2000s to satisfy the French public's taste for exotic fiction. In their focus on exotic identity such collections are "sites of ghettoization and stigmatization" rather than literary recognition (Ducas 2013, 205). When African authors marketed as francophone win French literary prizes fur-thermore, they are often commended for their foreign flavor (Ducas 2013, 207). It is significant that Lopes would publish his novel in France rather than Africa. Authors who reside in France can attract French publishers' attention more easily than Africa-based authors can. Lopes belongs to the African cultural elite and has served as Congo's ambassador to France since 1998. He has also published numerous fictional works centered on hybridity. An already consecrated writer—he received the 1993 Grand Prix de la Francophonie de l'Académie française—Lopes possesses the cultural capital to be coveted by major French publishers and to stand out in literary prize competitions.

Une enfant de Poto-Poto depicts a love triangle involving a literature teacher and writer, Émile Franceschini, and two friends and rivals: Péla-gie, who becomes his wife, and Kimia, who will intermittently be his lover. Set during Congo and Brazzaville's decolonization period (from the 1960s to the present), the text examines issues related to the coun-try's cultural and linguistic independence: the difficult choice between French and Lingala in the public sphere, as well as Congolese students' thwarted dreams of studying in France. Kimia—the novel's first-person narrator, an emerging writer in Congo and abroad—is Lopes's fictional alter ego. Influenced by her literary mentor Franceschini, she becomes aware of the condition that plagues postcolonial authors like her: she is torn between loyalty to her ethnic origins and the embrace of a universal, rootless conception of literature, and between eschewing and exploring hybridity in her work. Franceschini himself is an ambivalent authorial role model. He passes as white but is a racially mixed and ardent supporter of African languages and cultures. In his literature classes he extols the power of indigenous languages to capture African realities and posit an alternative to African writers' slavish imitation of French and European literary models. White skin, black mask—to reverse Franz Fanon's famous terms—could aptly depict a man who, as Lopes (2012) writes, "wanted to belong to this country. If there had been beauty products to blacken his skin and make his hair frizzy, he would have ruined himself" (263). Yet Franceschini is also wary of the risk of political and literary nationalisms. As Kimia points out, "at the same time, he taught us to become human beings. From here and elsewhere" (263).

Both Franceschini and Kimia strive to be plural while black and to accommodate their hybridity and African roots in their literary works. In focusing on Kimia's successful literary career in the United States, the novel draws attention to the symbolic value of African authors' literary identity in the French-language marketplace and to their strategic self-positioning vis-à-vis institutional pressures. Kimia's dilemma, which resonates with many diasporic authors, is how to position herself in both the national and global literary spheres. On the one hand she wonders how to be a francophone author in an anglophone country like the United States, where her Africanness differs from the local African American identity. On the other she searches for ways of being a francophone author in postcolonial Africa. In Congo, for instance, it is her elite Parisian accent that sets her apart from her fellow Congolese and their hybridized French.

The second half of the novel explores Kimia's simultaneous resentment of the global market's demands of exoticism and the concomitant temptations to benefit from the lucre her perceived exoticism begets. Scenes featuring editors' pressures and readers' expectations abound. Kimia's media appearances, global book tours, and lectures on African identity contribute to the pressures she feels to produce consumable fiction. To increase readership, her agent dramatically markets her biography as that of "a black woman from a former French colony, who immigrated in the United States because France refused her right to asylum" (153). Kimia's angry retort to a routine journalistic question—she describes herself as "a writer *tout court*" rather than "a Congolese, African, American, French, or francophone writer" (170)—proves a boon to her career moreover, as scandals boost sales. Aware that her ethnic origin represents cultural capital in the Global North–dominated literary marketplace, Kimia ponders the weight of literary labels on her creative freedom and the way they affect her view of readers. She deplores the fact that "today, it's through the mass media that authors capture readers. They're interested in our persona, not in our work" (204). Moreover, to her, book-signing sessions turn the author-reader relationship into a prostitute-client transaction (172). Kimia deplores the current condition of the novelist, whose image is constructed by agents and intensely mediatized. She insists that authors should be consecrated by their works, not their biography. Yet Kimia's novels, which deliberately "cultivate Congolese terms," cannot easily be read outside of the framework of identity politics (129). It is a dilemma to which Lopes himself can easily relate.

The questions the novel asks, through Kimia's case, speak to the current issues of literary commodification and prize culture. But the text's self-reflexivity and linguistically hybrid style are themselves salable in the literary marketplace (Brouillette 2011, 5). Despite Lopes's aim to contest the rigid literary categories defined within the traditional francophone context of production and reception, his novel was nevertheless chosen for being written, as several Prix littéraire de la Porte Dorée jury members put it, "in a 'Congolized' French language," "in a French lightly colored by exotic touches," and "in a classical and elegant style."[15] Reviewers moreover underscored the novel's optimistic approach, timely themes, and ambition to offer "a lesson of History and hope."[16]

In truth Lopes himself does little to prevent exotic readings; instead he meets readers' expectations when he inserts etymological explanations of italicized Lingala terms for non-African publics: "*dipanda*, an invented word to translate independence in *our language*" (9), "the

Mindélés (white people)" (13), or "'Quitte-là' ['Leave it'] doesn't have the meaning it has in France. In Congo, this means 'Stop talking nonsense' or 'Who do you take me for?'" (100). Through a didactic tone Lopes addresses an imagined general public that needs instruction on Congolese culture. His self-reflexivity also points to an implied academic readership, itself highly aware of its ways of consuming culturally hybrid writers and texts. Lopes faces an aporetic situation; all he can do is look forward to a future free of identity politics, when hybridity will be a moot point. As Kimia anticipates, "[i]n a few decades, maybe in less than a century, there will no longer be mixed people, but French, Congolese, Senegalese, American, white, black, brown people. . . . People of 'pure' origins will no longer dare to praise what will become the norm" (235). Hybridity will no longer be exotic in a world in which mixed national and racial identities are fully recognized. For now Lopes's novel must walk the seemingly contradictory line between praising hybridity as a mark of cultural enrichment and critiquing its exoticization by the forces of the marketplace.

DEBOUT-PAYÉ AND THE BEST-SELLER LIST

Clotilde Coquet's *Parle-moi du sous-sol* (2014), Bruno Deniel-Laurent's *L'Idiot du palais* (2014), Gauz's *Debout-payé* (2014), and Sylvain Pattieu's *Beauté parade* (2015) have woven their stories around working-class characters such as cashiers, security guards, and cosmeticians in the hypercommercial world of department stores and beauty salons. Although they all explore to varying degrees the links between labor, immigration, and consumerism, it was *Debout-payé* that became a best seller and media phenomenon. *Debout-payé* was chosen as the best debut novel in *Lire*'s 2014 list of the best books of the year, and it occupied sixteenth place on *Lire*'s best-seller list for the month from September 15 to October 12, 2014, and seventeenth place on *Livres Hebdo*'s list of the fifty best-selling novels for the week of September 22–28, 2014 (while remaining on the list for fifteen more weeks in 2014). What were the chances for a first novel by an unknown author from a small press to be a best seller? The achievement was in large part due to the marketing strategies and publicity campaign of Benoît Virot, the editor of Le Nouvel Attila, a small press founded in 2007 under the name Éditions Attila and revamped in 2013. Le Nouvel Attila specializes in contemporary French literature, especially hybrid or unclassifiable genres, and publishes only a few carefully selected and exquisitely designed books a year. Great attention to format and cover design went into the production of *Debout-payé*, which, according to the house's promotional material, had been reprinted nine times and had sold fifty-five thousand copies by 2015. The savvy marketing has paid off, as the novel has earned Le Nouvel Attila both financial return and cultural legitimation, while making Virot well known primarily as "Gauz's publisher."[17]

Debout-payé recounts the story of two generations of Ivorian immigrants in France, from the 1960s to the early 2000s, against the backdrop of changing immigration policies. The characters André and Ferdinand immigrated in search of a better education in the 1960s and 1970s, before the hardening of immigration laws during the Giscard d'Estaing presidency. As the narrator puts it, with the introduction of the *carte de séjour* (residency card) in 1974, "[a] new breed of citizens has been created overnight: the sans-papiers" (59). The characters Ossiri and Kassoum, by contrast, left for France in the 1990s to explore the world and escape poverty, respectively. Gauz playfully organizes the history of African immigration to France by "ages"—"The Bronze Age 1960–1980" (39), "the Golden Age 1990–2000" (85), and the post–September 2011 "Lead Age" (137). Later generations follow in their predecessors' footsteps: they too become low-income security guards and experience French racism. The novel inscribes the story of this "inherited" occupation in the broader history of African immigration to France, while drawing the portrait of a community of mostly undocumented immigrants whose employment renders them invisible observers of French society. In particular through the character of Ossiri, who works at the women's clothing store Camaïeu and at Sephora on the Champs-Élysées, Gauz satirizes today's materialistic society. Wealthy French and international customers flock to these stores to try, buy, and sometimes steal their products, while security guards—the marginalized and the dispossessed—are there to protect what is for them unattainable. It is an intertwined narrative of immigration and globalization in which commodities and the global elite traverse borders that the sans-papiers (poor, black, unskilled) cannot.

Despite the dark theme, *Debout-payé* inserts Ossiri's comic observations into the narrative. Written in the form of brief notes, which appear to have been jotted down quickly, the observations run the gamut from customer conversations to retail branding techniques to the buying practices of different nationalities. Ossiri's reflections bring out the contrast between his invisibility (to customers) as a security guard and the vividness of his imagination: "THEORY OF HAIR ENVY. Hair envy gradually spreads from south to north: the Maghrebi [*la Beurette*], south of the Viking [*la Viking*], wants the latter's straight, blond hair; the Sub-Saharan [*la Tropiquette*], south of the Maghrebi, wants the latter's curly hair" (22). The lighthearted yet punchy tone of these vignettes highlights Gauz's linguistic talent. His language often draws on stereotypes, which spare no one: blacks and whites, women and men, French and foreigners, Muslims and Christians. Even Ossiri embodies the age-old image of the frightening, strong black man. The vignettes are dressed with words from the Ivorian Creole language of Nouchi. In an excerpt called "VOCABULARY" (23), Gauz explains that *DEBOUT-PAYÉ* means "all the jobs where one must stand to make a living," and that *ZAGOLI* means security guard (24). He also translates Nouchi terms in footnotes, placing himself in the role of native informant. Gauz's novel does not shy away from the markers of exoticism and their appeal to French readers.

Debout-payé's sociohistorical content contributed to its immediate acceptance. It tells a diachronic story of African immigration to France in a colorful, hybridized French. While depicting immigrants' difficulties in France, *Debout-payé*, like francophone literature before it, also addresses French colonialism in Africa and Ivory Coast's status as a former colony. In this sense Aurélie Pasquelin considers the novel "[a] real gem that is both hilarious and critical of the relationships between France and the African continent."[18] The novel offers moreover a fresh look at French society through the eyes of a foreigner, in the style of Montesquieu's *Lettres persanes* (1721). The particularly French sensitivity to how others view France betrays a concern for the country's image in the global sphere.

The *Mediapart* journalist Lucie Delaporte writes, for example, that the novel's character "sees all our contemporary follies," while the blogger of *Lecture/Écriture* states that "[t]here is nothing like a foreign gaze to reconsider our French society."[19] The novel's ethnographic stance does not, however, aim to elucidate how to become French, as is the case with *Lettres persanes*.[20] It tackles instead, from the perspective of the immigrant, the restrictive politics of French immigration over several decades. It underscores the honesty and dignity of the undocumented immigrant in opposition to mainstream racism and crass materialism. Critics have highlighted precisely this positive message and praised the novel for giving voice to the subaltern.[21]

The publisher's decisions about the book's title, cover design, and distribution networks had much to do with the novel's success. The title expression, which refers to security guards' "*standing* [*debout*] all day long" to be "*paid* [*payé*] at the end of the month," is grammatically truncated, arresting readers' attention (8, emphasis added). The title stands out typographically as the long (and only) black line on the white front cover. It is sandwiched between the author's enigmatic name (Gauz is the penname of Armand Patrick Gbaka-Brédé) and the genre specification ("roman" [novel], in a smaller font), both printed in red. As Virot explains, Le Nouvel Attila's sales department seized upon the novel's "mysterious and provocative" title to capture reader attention, dissuading Gauz from adding the subtitle "The Security Guard's Inner Life," as he had wished.[22] Equally playful, the detachable dust jacket features a young black man, his face half concealed by a red cap, contorting his body to reach a shampoo bottle from one of the many supermarket shelves that form the background. The ambiguous image piques the reader's interest (those who do not know the plot cannot yet identify the man as a thief). The detachable jacket reveals, on its back flap, an excerpt in white whose lines are printed vertically (bottom to top) on a bright red background, forcing readers to tilt their head. It is a fragment of the author's biography, written in tongue-in-cheek prose that can be read in full in the novel's final chapter. The book's front and back covers follow a similar design. Printed vertically in red on white background are the novel's opening words. To read them requires flipping the book ninety degrees and starting on the back cover before turning to the front cover. In this way, readers are invited to engage with the materiality of the book and to consider the novel not only as signification, or as a good story, but also as a ludic artifact. While the dust jacket targets more playful readers, the book's pages—where long and short paragraphs alternate, and words in italic, boldface, and underscored fonts catch the eye—give the impression of a fun and easy read for "average" readers.

An enticing book jacket was not the only way to launch the novel of an unknown writer. An authorial image was also created. The press prepared a poster for bookstores throughout the country. An example of "the publisher's epitext," the poster featured a black-and-red image of the author, whose gaze firmly meets the onlooker's (Genette 1997, 347). A stylized map of Paris indicating the eleventh and twelfth *arrondissements*, where the character Ossiri lives and works, appears on Gauz's face. Underneath are the author's name, the book title, and an excerpt from the novel. In an age when readers are drawn to already-established authors (Squires 2009, 87), whom booksellers promote as "safe bets," Le Nouvel Attila's poster put a face to a mysterious name. No mere branding technique, the poster also lent authenticity; Gauz, who immigrated to France in 1999, bases the narrative on his own experience as a security guard in two stores of Parisian haute couture.

The novel's press reviews use these autobiographical elements and the African characters' critical gaze on French society for further promotion. *Debout-payé*'s *succès de presse* (media success) started with laudatory reviews in the well-respected *Le Monde des livres*, where Jean Birnbaum declared the novel was "[o]ne of the most pleasant surprises of the [fall] publishing season," and in *L'Express*, where Marianne Payot confirmed the realistic portrayal of the lives of security guards by highlighting Gauz's biography.[23] Such comments had a reverberating effect in the printed press, as more reviews followed in *Libération*, *Le Figaro*, *La Croix*, *Le Nouvel Observateur*, *L'Humanité*, *Le Journal de Dimanche*, and *Elle*, among others. The *Le Point* review included excerpts from the novel. Gauz also spoke about his writing and personal history on France Inter, France 3, France 5, Canal Plus,

ARTE, and TF1 radio and television programs. On his show *Boomerang* broadcast on France Inter, Augustin Trapenard applauded the novel and encouraged viewers to buy it and spread the word.

The novel's popularity also benefited from Gauz's "flamboyant personality," regarded as one of the ingredients of a debut novel's success in addition to booksellers' support, media reception, and literary awards, even though it is difficult to accurately predict a book's achievement in the marketplace.[24] In promoting his work in the audiovisual media, Gauz frequently recounted how he would furtively take notes for his novel while on duty as a security guard. Yet at the same time he is careful to present himself primarily as an author who writes in a literary tradition, his models being Louis-Ferdinand Céline and Ahmadou Kourouma, the latter an Ivorian author of acclaim in France. Gauz thus positions himself in a "double culture," as he calls it, meaning an identification with both French and Ivorian cultures.[25]

Booksellers highly praised *Debout-payé* on their websites, especially on Le choix des libraires (lechoixdeslibraires.com), a site that valorizes booksellers' recommendations. As mediators between authors and readers and with strong ties to publishers, booksellers are a key player in the game of literary recognition. Gauz was not only invited to readings and meet-the-author events in bookstores across the country but also won the fledgling Prix des libraires Gibert Joseph, awarded by the Gibert Joseph bookstore chain starting in 2014. Gauz also won the November 2014 Prix du Roman du mois des Espaces Culturels E. Leclerc et Télé 7 Jours (a monthly literary award founded by a bookstore and weekly magazine), the 2015 Grand prix Kaïlcedra des lycées et collèges in Ivory Coast, and the 2015–16 Prix littéraire des lycéens, apprentis et stagiaires de la formation professionnelle en Yvelines. Except for the Prix littéraire de la Porte Dorée, for which *Debout-payé* was a finalist in 2015, these are not France's most prestigious literary prizes. They represent instead a new trend of alternative juries and agents (booksellers, bookstore members, and students) who participate alongside traditional institutions in the process of literary recognition. These popular awards are the symptom of a more "direct" and non-elitist form of consecration involving bookstores and media outlets that are closer to the public's tastes and motivated to discover new talents (Ducas 2013, 131). Reviews, author interviews, and literary prizes created an eager audience of both professional and "common" readers. As for the novel itself, it is the combination of postcolonial history, innovative language and theme, and liberal politics that has given *Debout-payé* the competitive edge in the marketplace that Coquet's, Deniel-Laurent's, and Pattieu's novels lacked.

THE AUTHORIAL CRAFT IN *ULYSSE FROM BAGDAD*

Published by Albin Michel in fall 2008, six weeks after the start of the *rentrée littéraire d'automne*, *Ulysse from Bagdad* was rapidly acclaimed in literary venues such as *Le Figaro*, *Télérama*, and *L'Express*, which also published an excerpt. It remained on *Livres Hebdo*'s list of fifty best sellers for several months in 2008 and 2009, won the Prix des Grands Espaces in 2009, and, as a sign of its mass appeal, was issued in paperback by Le Livre de Poche in 2010. Equally successful abroad, *Ulysse from Bagdad* has been translated into more than a dozen languages. Its author, Éric-Emmanuel Schmitt, is not only a best-selling novelist but also a reputable playwright and holder of a doctorate in philosophy. He narrates stories about the human condition in erudite yet accessible ways. The novel's first paperback edition illustrates Pouly's (2016) paradoxical concept of the "literary bestseller," in which thought-provoking content merges with a commercially designed paratextual apparatus. The text (a humanist novel about the difficulties of illegal immigrants) and the paratext (the front cover featuring a car moving in a cloud of dust, reminiscent of Hollywood road movies), though ostensibly at odds, encourage a double reading: one for literary complexity and one for pleasure.

In May 2016 Le Livre de Poche reissued *Ulysse from Bagdad* with a new cover trumpeting its inclusion of "the author's 'before' and 'after' writing journal," that is, Schmitt's private musings from before and after the novel's initial publication. More than simply a publisher's marketing tool, Schmitt's journal brings the current European migrant crisis to bear on his 2008 fictional narrative, inviting us to reconsider it alongside his reflections on the current state of literature, media, and politics. In so doing he reaffirms both the migrant genre's urgency and literature's capacity to offer alternative models of political engagement. Taking up Sartre's notion of *engagement* (political commitment), the journal asks not what literature is but what it can do in times of humanitarian crisis. By editorial decision the author's journal thus intervenes in interpretations of the novel, adding political value to its already acquired symbolic and commercial capital. The journal recasts *Ulysse from Bagdad* not merely as a "feel-good novel," as Marianne Payot states, but also as a politically engaged novel.[26]

Ulysse from Bagdad explores the ties between literature and life in two ways. One is through the Homerian intertext, which provides a model of resourcefulness for Schmitt's character. The other is through the discourse on European hospitality that emerges from various didactic scenes and dialogues. Saad Saad—whose name means "Hope Hope" in Arabic and "Sad Sad" in English (9)—is a young Iraqi forced to leave his war-ravaged country to provide for his impoverished family. He chooses England as his destination due to his long-standing fascination with Agatha Christie novels. Saad has learned to associate literature with freedom because of his childhood immersion in his father's clandestine library of European masterpieces. The father's ghost, who accompanies Saad on his journey and cheers him on, embraces literature's power to offer solutions to real-world problems. It is not surprisingly *The Odyssey* that inspires Schmitt's hero to escape. Saad evades the grip of the Lotus-Eaters, two drug traffickers who smuggle him to Egypt; travels freely with the Sirens, a heavy metal band; escapes a Maltese detention center (in a dream) by wounding the Cyclop, its guardian; and arrives in France tucked underneath a truck, just as Ulysses clung to the belly of a sheep to exit Polyphemus's cave. These *Odyssey*-inspired episodes provide comic relief to an otherwise serious topic, but what is more important, they stress that present-day migrants face challenges as daunting as Ulysses faced. As Schmitt explains in his writing journal, Homer's epic allows him to stress that illegal immigrants are "the heroes of our time" (278).

Centered as it is on the courage of migrants under harsh circumstances, *Ulysse from Bagdad* is an apology for hospitality. The greatest challenge to the theory and practice of hospitality, the novel suggests, is the presence of illegal immigrants on European soil. These noncitizens embody not merely cultural and racial otherness; they are the absolute, ultimate Other because they are deprived of any legal rights. More than a stigma, then, illegal status becomes for Saad an identity he internalizes. In many self-transformations he experiences along the way—from refugee, migrant, and beggar to "illegal immigrant" (*clandestin*) (11)—Saad regards the last as the most degrading condition of all because it reduces him to "an inferior being" or "a sub-human" (219). As he states, "I don't belong to any nation, neither to the country I have fled nor to the country that I wish to reach, even less to the countries I pass through. Illegal immigrant. Just an illegal immigrant. Welcome nowhere. A stranger everywhere" (11). "Illegal" is a condition that gradually conquers all other facets of his identity. At journey's end, despite being Iraqi, Arab, Muslim, Democrat, son, student, and lover (41), Saad introduces himself as "Nobody" to the customs officers who interrogate him (222). More than a ruse, Ulysses' pseudonym underscores Saad's profound sense of alienation as "a stranger to the human species" (11). Saad's embrace of this radical nonidentity, "Nobody," moreover speaks to the marginalized immigrant's view of a Europe that chooses to "remain an unassailable fortress, protected by its walls of waves" (148).

The encounter between clandestine immigrants and Europeans, the novel suggests, disturbs the foundation on which European (or any) identity is based. Uprooted outsiders confront Europeans with the randomness of birth and the mythology of their own identitarian origin. Nation-state, religion, and ethnic community, as Europeans possess, are mere constructions designed to ward off fears of nothingness. Saad sees that Europeans fear him, the clandestine immigrant, because he dispels the illusion of their consistency, reminding them that they are "but the sand that was poured into [them]; [that] in and of [them]selves, [they are] nothing" (228). Some characters, however, offer a more pointed critique of European borders and inhospitality toward foreigners. An Italian police officer, for whom human history is nothing but an arbitrary "history of shifting borders," lets Saad escape (223). The police officer envisions a utopian project wherein political borders gradually disappear and only natural ones—seas and continents—remain. He proposes moreover a redefinition of community in humanist terms—as "we, human beings"—rather than along lines of nationality, ethnicity, religion, or language (224). In similar fashion Dr. Schoelcher, the mayor of a small French town, explains to Saad that, historically speaking, identity constructions have always been founded on the exclusion of others. In the doctor's view, narrow conceptions of identity make people forget they are "butterflies who think they are flowers" (244).

Ulysse from Bagdad argues that the "stateless" world that Saad imagines can be made possible through a humanist gaze on the displaced and dispossessed (238). The officer and the doctor, for example, propose that identity-based definitions of Europe be replaced with conceptions stressing the elasticity, or even dissolution, of borders. Thus reenvisioned, Europe "fosters Saad's enduring belief in the connection between *humanitas* and humanistic culture as a promoter of diversity across geographical and ideological barriers" (Pireddu 2015, 282). Indeed numerous events of Saad's arduous journey reinforce and challenge his conviction that literature can alter reactionary outlooks. Saad concludes in a moment of dejection that "writers are charlatans. They try to sell us the world for what it is not, orderly, fair, moral" (261). However, his father maintains that "[w]riters do not depict the world as it is, but as people could make it" (262). This and other didactic moments in the text draw readers' attention away from the plot, inviting them to reflect on the novel's larger message. *Ulysse from Bagdad* offers a utopian model of a postnational and cosmopolitan Europe in which humanist principles are the best tools for addressing humanitarian predicaments.

Schmitt's writing journal reinforces the notion of literature's real-life potential. Composed as a triptych, it covers the history of the novel from its conception to its reception. The "'before writing' journal (2007)" locates its genesis in Schmitt's feelings of shame and indignation after hearing a piece of news that dehumanized illegal immigrants (273). Seeing parallels with Nazi depictions of the Jews, Schmitt "had to write" because, for him, "to write is to act" (274). *Ulysse from Bagdad* is thus an act of rebellion. Schmitt also mentions the inspiration for his hero's name and the deliberately bilingual (French and English) title, as well as his conversations with immigrants in Bruxelles, which enabled him to "adopt the gaze of a sans-papiers" (275). Schmitt's "'during writing' journal (2008)" presents his art of the novel, which he views as a ludic genre and not surprisingly as palimpsestic, given his framing device of *The Odyssey* (281). But more than a playful intertext, he writes, Homer's epic informs his novel because it presents the concept of identity as place-bound, while also undermining it through Odysseus's wanderings. What better starting point than *The Odyssey* to explore contemporary travel and hospitality? In his "'after writing' journal (2009–15)" the author attributes the novel's positive reception to his capacity for empathy and the text's personalization of the illegal immigrants' story, in contrast with the dehumanizing journalistic accounts that have dominated the public sphere (295).

Although Schmitt's writing journal reveals a few authorial choices, as well as musings on the accidental nature of birth and the constructedness of identity, it does not shed much light on the creative process. Instead Schmitt states that "[t]he book is writing itself more than I'm writing it" (281). Intimations of creative labor, writer's block, or other challenges of craft are absent. The journal's form is hardly diarylike. Its entries are undated, and its generic mixture of essay, autobiography, polemic, and manifesto makes it hard to define. In short it reads more like a postscript than a journal. Schmitt's diary underwhelms in ways foreseen by Genette. As Genette (1997) points out, "the intimate epitext," as he calls a writing journal, usually offers sparing comments on an author's work (372). Writers either use it as a relief from their main work, in which case they record external events, reserving the labor of writing for rough drafts, or, if the writing is going well, do not feel the need to comment on the process (392). For these reasons, Genette concludes, "the 'logbook' aspect of writers' journals is often fairly limited" (392).

As a general rule, authors address private journals to themselves, even if their intention is to make them public. Schmitt's "during writing" journal offers a rare window onto his conflicted feelings about the sans-papiers. On the one hand his humanist beliefs dispose him toward a hospitable attitude that welcomes all immigrants regardless of political or economic status. On the other hand his civic responsibility alerts him to the burden that immigrants, especially when arriving in great numbers, can represent for a nation-state's limited resources. Schmitt depicts this tension between cosmopolitanism and patriotism, or between his "ethics of belief" (*éthique de conviction*) and his "ethics of responsibility" (*éthique de responsabilité*) as an irresolvable tension and source of inner turmoil (294). This then is the special insight his journal brings. It offers Schmitt a space for articulating a notion of hospitality that is both an aesthetic and a social practice.

For the author, aesthetics and social practice are inextricably linked. Life imitates literature not only within the novel, as we have seen, but in the real-life public sphere as well. In his "after writing" journal Schmitt recounts a confession that the president of the European Council, Herman Van Rompuy, shared with him after reading *Ulysse from Bagdad*. The novel, Van Rompuy confessed, had made him determined to "introduce the maximum of humanity" in the new laws to safeguard asylum rights (299). That the novel's hospitable ethos translated into political gestures of hospitality is for Schmitt an affirmation of literature's agency. The author's writing journal is thus more than a critical apparatus. It repositions *Ulysse from Bagdad* as a text that, while successful in the marketplace, also intervenes in the public sphere. Schmitt invites the new readers of his 2016 edition to reflect on migrant literature's continued potential to connect aesthetics and politics, relating *Ulysse from Bagdad*, in his journal's last pages, to the recent plight of the Syrian refugees and the challenges they pose to Europe's notions of hospitality.

The three case studies examined have shown how editorial interventions into the marketing of migrant texts are crucial to constructions of meaning and value. An identitarian, francophone series such as Continents noirs activates readings that emphasize authorial identity rather than the text. Creative paratextual strategies can assure a debut novel's placement on best-seller lists. Finally, the inclusion of an author's writing journal in a new edition can reposition a novel in relation to current political events. This chapter has by and large emphasized the agency of editors and authors. The various marketing techniques developed by editors and authors are designed to attract readers. But precisely who reads migrant literature and how they construct its value is a question that still needs to be answered.

2

———

RECEPTION

Online Readers in the Global
Literary Marketplace

Migrant literary texts capture both academic and nonacademic audiences through publishers' marketing strategies and internal narrative techniques. The present chapter examines the ways in which audiences respond to migrant novels and their paratextual elements, thereby participating in the legitimation of migrant literature. Whereas scholars of various types of readership have largely focused on elite audiences and professional modes of literary consecration, the following discussion addresses a particular type of reader and critical discourse—online readers and their book reviews—to offer a better understanding of how lay values and expectations shape the reception of the migrant genre. The surge in online reviews, which have been associated with a "participatory culture" (Jenkins et al. 2016, 2) and the "democratization of the reading and evaluation of literature" (Steiner 2008), speaks to common readers' need for alternative modes of literary legitimation. Indeed "lay" readers have newfound authority as tastemakers via commercial websites such as Amazon and noncommercial book review forums such as Babelio, Critiques Libres, Lecteurs, and SensCritique (Guillory 2000, 33). Such forums have created communities of like-minded book aficionados, hosted debates on literary value, and enabled readers to validate migrant texts through literary prize competitions in which they participate as jury members. Readers are no longer passive consumers. They have entered the game of literary consecration as producers of literary meaning and value.[1] They are thus fulfilling the role, once exclusive to professional critics, of determining aesthetic value. Online reviews are a valuable source of information about present-day readers and the part they play in creating a taste for migrant literature through their newfound critical practices.

The digital space of websites, blogs, and review forums constitutes a radical change in the processes of literary consecration, as it directs attention away from authorial and textual singularity toward the large-scale circulation and consumption of literary works. Online readers, who perform acts of literary criticism in their own right, offer added value as consumers of literary fiction by revealing the mechanisms through which books find readers in today's commodity culture. Online reviewers are thus a sounding board for testing the strategies of marketers (they review books that publishers distribute to members of reading forums), the effects of institutional consecration (they admit to purchasing books that won literary prizes), and alternative promotional techniques (they are often guided in their choices by word-of-mouth communication and blog posts). Lay discourse on migrant fiction, produced by readers through digital media, merits critical attention. It is a frequently overlooked, yet vital source for the study of changing hierarchies of legitimacy and taste in contemporary French as well as global culture.

This chapter draws on the fields of reception theory, online audience studies, and discourse analysis to examine the online response to two novels of the "return" or "homecoming" subgenre of migrant literature: Milan Kundera's *L'Ignorance* (*Ignorance*) and Andreï Makine's *La Vie d'un homme inconnu* (*The Life of an Unknown Man*). These novels are "crossover narratives"—fictions that are "receptive to both professional/academic and everyday audiences" (Procter and Benwell 2015, 11)—that are typical of contemporary migrant texts.[2] The two novels moreover make ideal case studies insofar as they address issues of literary commodification and represent canonized authors who also have a broad readership.

Reading texts by so-called elitist authors who are anxious about their lay reception alongside reviews by lay readers themselves yields productive insights. Analysis of online discourses about migrant texts shows that lay and professional modes of reading overlap. Lay readers consume books for pleasure and are generally drawn to realist narratives, in opposition to "professional readers," who are trained to look for textual complexity (Guillory 2000, 33). Online reviewers, however, oscillate between the expectation that literary texts provide simply pleasure and escape versus the demands that texts challenge them through their literary sophistication. They insist on the criteria of spontaneity, orality, reading experience, and the pleasure of sharing their opinions and feelings about books, while simultaneously drawing on aesthetic criteria and the rhetoric of evaluation employed in the academy. In other words the online readers perform discrepant readings that position Kundera's and Makine's novels between what John Frow (1995) has termed distinct "regimes of value" (144). Frow's concept refers to a set of criteria, mechanisms of signification, and codes of value that determine what constitutes "good" literature and who can make judgments of value. In proposing this notion, Frow draws on Tony Bennett's concept of "reading formation"—"a semiotic apparatus" or network that organizes the relations between texts and readers in ways that situate value formation not so much in relation to texts' inherent properties but to contingent social and institutional conditions (quoted in Frow 1995, 145). Frow's and Bennett's concepts help us to understand book reviews as heterogeneous practices that situate migrant literature between distinct evaluative norms. Online reviewers adopt the protocols of reading pertaining to regimes of both high and popular culture by positing migrant novels as commodities that are endowed with aesthetic and ethical value.

Different regimes of value generate different kinds of readings. It is therefore important to ask who online readers are and how they position themselves vis-à-vis literary texts, their institutional recognition, and other members of the online community. "Online readers" is a capacious category, encompassing nonacademic audiences as well as authors, editors, publishers, and critics who review behind the veil of anonymity. Since the online medium allows for reader anonymity, ethnographic data are generally scant. The little biographical information available suggests an acutely heterogeneous readership, differentiated along national, ethnic, social, and gendered lines, among other factors. Babelio and Critiques Libres users often include information about their location that shows that readers are national (based in France or Belgium) and global (situated in francophone territories outside the countries in which these websites were created). Online readers also diverge in terms of literary taste and expertise—criteria that signal a hierarchy of values based on critical competence and literary preference. How do online readers' expertise, desires, and expectations fit into authorial agency, institutional contexts of consecration, market pressures, and the constraints of digital media to constitute the particular reading formation born of Kundera's and Makine's texts? We begin with recent shifts in the literary field before turning to the online discourse on Kundera's and Makine's novels.

DIGITAL AUDIENCES AS CONSECRATING AUTHORITIES

In France the technological shifts that have empowered lay readers to participate in literary legitimation began rather recently, in the first decade of the twenty-first century, with the creation of Amazon.fr and forums such as Babelio, Critiques Libres, Lecteurs, and SensCritique. However, the rise of a mass readership, and its importance to authors, publishers, and booksellers, is not a recent phenomenon. Sylvie Ducas (2013) traces the shift from elite to mass readership in France to the beginning of the twentieth century, when developments in technology, literacy, infrastructure, and editorial policies led to the emergence of a bourgeois public avid for reading and instruction (22). Since the 1960s and 1970s book clubs such as France Loisirs and Le Grand Livre du mois have engaged French readers in collective and public acts of literary criticism, and the French media (newspapers, magazines, and radio stations) endowed readers with added consecrating authority by creating literary prizes such as the Prix des Lectrices de *Elle* and the Prix du Livre Inter et de RTL/Grand public, whose juries were composed of lay readers. Online prizes and reviews signal not only a change in the criteria of literary consecration but also the increased power of lay readers to designate literary value insofar as they measure works' success by their popularity within a community of shared tastes. The shift from elite to popular, print to digital, and from individual to collective forms of consecration has brought changes in literary consecration to even greater heights. In what follows we will see how lay readers deploy their newfound consecrating power in digital reading forums.

Online review forums conflate old and new media. They draw at once on "historically developed professional criticism" and older practices such as diary and letter writing, as well as "a rapidly developing blog culture" that foregrounds "self-expressiveness, intimate language, and self-exposing details" (Steiner 2008). Blogging practices cultivate reviewers' personae as never before, situating members of online communities in relation to each other and fostering a relational understanding of their new cultural authority. In fact these sites' appeal is that they embed readers in "a community of shared tastes," where the criteria of readerly pleasure, sincerely expressed emotions, and "belonging and complicity" often prevail over that of literary excellence (Ducas 2013, 143). Online commentaries thus focus on the reading experience, or the effects of reading on reviewers, and not solely on textual features. Reviewers generally comment on both the authors (by specifying their degree of familiarity with authorial biography and oeuvre) and the texts themselves (by focusing on internal elements such as plot, characters, themes, and style). Readers' proffered comparisons to other authors and texts within the same genre serve to display their literary knowledge and establish their literary authority vis-à-vis their peers. Reviewers also debate the conditions of book purchasing and consumption. They write about their reasons for buying, the reading experience, and the relationship between quality and price, thereby underscoring the status of contemporary novels as commodities.

Take, for example, the sophistication of Babelio reviews on popular authors and genres such as Marc Levy's and Guillaume Musso's mass-market romances, Anna Gavalda's "chick lit" novels (which veer toward literary fiction), and Fred Vargas's detective novels. Readers are acutely aware of literary hierarchies (i.e., what constitutes "good" literature) and generic boundaries (they point out authors' deviations from genre conventions such as optimism, sentimentality, and suspense). In the case of Levy's, Musso's, and Gavalda's texts reviewers generally read for empathy, relaxation, and therapy. Some stress their emotional connections with the novels and appreciate them for advocating values—friendship, love, and solidarity, in Gavalda's case—and providing entertainment and respite from pain or stress, even though they lack original plots, complex characters, and sophisticated styles. Others dismiss these "feel-good" novels as holiday reading (to be read on the beach and in airports), objecting to their media hype and questioning the genre's popularity among large audiences. Discussions about the state of the contemporary literary industries and about aesthetic value thus ensue, even in the case of popular fiction. Fred Vargas readers, consisting mostly of fans who eagerly await each new release of the author's work, praise her for creating an idiosyncratic literary universe, with colorful and recurrent characters and unpredictable plot twists. Some even credit her distinctive style and atypical detective novels for awakening their passion for the genre. Although they acknowledge that Vargas's thrillers encourage recreational reading, reviewers still underscore their "literary" qualities. Far from being mere mindless consumers, the Babelio readers of these novels defend pleasure reading and underscore its value in their lives. Their commentaries offer conflicting perspectives on the uses of popular fiction and hierarchies of value in today's literary industries. They provide a forum for exploring "the relationship between literary and popular taste"—a major concern in reviews of migrant literary texts as well (Holmes 2010, 287).

Consider also the commentaries from Amazon.fr, Babelio, and SensCritique on recent novels about clandestine migration to Europe: Laurent Gaudé's *Eldorado* (2006), Olivier Adam's *À l'abri de rien* (2007), Éric-Emmanuel Schmitt's *Ulysse from Bagdad* ([2008] 2016), Maylis de Kerangal's *À ce stade de la nuit* (2015), and Pascal Manoukian's *Les Échoués* (2015). Reviewers not only draw attention to a newly emerging subgenre of migrant literature but also distinguish between different texts of the same subgenre. They identify the novels' timeliness as their greatest strength and their appeal to readers' empathy and humanitarianism as their greatest weakness. They draw distinctions between politically engaged texts (Adam, Manoukian), popular or commercial novels (Gaudé, Schmitt), and texts endowed with aesthetic value (de Kerangal). They also respond to migrant novels whose serious themes are at odds with their overly lyrical style, while comparing them to other texts whose content and form go hand in glove. Online readers are surprisingly protective of the conventions and boundaries of the migrant genre and judge works according to their degree of conformity to or deviation from it. The same mechanisms apply to Kundera's and Makine's novels. The reviews of *L'Ignorance* and *La Vie d'un homme inconnu* single out migration among the multiple themes the novels address. Readers make generic discriminations, judgments of literary value, and comparisons to similar novels, and they help to market the two novels by insisting on their timeliness and powerful emotional effects on readers. Overall their comments are a great source of information about how online audiences understand and describe migrant texts outside or in addition to the criteria and classifications proposed by professional critics and literary institutions. Online reviews are key sites of meaning production around migrant literature.

Online readers also assume the power to consecrate authors and books in their capacity as juries of literary prizes, which are awarded by Critiques Libres, Lecteurs, and other digital sites. Since 2008 the Prix des Lecteurs/Lectrices de Critiques Libres has spotlighted underappreciated literary works that were published during the previous three years by small presses but failed to earn literary prizes and thus the publicity and increased readership such awards would have generated. The award differs from major French prizes through its open membership, democratic deliberation process, and disinterested character. Any registered Critiques Libres member can suggest works and participate in forum debates, and laureates are chosen by popular vote tallied directly on the site. In turn the Prix Orange du Livre has since 2009 been awarded by Lecteurs to a French novel published during France's *rentrée littéraire d'hiver*. Its process is likewise democratic, involving seven web users who serve on the jury alongside established authors and booksellers. Such readers' choice awards in the digital sphere strive to "impose a new legitimate definition of literature, as dictated by 'I like/I don't like' statements that characterize sincere or passionate readings" (Ducas 2013, 141). In other words, while still committed to aesthetic quality, online reviewers privilege readerly pleasure and textual accessibility in the evaluation of literary works.

In 2016 Éditions Gallimard partnered with Babelio to organize the first Prix des lecteurs Gallimard, a book competition in which readers chose their favorite book from a pre-established list of books published by Gallimard in 2016. Readers were encouraged to consult the list (available on both the Gallimard and the Babelio websites), email their vote to the publisher, and write a review to justify their choice. The contest rewarded both readers and books. Selected participants won a free copy of a Daniel Pennac novel, while numerous others, chosen by a Gallimard jury, were invited to attend the award ceremony celebrating the winner—Leïla Slimani's *Chanson douce*—at Gallimard's headquarters in January 2017. An elite publisher, Gallimard nonetheless assures the promotion and consumption of its books by encouraging lay forms of consecration. In digital book reviews lay readers' aesthetic interests and publishers' commercial goals intertwine.

BOOK REVIEW FORUMS AS PROMOTIONAL TOOLS

An examination of commercial and noncommercial digital spaces such as Amazon and French-language reading networks shows how reviewing practices are inevitably embedded in the medium in which they are produced and how literature and commerce are inextricably linked. On Amazon—the largest digital bookstore in the global literary marketplace—book reviews are effective and inexpensive promotional tools designed to maximize sales. They provide information about books, their purportedly beneficial effects on readers, and the conditions of book distribution and reception. One aim and upshot of customer reviews is to help other buyers make informed choices and optimize their reading experience by taking into account nonliterary factors such as money, reading time, and the speed of the shipping service. Paradoxically reviews also allow Amazon to appear as "a customer-oriented, non-commercial site"; the commentaries posted by customers do not resemble marketing but rather "the real thing—authentic readers commenting on books they have actually read" (Steiner 2008). The fact that these reviews are provided by common readers for other consumers also reinforces the impression, noted by Mary Leontsini and Jean-Marc Leveratto (2006), that "web users and potential buyers are in a relation of solidarity with each other, offering mutual help to facilitate safe choices." Leontsini and Leveratto continue: "[t]he idea of the safe choice based upon personalized criteria and user-centered priorities enhances trust in the web activity, and thus . . . its host or owner" (167).

Amazon's discursive space, in which readers freely express opinions and make reading choices based on the views of like-minded readers, is nevertheless a commercial setting that places constraints on its users. For example, the Amazon rating system, in which users can give a book from one to five stars, allows readers to evaluate a book based on subjective criteria and then gives other users the option to indicate the degree of usefulness of the review. The rating service strengthens the impression that books are highly debated because they are aesthetically valuable or pleasant to read (Leontsini and Leveratto 2006, 168). However, it is also meant to stimulate purchase by creating the illusion of a given book's aesthetic or commercial achievement among similar readers. A book's numerous ratings indicate reader interest and reactivate "an old widespread notion of a 'classic' of enduring literary value" (168). Amazon's mechanisms enable reviewing practices that conflate the ideas of literary autonomy and commerce. The site's classification of reviews as positive or "critical" (negative) is moreover seemingly objective insofar as it gives equal consideration to diverse and even opposing opinions. Amazon thus appears as a democratic discursive space where readers are free to express their impressions without aesthetic constraints or professional criteria associated with academic forms of interpretation. In fact it is a carefully orchestrated commercial strategy. Books' editorial blurbs are designed to cue readings and customers' reviews, visits to authors' Amazon pages, and perusal of books other customers have bought.

The nonprofit French-language community platforms that began springing up in the first decade of the twenty-first century are similarly implicated in the commercial realities of the literary marketplace. Babelio (the first online reading community in France, created in 2007), Critiques Libres (a Belgian site founded in 2008), and other French community platforms, such as Lecteurs (2009) and SensCritique (2010), have altered literary distribution and criticism by shifting authority from professional critics to lay readers. Most of these sites enable members to share readings, discover new books, keep up with the latest releases, participate in quizzes and contests, and serve on literary prize juries. Yet it is their capacity as book reviewers that implicates the editorial field. French presses supply readers with books in exchange for online reviews, as these constitute free publicity for authors and publishers, all in the name of expanding the buying public. Babelio and SensCritique readers, for instance, receive books for review ahead of their publication date—a means for editors to spark interest, build excitement, and ensure future book sales. Although most of these sites are "noncommercial," they offer suggestions for gifts, invite readers to make lists for future purchases, feature lists of France's weekly best sellers, and provide links to sites such as French online bookstores or Amazon.

For all their efforts to preserve some autonomy from the marketplace and celebrate the agency of lay readers, such online platforms nonetheless borrow from classificatory practices employed by professional critics and cultural institutions. The thematic lists created by Lecteurs users (divided by theme, year, format [e.g., paperback], genre, and nationality) and Babelio users (from "The Body in Literature" and "Novels Adapted to Screen") obey the same critical principle of segmenting the literary market into niche products, orienting readers, and influencing their choices. Babelio users have compiled numerous lists about migrant literature, comprising more than two hundred books: "Émigration—Immigration," "Migrations," "L'immigration en littérature," "Venus d'ailleurs," "Immigration et jeunes héros: quand la littérature jeunesse interroge," "Différence, immigration, tolérance," "Exils multiples . . . intérieurs, politiques ou sociaux," "Exils et migrations," "Immigration," and "Ces Français partis vivre à l'étranger." Classifications such as these signal that migrant literature occupies a recognizable niche in the francophone literary marketplace. Lists of migrant texts and online reviews have done much to promote the migrant genre in an oversaturated literary market.

In particular digital platforms influence the literary field by making a selection in the plethora of books made available during France's *rentrée littéraire*. The sites' administrators and members organize literary challenges wherein they aim to discover new books according to their own interests rather than those of critics and journalists. For example, to make sense of the five-hundred-odd forthcoming books in France's 2016 *rentrée d'automne*, Lecteurs chose fifty "explorers," each of whom read three to four books from a pre-established list, reviewed them for other community members, and assembled a best-books-of-the-year list. To counter the clout of top presses, Babelio tackled the overabundance of yearly publications by focusing on marginal books that have escaped the notice of literary authorities. A literary challenge such as the "68 First Times," initiated by a Babelio member in 2015, had a team read sixty-eight novels by first-time authors from the fall publishing season and then pick the ones they believed merited wider dissemination and promotion. Her challenge invited not only other bloggers to join the endeavor but also publishers, who provided review copies of the books. Like Lecteurs members, Babelio readers made individual top lists, reviewed their choices online, and met their favorite authors during a closing-night event that assured publicity and book sales.

For these sites readers are not merely consumers. They are active participants in cultural production who engage in reading as a social, as much as literary, practice. In this sense these online sites perform important cultural work by proposing alternative criteria for shaping the critical discourse on literary production. They elevate word-of-mouth promotion and oral style—as opposed to printed and polished book reviews found in daily newspapers and media advertisements—as a more effective way of disseminating books and making reading choices. The sites' emphasis on hearsay also celebrates the personal tastes, critical judgment, and writing of anonymous readers. For instance, Critiques Libres asks readers to rate the book they review, which causes members to justify their ratings in the reviews themselves.[3] In turn Babelio classifies and showcases readers according to their membership and reviewing practices. It establishes categories for the oldest, newest, and best reviewers (judged according to the quality of their writing and the diversity of the books they review), compulsive reviewers (those who type the lengthiest commentaries), and *Babeliothécaires* (or Babelio librarians, who enrich the site's bibliographic content with their book suggestions). The site thus involves its members in a "community of practice" to render them loyal to its literary activities and commercial transactions (Procter and Benwell 2015, 27).

In light of the reconfiguration of the process of literary consecration in twenty-first-century France, Kundera's and Makine's novels display unease about the power of lay readers to determine literary value and impose literary classifications. They deplore these new modes of meaning production and lay readers' powers as new tastemakers that have contributed to the authors' desacralization in today's literary culture. The authors' decisions about the content and publication venues of their novels underscore their attempts to assert authorial agency and to forestall what they regard as narrow critical interpretations of their works. For example, the publishing history of Kundera's French-language novels *La Lenteur* (1995; released in translation in 1996 as *Slowness*), *L'Identité* (1998; released in translation as *Identity*, 1998), and *L'Ignorance* (2000/2003) attests to their initially lukewarm and then outright negative reception in the French press. Kundera's refusal to praise the genius and universality of the French language contributed to this negative assessment. To punish hostile French critics for what he saw as their narrow expectations of migrant authors and then to divest them of their authority to judge his works, the author published *L'Ignorance* in Spanish, Catalan, German, and Italian translations in 2000 before releasing the work in its original French with Éditions Gallimard three years later. Kundera's translation strategy flew in the face of nationalistic appropriations by those who deemed him a Czech dissident author who should continue to write only about communist themes, long after his French naturalization. It also suggested, in the author's view, that only transnational legitimation could do justice to his works. In a similar way

Makine's resounding critical and commercial success in his 1995 Médicis-winning novel *Le Testament français* (*Dreams of My Russian Summer*, 1997) was followed by scathing reviews of his subsequent novels, in which he deviated from established themes—France as a literary country and French as a poetic language—and took up darker Russian themes.[4] His later work, *La Vie d'un homme inconnu*, responds directly to this reductive reception and French critics' expectations that Makine continue to deliver hymns to French culture.

It is important to take into account literary critics' horizon of expectations regarding Kundera's and Makine's fictions and the novels' retort to French consecrating authorities when examining Amazon, Babelio, Critiques Libres, and SensCritique reviews. Online readers negotiate the novels' literary value in relation to larger contexts of production, circulation, and reception, rather than viewing them as autonomous texts. Judging by the novels' numerous reviews between 2000 and 2017, digital audiences position themselves vis-à-vis authorial agency and professional criticism, in addition to other members' literary expertise.[5] The following sections provide qualitative analysis of online reviews to elucidate these mediations between authors, texts, and different consecrating agents.

L'IGNORANCE'S HETEROGENEOUS PUBLICS

L'Ignorance (2000/2003), as well as the English translation, *Ignorance* (2002), presents a complex portrait of emigration and return through the intertwined stories of Irena and Josef—two Czech émigrés who live for twenty years in France and Denmark, then return to Prague after the fall of communism. Although Kundera frames his narrative through references to Homer's *Odyssey*, he interrogates conventional views of émigrés as invariably nostalgic for home, and of return as nothing but joyful. As "the founding epic of nostalgia" (7), as well as a recurrent intertext in migrant literature, *The Odyssey* has articulated powerful concepts—Ithaca, *nostos*, *algos* (5)—that have shaped the European cultural imaginary and led to the privileging of home and rootedness over endless drifting. Having imposed "a moral hierarchy of emotions" (9), with nostalgia at its peak, *The Odyssey* represents the literary yardstick by which one measures émigrés' degree of loyalty to their roots and their suffering of forced separation: they are "either the Great Traitor or the Great Victim" (30). The novel, however, disables these stereotypes by exposing both French and Czech perceptions of émigrés as exotic and provincial, respectively.[6] Whereas in France Irena is valuable insofar as she can be safely labeled a foreigner, in the Czech Republic her friends' lack of interest in her time in France "amputated twenty years from her life" (43). Josef has a similar experience of return. His family and friends ignore his émigré life, treating him not as a foreigner but as a native, just like Odysseus's compatriots did, even as he aches to recount his adventures abroad because "the very essence of his life, its center, its treasure, lay outside Ithaca, in the twenty years of his wanderings" (34). The protagonists perceive exile and return as an ontological rupture that severs their life into irreconcilable halves. Contemporary incarnations of Odysseus, Irena and Josef experience "the horror of [. . .] return" instead of the joy of homecoming (15). The novel debunks accepted notions of emigration as a tragic uprooting and transcends national frameworks by featuring cosmopolitan protagonists whose flexible sense of belonging invalidates the myth of the "Great Return" (4).

Through the French and Czech reactions to the protagonists' return, Kundera satirizes French and Czech readers' reductive judgments of émigrés, which are based on the Romantic idealization of national belonging—a notion the novel's opening conversation between Irena and her friend Sylvie exemplifies. Sylvie's urging Irena to return to "[her] own country" (3) "when great events are happening" (4) points to French exotic views of central European dissidents and the limitations of French hospitality. Whereas during communism Sylvie regarded her friend as "the embodiment of an émigré's suffering," she lost interest in her when the figure of the émigré began to fade from the collective unconscious (169). As a result Irena felt "duped" because "up till then [she]'d thought they loved [her] not for [her] suffering but for [her] self" (169). The novel critiques the ways in which, in France, émigrés' cultural capital hinges on their political ties to their native country rather than their individuality. In light of Kundera's French reception, it is impossible not to hear autobiographical echoes in these remarks. To "love" the author for himself rather than his Czechness means reading his works for their aesthetic value, that is, independently of his authorial biography or the host country's ideological principles.

For Kundera (2006) "the *large context* of world literature" is "the only approach that can bring out a novel's *aesthetic value*" (36, original emphasis). Two intratextual strategies orient our reading toward transnational contexts. One is the novel's reference to a canonical work of European and world literature. *The Odyssey* is present in *Ignorance* not only as a literary topos but also as a material object; a Danish-language copy of the epic rests on the night table of the protagonists' hotel room. To read *Ignorance* through the prism of a text that started in ancient Greece and traveled in many languages, Kundera suggests, is to read *Ignorance* as a work of world literature. The *mise en abyme* of the transnational circulation of canonical texts could not be more explicit. The second tactic consists of an etymology lesson. The narrator traces the Greek and Latin roots of the term "nostalgia" in several European languages, defining it not only in relation to the suffering—*algos*—caused by physical distance but also to the ignoring of, or not missing—*ignorare*—one's faraway country (6). The title's conflation of etymologies deemphasizes national linguistic attachments in favor of translatability or movement across languages. Extratextually moreover the novel's near-simultaneous publication in multiple languages—an example of what Rebecca Walkowitz (2015) terms "born-translated" novels (3)—invites transnational readings. *Ignorance* refuses to be grounded in a single national and linguistic context; it embraces world circulation and envisions cosmopolitan readers who embrace border-crossing texts.

What do readers seek in Kundera's novel? What do they find? Online reviews show that contextual elements—the author's biography, his art of fiction, and his previous novels—are, for readers, critical. The majority of the reviews came from those who were acquainted with his previous works and brought expectations about content and style to their reading of *Ignorance*. A smaller number came from first-time Kundera readers who were either indifferent to or confused by the formal density of the novel, the philosophical, historical, and etymological digressions of which prevented them from enjoying "a good read." Sometimes detailed and insightful, other times superficial and repetitive, these reviews display patterns as well as disagreements. There are four recurrent issues they touch upon: Kundera's biography, the migrant genre, the novel itself (its content, form, literary value, and placement within the author's oeuvre), and reviewers' speculations about its implied readership.

Readers who took into account Kundera's biographical context often ponder whether his migrant trajectory has inflected *Ignorance*'s content and style. Kundera immigrated to France in 1975 and gained recognition for his Czech-language novels, but after the collapse of communism he sought to "remain relevant" by writing in French and employing intertextual allusions to French and European literature (Wachtel 2006, 218). The new language and use of European literary history enabled him to shed his image as a Czech dissident and style himself as a European author concerned with purely aesthetic issues. Wondering how best to position Kundera within literary and linguistic traditions, some readers divide the author's literary oeuvre, perhaps artificially, into two halves—his "Czech cycle" and his "French cycle," as the literary critic François Ricard (2003) calls them (232). They question Kundera's motives for adopting French and his capacity to write equally well in his adopted language. Amazon.fr customer Filo, for instance, asserts that Kundera lost his genius after his emigration, while an Amazon.ca reader similarly opines that "Kundera seems to write better [. . .] in his native Czech than in French," even though the reviewer finds the author's language switch understandable.[7] The rhetoric of these reviews echoes that of the negative reviews Kundera has received in the French media, hinting that the author's journalistic reception may guide lay reader expectations.[8] Such judgments assume that migrant authors use their native language more effectively and should draw on native themes and literary models to preserve literary force and authenticity. These two online reviewers, who wrote their comments in French and English, respectively, do not mention the language in which they read Kundera's novel. Yet they privilege the native over the adopted language, as well as interpret *Ignorance* through the aesthetic codes of French literature, in opposition both to Kundera's attempt to blur the boundary between original and translation and to the novel's global circulation, as its multilingual reviews on different Amazon sites attest. In so doing they inadvertently tie migrant authors and texts to national, rather than more befitting global contexts, and show the extent to which the language of publication and of reading shape the reception of migrant texts.

Ignorance, however, has also gained sympathetic readers. Aesthetic criteria aside, some view the author's choice to write in French shortly after his emigration as a deliberate strategy to position himself within French literature. For online reviewer A. Peel there is no doubt that Kundera has earned his status as a French novelist. A. Peel writes that, although Kundera beautifully captured divergent perceptions of émigrés in their home and host countries, Kundera's decision to write *Ignorance* in French shows "how much he, the author, and the characters through him, have absorbed the French culture. His identity has evolved far beyond [French] perception of it."[9] M. Benet shares this view, acknowledging Kundera's dilemma as an author from a small central European country and as one who struggles against conceptions of authorship based on national identity: "Kundera is wrestling with the fiery dragon of the [R]omantic legacy in which identity was always rooted in the fertile soil of a distinct homeland from which one was sprung and for which one was willing to die."[10] Both commenters eschew exotic and nationalist criteria for situating migrant authors' works and see Kundera's flexible trajectory in a positive light.

Despite Kundera's claim to literary autonomy, some reviewers consider the novel, in its historical and political context, as an authentic representation of the author's migrant experiences, tying authorial biography to the generic conventions of migrant novels. Reviewers often identify *Ignorance* with the migrant genre through its themes, even though they may not use the critical labels (e.g., migrant literature) commonly employed by professional critics. In their words *Ignorance* is "a novel about exile par excellence" (Hadeel Altreikion), "a book about immigration" (Hana), "a tale of homecoming" (A. Peel), "an account of the move from one world to another" (Rev Kurt), and "a 20th century tale of emigration and return" (Teresa Neeman).[11] Readers Syd Dithers and lDavidl cite migration and return as the topics that made them pick up Kundera's novel.[12] Migration and return are issues that also resonate with readers due to personal migrant stories, be they their parents' or their own (bibliovegevore, Loly Perez, Soleada).[13]

For such reviewers, the personal experience of migration underpins any "true" understanding or writing of "authentic" migrant novels. In this sense they invoke their own and Kundera's migrant biographies to confirm the truthfulness of the migrant experiences of his characters. "As somebody who has experienced this, I can see firsthand much of what he is talking about in this book, but then again, Kundera also has experienced this, and it seems as if he is talking about issues straight out of his own experiences," states one reviewer.[14] Another similarly compares Irena and Josef's return to the Czech Republic to his or her own return to Hungary, concluding that "[t]he author's words ring extremely true. This isn't the type of book I normally read and I appreciated learning from the author's point of view."[15] Comparing Kundera's *Ignorance* to novels by migrant authors such as W. G. Sebald and Nancy Huston, readers situate the achievement of Kundera's work in relation to the common themes of the genre. In this way they negotiate its value in the migrant literary marketplace. At the same time, they measure the novel's aesthetic accomplishment against their own politicized views about the stories that migrant novels should tell. These personal views represent an alternative criterion for validating migrant literature, one usually absent from professional mechanisms of consecration. By and large readers unacquainted with Kundera's broader literary output ascribe truth-value to his migrant narrative, reading it for its biographical, mimetic, and didactic aspects. It is no small irony that these are precisely readings that Kundera's novelistic theories actively discourage.[16]

Reviewers also focus their debates on specific aspects of *Ignorance* itself. Readers show a keen sense of the richness of Kundera's literary oeuvre and of the novel's place within it. Audiences rate *Ignorance* as a less accomplished novel by drawing on knowledge and critical appreciation of Kundera's previous Czech-language novels, as well as his French-language novels *La Lenteur* and *L'Identité*. For many readers *Ignorance* disappoints in comparison with Kundera's better-known *The Joke*, *The Unbearable Lightness of Being*, and *The Book of Laughter and Forgetting*.[17] They lament Kundera's sparse prose and roughly drawn characters, which are features that stand in marked contrast with the ornate style and character development of his Czech novels. Other readers, by contrast, call such division of

Kundera's works arbitrary, identifying the author's unique style in his latest novels. Indeed Kundera's French novels are only superficially different; they take up the same themes (memory, forgetting, identity, language, and the defense of the individual before the totalitarian state). In the words of Rouchka1344, "To read a Kundera book is to reread his previous books."[18] The repetition of familiar themes disappoints some readers.[19] However, the reviewer le dernier carré expresses ambivalence about the thin line separating Kundera's Czech and French periods: "*Ignorance* is disappointing for the pre-exile Kundera fan that I am. Of course, we recognize Kundera's style and narration from his 'great period,' but I'm less likely to succumb to his charm. He doesn't renew himself. [...] We find the author-demiurge who looks down on his token creatures, but this time his kindness has turned into bitterness. A good thing, though: it's a fast read. We feel nostalgic for a different Kundera, the one who wrote through difficult times."[20] This reader places two contradictory demands on Kundera: that he renew himself thematically and stylistically after emigration and that he remain recognizable as the determinedly Czech writer he once was. The exotic value of the Eastern Bloc writer dies hard.[21] Yet it is precisely this desired image—the heroic émigré, liberated from communism—that *Ignorance* aims to undermine.

Kundera's French prose style is another key point of discussion. On one side are those who appreciated Kundera's literary digressions, philosophical reflections, and authorial interventions in the text, and on the other are those who found that his theorizations disrupted the linearity of the plot.[22] Some readers eagerly take on Kundera's challenging plot, creating meaning out of the "elliptically composed" novel "in regard to the story line" (Frank 2008, 117). Stewart, for instance, confesses that "for me, the true thrill was watching how the philosophical and historical asides came together to complete the novel, and reinforce the characters' feelings."[23] Like Wolfgang Iser's implied reader, he reads between the textual gaps and discerns a pattern in the novel's loosely connected parts.[24] M. A Netzley is representative of the positive reviewers: "[A]s we would expect, Kundera weaves a tale of commentary, quotes, history, and the main narrative to make his point. He moves and quotes much like a jazz musician. At first I wondered if I would be disappointed by the same old literary techniques Kundera has been using for years. Let me answer my own concerns with a firm 'no!' [. . .] As always, Kundera makes us think."[25] It is that very form on which negative reviewers base their complaints: "Heavy, clumsy, disorganized, disarticulated, sometimes trivial, sometimes a mythological or sociopolitical analysis." Another reader "[finds] [her]self just flipping through the pages and skipping most of the text to read a few sentences that may or may not be worth reading."[26] The opposing views reflect the different regimes of value in which they operate: professional criticism and reading for pleasure. The taste for formal experimentation on the one hand and the need for accessibility on the other divide Kundera's readers into two separate camps. The fact that the same text elicits divergent readings locates *Ignorance* in an online space of debate that conflates high and low regimes of value.

In his afterword to the novel's French-language edition, Ricard (2003) alludes to the novel's implied readers, suggesting that Kundera devised a form capable of seducing both professional and lay readers: "semantic density in minimal space" (237). Kundera regards conciseness as the antidote to a major problem of the novelistic genre: "readers' limited and faulty memory," which prevents them from retaining a complete and detailed picture of the novel after reaching its end (237). For "shortsighted and distracted readers," who tend to "devour" his texts, Kundera "reduce[s] the reading time to an extreme, but without sacrificing the richness and diversity of the novelistic material" (237). By allowing both fast and slow readings, depending on readers' tolerance of formal experimentation, Kundera markets his novel to more than one type of audience.

The online reviewer Trevor Kettlewell raises the issue of class when discussing the novel's density, as valued by Kundera. He underrates the author's prose style for its formal tricks and "trademark" erotic themes, which for Kettlewell are a mark of "European sophistication" and a privileged, white, European background, unlike those of racial minorities in France and Europe. As he puts it, Kundera seduces readers with "his assured prose style; educated description of subtleties of how different languages deal with the term 'nostalgia'; and the classical motif of Odysseus," but all this "shows more about class than insight."[27] Kettlewell infers that national differences are as crucial to reception and interpretation as questions of literary aesthetics. Indeed intertextual references to Homer's epic and a penchant for eroticism make Kundera particularly amenable to European literary canonization. The policing of European borders and the plight of the refugees are not, after all, his novel's focus. Kundera's (2006) work moves to erase the cultural boundary between western and central Europe by claiming the latter to be "the easternmost edge of the West" (160). He defends a primarily cultural vision of Europe, anchored in Renaissance humanism and Enlightenment cosmopolitanism but marked as much by central European novelists like Kafka and Robert Musil as by western European figures such as Diderot, Flaubert, Sterne, and Joyce. Kundera sanctions a conservative notion of Europe understood as a cosmopolitan community of great European writers, whose literary inheritance he revives and claims through his own writing.[28]

With this arguably elitist vision of Europe, Kundera presents himself as a creator of highbrow literature for a cultured public. Online reviewers acknowledge this tactic, yet nevertheless insist on viewing his novel also as a commercial product that should aim to satisfy consumers. On Amazon.ca a passionate debate on the novel's packaging has flourished. The online reviewer Victor Cresskill dismisses *Ignorance*'s brevity as a commercial trick: "the type is way too large, the margins way too wide, the price way too high for a book whose landscapes and interiors are mostly white space, whose characters are virtually featureless and faceless, and whose prose is bland enough to match." Reacting to Cresskill's attention to marketing aspects such as typeset, layout, and price, "A customer" writes, "[H]ow a book is set and how much it is sold for are not matters for literary criticism to contend with."[29] This reviewer, self-associating with professional modes of reading and questions of abstract value, invites other readers to turn to Kundera's previous French novels and novelistic theories for a deeper understanding of *Ignorance*. Still another reviewer takes issue with contextual readings of *Ignorance*, suggesting that readers should "judge it on its own terms" rather than in relation to the author's work as a whole: "Are we blind to bland [writing] because Kundera's name is attached to it? Large margins and type and a fat price tag might not be for critics to contend with, but most of us are also buyers." In his or her view Kundera's celebrity should not obscure the fact that his novel "fails to do" what "any good book" should do: "create a world" and "transport the reader to that world."[30] Crediting Kundera's fame for overly high expectations of his works, another reviewer scoffs at the previous reader's amateur approach and defends Kundera's aesthetics: "Judging a work on its own terms means not faulting *Ignorance* for neglecting to describe the physical appearance of its characters where that would be irrelevant (as Kundera, and Kafka too, characteristically do not)."[31] For this reviewer *Ignorance* is not simply a page-turner.

These exchanges illustrate the "contingencies of reading," whereby external sources such as the author's biography, the price, or other works prompt interpretation and animate debate (Procter and Benwell 2015, 18). The above-mentioned reviews debate the right way to read. Should one focus on a novel's intrinsic value, draw on paratextual elements and comparable works, or judge it as a commodity? Although they are conscious of their status as consumers, they do not completely challenge modes of critical evaluation based on the belief in texts' intrinsic value. Online readers generally have difficulty envisaging Kundera's novel as a commodity that instructs and entertains.

Finally, online reviewers speculate about the novel's intended audience. Some envision dual national audiences: "Milan Kundera wrote this book at once for the French, who think they know the suffering of exiles [. . .] and for the Czechs who stayed in their country and who don't know anything about life in exile."[32] Others imagine migrant publics and students of migration as the novel's ideal readers: "This book speaks to all exiles," "To [be] read especially by all those with an expatriate experience," and "I recommend this reading to those interested in questions of immigration."[33] Nevertheless there are others who emphasize the text's universal potential: "It will surely be a delightful read for those living away from their home countries. But the issues are universal."[34] One such issue is "lost love," which "allows Kundera to connect with the everyday reader."[35] Despite the novel's all-encompassing themes likely to appeal to wide readerships, many reviewers suggest that *Ignorance* presents interpretive challenges to those unfamiliar with Kundera's works: "If you're a fan of Kundera, then this book is for you [. . .] but is a poor selection if you're unaccustomed to his prose."[36] In a similar vein other reviews establish the novel as a highbrow literary work that only a few sophisticated readers can appreciate: "it may not be to the tastes of all (i.e. those seeking action)," "probably not for a wide audience," and "everyone who is into high literature should read this book."[37]

Ignorance appeals to heterogeneous publics who bring different levels of critical competence to the novel. Some draw on their knowledge of Kundera and his oeuvre to interpret the novel, while others display a lack of familiarity with Kundera's literary universe and skepticism about the literary hype attached to the author and his novels. All in all, digital audiences who debate the literary value of *Ignorance* struggle to reconcile the novel's aesthetic and commercial value—a tension also present in online discourses about Makine's novel.

LA VIE BETWEEN CULTURE AND COMMERCE

La Vie d'un homme inconnu (2009), published in English as *The Life of an Unknown Man* (2012), recounts the story of Ivan Shutov, a middle-aged Russian author who immigrates to France in the 1980s and returns to Russia after twenty years. A marginal literary figure in France, he rejects and at last leaves behind contemporary French literature's trend toward the commodification of ethnic difference. Yet his arrival in Saint Petersburg quickly dispels his illusion that contemporary Russian authors enjoy literary autonomy and need not write for the market. In fact post-Soviet Russia is a materialistic society in thrall to American capitalism, where "high" art and literature have been replaced by Russian brands of the global literary marketplace. Contemporary France and Russia, and their respective literary industries, are presented as mirror images of each other. The myth of the migrant return is no more, alongside the ideal of a non-Western space of literature that operates in isolation from political and economic constraints. Shutov's quest to address deep human issues beyond the commercial leads him to Guéorgui Lvovitch Volsky. Volsky, from his sickbed, recounts his life as a World War II veteran who has survived the horrors of Stalin and the siege of Leningrad (1941–44). His story highlights the heroism of ordinary citizens and the power of culture to counter the atrocities of war. Volsky makes Shutov a witness to his account of a Soviet era whose virtues have been all but forgotten in contemporary Russia. Shutov's self-identification as "Soviet" provides him with a new literary mission: to rewrite History in ways that account for anonymous and forgotten figures like Volsky (33).

The Life of an Unknown Man leaves no doubt about the aesthetic and political value of Volsky's account, while attacking contemporary French novels (chief among them Kundera's) as self-absorbed and commercially oriented. Among the main targets of Shutov's criticism are Kundera's novels, which he mockingly discusses with his French lover, Léa. Shutov cites a passage from *Identity*, which describes the passing of saliva from lovers to other people and objects. Shutov deems the excerpt "[r]evolting [. . .] Formulated by a writer whom Léa idolizes and whom Shutov regards as drearily pretentious. A far cry from Chekhov. Nowadays a hero has to be neurotic, cynical, impatient to share his unsavory obsessions with us" (6). Makine's attack on his fellow migrant writer through Shutov ignores Kundera's similar battle: he, too, deplores the state of contemporary literature and looks back nostalgically at a period in European literary history when literature was not wedded to the demands of the marketplace. Makine furthermore obliquely mocks another Kundera novel through Shutov's remark that French critics and readers appreciate "one of those little stories that crowd the bookstore shelves: two characters meet, fall in love, laugh, weep, part, are reunited, and then she leaves or kills herself (according to taste) while he, with a tormented but handsome face, drives away into the night along an *autoroute*, heading for Paris, for oblivion" (14–15). This passage—especially if read in light of Makine's earlier citing of *Identity*—recalls Kundera's *Slowness*, in which Vincent rushes to Paris on his motorcycle after failing to make love to Julie. Makine's veiled criticism overlooks the fact that Kundera's novel also stages the clash between two epochs—the eighteenth century and the contemporary period—clearly showing its preference for the former, much like Makine's novel highlights a forgotten historical period that deserves to be remembered and that comes to life in Volsky's narration.

Makine's biography and *The Life of an Unknown Man* share much with Kundera's biography and work. Both authors hail from nonfrancophone eastern European countries (Makine immigrated to France in 1987) and adopt assimilationist strategies by writing about their native cultures in French, for French audiences, and with reference to French culture. They also uphold a conservative view both of literary value, as rooted in autonomous principles of pure aesthetics, and of French and European literary history. In Makine's case this conception is visible in his debut novel, *Le Testament français*, which deliberately exalts the prestige of French literature and the genius of the French language. While the two authors' receptions in France follow the same path of initial celebration followed by subsequent critique, they nevertheless remain central literary figures in France, as their institutional recognition attests; Kundera and Makine won both French literary prizes (the Goncourt, the Médicis) and the international Prix mondial Cino Del Luca in 2009 and 2014, respectively. In addition Kundera's oeuvre was published in Éditions Gallimard's prestigious Bibliothèque de la Pléiade series in 2011, and Makine joined the Académie française in 2016. Like those who commented on *Ignorance*, online reviewers of *The Life of an Unknown Man* focused on the author's biography, the impact of his migrant experiences, critical celebrity, expectations of literary excellence, and the novel in the context of his oeuvre in general. The most striking topic of these debates—the novel's atypical structure—raises new questions about the professionalization of lay readers in online communities.

Volsky's story is a novel within a novel; it is placed in the middle of Makine's text and bookended by Shutov's departure from and return to France. Its lyrical and lofty tone contrasts sharply with the sarcastic tone Shutov harnesses to critique French society. *The Life of an Unknown Man*'s structure and tone match its content; it stages a clash between aesthetic and commercial visions of literature, whether French or Russian, and between commercial authors and those socially committed. Yet the framing device serves another purpose: to build momentum for Volsky's tale and humanist vision of war. Through these narrative techniques, Makine triggers emotional reactions in his readers, who cannot but be moved by the resilience of ordinary people under extreme physical and psychological hardship. This discord between Makine's trademark style, which he preserves in Volsky's sentimentalized narrative, and *The Life of an Unknown Man*'s experimental structure has provoked confusion among online readers. Their debates over the merits of the novel's structure offer useful tools for analyzing the ways in which formal aspects condition readings.

Most reviewers who engaged with the novel's bipartite structure hold contrasting views. They find the first part (the critique of French society and literature) either superfluous or, on the contrary, necessary to the second (Volsky's war narrative). Lay readers have difficulty connecting the novel's parallel threads. Indeed Makine tackles several different themes simultaneously: an exile's homecoming; cultural globalization and literary commodification; parallel love stories taking place in Russia and France, before and after Shutov's emigration, in literature and real life; and the effects of war on individuals. Online audiences perform selective readings, highlighting a particular theme that resonates with them personally (e.g., an exile's return) or that makes an emotional impact (e.g., Russians' resilience during the siege of Leningrad). As Mandarine puts it, "I find the first part a little long because everything is not essential for me."[38] In a similar vein another reader states, "The first part did not interest me very much, but Volsky's story is really touching."[39] Many debate the novel's true subject matter. In reviews it appears as a migrant novel ("an exiled dissident's discovery of what Russia has become," "a beautiful text about exile"), a testimony of war in Soviet times ("A book about Russia"), and a universal love story ("an absolute love story").[40] Few notice Makine's critique of the contemporary French and Russian literary establishments or his reference to Kundera's *Identity*, focusing instead on Volsky's story. Makine thus appeals to professional readers, who are aware of the author's previous reception by French critics and the literary expectations placed on migrant writers in France, as well as lay readers, who seek in this novel "beautiful images" (Nathafi), "poetry" (Pucksimberg), dark Russian themes (CoupdeSoleil), and compassionate characters (Alma).[41]

Not all online commenters ignore the necessity of the framing structure. Alma, for instance, reads Shutov's disenchantment with the state of the French publishing industry and mass media, as well as his search for cultural values in contemporary Russia, as "two necessary steps" that introduce Volsky's narrative. As she puts it, "to suppress the beginning and the end of the novel would deprive it of an indispensable dimension."[42] For the online reviewer soleil, the middle part, in which Shutov returns to Saint Petersburg, underscores his in-between identity position: neither French nor Russian.[43] Isad similarly deems the first part relevant to the relationship between the protagonists, because the contrast between France and Russia, and Shutov's exilic life and his return experience, helps to develop Volsky as Shutov's foil. As Isad explains, only through his encounter with Volsky can one interpret Shutov's migrant return as a voyage of initiation from which he emerges revitalized.[44] To put it differently, "[I]f the story within the story had stood on its own," the novel could not be read as a migrant novel, and the "cultural difference between Soviet and new Russia" would not have been so poignant.[45]

The novel's frame is clearly indispensable, for besides creating momentum for Volsky's Soviet experiences it highlights the commodifying context in which literary works—especially those by migrant and diasporic authors—are consumed in the Global North. The frame sets up Makine's move from discussions of identity politics in the first part to debates about aesthetic value in the second. As a marginal writer in France, Shutov rails against politically correct and commercially oriented forms of literature, highlighting the dilemmas authors face today: to seek the spotlight or solitude, to write for mass or elite audiences. He abhors the role of the exotic Russian writer he plays in television interviews, where he, as well as the two black and Chinese francophone writers who join him, represent "[t]hree living proofs of the globalization of French literature" (26). Shutov prefers to remain an "[u]nusual" writer with "a limited readership," rather than embrace the latest trends (7, 15). His models are the nineteenth-century Chekhov and Tolstoy, and he marvels that "[t]hey could still write like that in the good old days" (i.e., obeying only aesthetic concerns) (6). It is a Romantic notion of authorial autonomy that conveniently ignores the part that literature and commerce also played in the period. Exile has no doubt shaped Shutov's idea of Russia as a literary country. Upon his return, however, he discovers a Russia of crass materialism, where the rich make the news and talk of money is the order of the day. Despite his Russian origins, Shutov remains a misfit here as well. And the state of Russian literature disappoints even more. The publishing house run by Vlad, the son of his former lover Iana, produces commercial novels and markets them aggressively, with sensational book jackets and catchy titles such as *Nicholas II, the Innocence of a Martyr* (62). As Vlad explains, these "brands" need not be historically accurate (61); on the contrary he and his staff manipulate historical truth through advertising to pique interest and increase commercial appeal. Shutov deplores the desacralization of authors and books, as well as readers' transformation into indiscriminate consumers of literature. For him, Vlad is "selling books like vacuum cleaners" (63).

Out of sync with the commercial logic that drives literary production, Shutov belongs to an earlier era, when fictional texts engaged with history in ways that underscored human beings as singular and heroic, rather than implausible, as in Vlad's Russian novels, or neurotic, as in contemporary French novels. Musing on the impact of history on literature, Shutov at first celebrates underground poetry—what Vlad mockingly calls "Great Literature" (63)—for its independence from the Soviet political agenda and the literary marketplace. Great literature in his view flourishes in times of censorship. Shutov prefers marginal subjects left out of official historical accounts. For him, Volsky's story represents a model of discourse that links suffering to authenticity and value. As a migrant author, Shutov positions himself not in relation to a multicultural model of identity politics but to an ideal of literary autonomy from politics and the market. He eschews the usual national identity categories devised by critics, opting for an aesthetic credo based on the writer's responsibility to correct historical gaps. Discarding Chekhov, a bourgeois author, as well as self-absorbed French writers, Shutov embraces instead Volsky, an ordinary storyteller, for the power of his words and emotions. Shutov's identification with the dark Soviet period evoked by Volsky suggests that his literary belonging should be understood in temporal rather than spatial terms. As an online reviewer put it, "his true homeland is not a territory but a bygone era."[46] Shutov's nostalgia for his native country is, in fact, "a yearning for a different time" (Boym 2001, xv)—a bygone era that preserved cultural values endangered by today's commodity culture. *The Life of an Unknown Man* makes a case for writing and reading literature outside of commercial contexts, but it also highlights the arbitrary factors involved in literary legitimation.

Online reviewers who privilege Volsky's narration over other parts of the novel demonstrate that the "Great Literature" of bygone eras does not appeal only to an elite public. Readers react emotionally to the long string of horrors as well as the hopeful moments in times of war. They are stunned by Volsky's strength, touched and revolted, at a loss for words, and "exhausted, trembling, with tears streaming down" their cheeks.[47] Other readers on the contrary express annoyance at the "childish emotionalism" deployed by the novel in its effort to appeal to "hypersensitive readers."[48] The success of the war narrative can be explained partly by the fact that Makine targets non-Russian readers whose lack of knowledge about Russian history prevents them from noticing the author's omission of dark aspects of the siege in favor of "the Leningraders' heroism, altruism and high level of culture" (Duffy 2015, 142). Reviewers who are drawn to the historical aspect of Volsky's story react according to their degree of familiarity with Russian history and the Gulag. For example, while some claim that the story within the story is "what saves the book," others—acquainted with authors such as "Solzhenitsyn, Axionov, Shalamov"—reproach the novel's "very banal generalities."[49] As a narrative of return to a country largely unknown to contemporary French readers, the novel estranges some reviewers, like Elya, who wishes the novel were written in a way more accessible to French audiences.[50]

Online commentaries on *The Life of an Unknown Man* demonstrate that reading is "a socially situated practice," meaning readers who differ in terms of social status, geographical location, and literary knowledge, among other extrinsic factors, offer divergent responses to the same text (Procter and Benwell 2015, 27). One such nonliterary factor is the novel's selection as a finalist for the 2012 Prix des Lecteurs/Lectrices de Critiques

Libres. That the novel was proposed for a literary prize endowed it with value, enticing readers to discover a new author. Elya, who dislikes the novel, would not have finished it if not for the award and finds in other members' ratings confirmation of her low impression. Another reader, Donatien, likewise invests other reviews with critical authority: "I borrowed this book after having read very laudatory comments." According to migo, existing critiques provided encouragement to fight through the challenges of a difficult-to-read novel: "Luckily after the first third of the novel I read the reviews of Babelio readers. So I got over the boredom of the first chapters. I was right to persevere."[51]

Readers thus often post comments about their reading experience, namely its relative easiness or difficulty. They obey the conventions of writing online reviews by not revealing spoilers or "aspects the reader might like."[52] They pay attention not only to other reviews but also to editors' and professional reviewers' blurbs and to novels' construction of implied readers. A reviewer writes that the jacket blurb of Makine's novel disappoints; it promises an unclichéd story of exilic return but banks on tired cultural stereotypes of Russia.[53] Online readers by and large display awareness of marketing techniques and the novels' own strategies to seduce readers. At the same time, they seek new forms of critical authority (those offered by their peers, members of online communities) and criteria of legitimation (sincere expressions of emotions and books' ability to offer a pleasurable reading experience). Reviewers' critical sensibility and affective responses substantiate the circulation of migrant literature as a commodity endowed with aesthetic value.

It is ironic that online reviewers would elect *The Life of an Unknown Man* for the Prix des Lecteurs/Lectrices de Critiques Libres, given the novel's rebuttal of modes of contemporary consecration and its ideal of literary legitimacy based on literary models of the past. The same can be said about *Ignorance*, with its cosmopolitan aims and intertextual ties to canonical literature such as *The Odyssey*. After all, they are novels that express fear of literature's appropriation by lay readerships. But the forms of online criticism propose new criteria of consecration that transcend the aesthetic/commercial binary. The new criticism encompasses aesthetic readings (in conformity with the authors' aims), biographical readings (through the recuperation of the authors' migrant trajectories), economic readings (in light of the novels' global circulation as literary commodities), and affective readings (born within communities of shared tastes). In doing so, online reviewers affirm their critical agency in ways that circumvent the prescribed readings of authors and professional critics. This chapter has explored digital audiences as newly empowered agents that wrestle with the meaning and value of migrant texts. The next chapter continues to pay attention to lay readers alongside other consecrating agents of the French literary field, namely a new literary prize.

3

CONSECRATION

The Prix littéraire de la Porte Dorée and Its Migrant Archive

Since the early 1980s French literary prizes have steadily celebrated migrant authors from former French colonies and nonfrancophone countries who have adopted the French language for their works.[1] This surge in recognition occurred at a time of increasing demand on the part of French editors, critics, and readers for migrant and diasporic fictional works that either critiqued the racism of French society (as Beur and African diasporic texts did) or praised the French language for its universality (a strategy adopted by nonfrancophone writers). These authors redefined French literature by infusing it with their own languages and cultures, even if their integration into the French literary field came about in ways that either exoticized or assimilated them. Given this increasing taste for migrant fiction, it is not surprising that the institutional celebration of migrant writers has continued in the 2000s as well. From 2000 to 2016 the growing number of literary prizes for migrant authors' works attests to the writers' mainstream position in the French literary field.[2] The surge in foreign-born prize winners did not escape the notice of the signatories of the 2007 manifesto "Pour une 'littérature-monde' en français," who asserted that the awarding of major French prizes in 2006 to writers outside of France marked a "Copernican revolution," in the sense that the peripheries now constitute the center.[3] If the authors of the manifesto regarded the middle of that first decade of the century as a historic moment, they could scarcely have foreseen that only a few years later another event would revolutionize the French literary prize system.

The creation of a literary award in 2010 that celebrates not only migrant authors and texts but the genre of migrant literature itself has changed the ways in which contemporary French literature is being produced, disseminated, and received both within and outside France. Established by Élisabeth Lesne under the auspices of the Musée national de l'histoire de l'immigration (National Museum of the History of Immigration), the Prix littéraire de la Porte Dorée (Golden Door Literary Prize) is awarded annually to a French-language fictional text about exile or immigration.[4] The eight winners to date (Alice Zeniter, Michaël Ferrier, Henri Lopes, Mathias Énard, Julien Delmaire, Sylvain Prudhomme, Doan Bui, and Négar Djavadi) have addressed topical issues such as Nicolas Sarkozy's debate on French national identity, clandestine Mediterranean crossings from the Maghreb and Sub-Saharan Africa, and the echoes of the Arab Spring in Europe, among others.[5] While celebrated for their testimonial, didactic, and exotic value, like works of migrant fiction before them, these prizewinning novels treat the political, social, and economic changes occurring in France, Europe, and around the globe in unprecedented ways. They underscore moreover the historical place of immigrants in the nation-state, revealing France to have always been a hybrid and plurilingual space. The Porte Dorée prize has seized upon these novels' timely themes and appeal to a general audience receptive to a type of fiction that promotes humanitarian values. In doing so it has shaped the terms in which they are being read.

The relationship between France's literary prize system and the literary market for migrant fiction has much to show us about how prizes influence literary production and canon formation. In selecting and consecrating fictional texts that conform to contemporary tastes, the Porte Dorée promotes a literary genre that is political in content, yet palatable and nonsubversive by virtue of its legitimation by a national institution and its conformity to a favorable horizon of expectations. To put the argument differently, through its focus on migrant literature the prize represents a belated acknowledgment of the centrality of immigration in contemporary France and French literature, while serving at the same time as an instrument of French cultural and linguistic hegemony: it sanctions fictional texts that conform to the ideology of the Musée national de l'histoire de l'immigration and that are published by top Parisian presses.

From the start of the twentieth century literary prizes have been directly implicated in the struggle to designate literary value. As one of the consecrating agents of the literary field, they perform several important functions. One key role is to classify literary works into recognizable labels. In this sense, as Sylvie Ducas (2013) argues in her richly documented *La Littérature à quel(s) prix? Histoire des prix littéraires*, French literary prizes function as "a salutary sorting and selection tool in the jungle of titles that inundate the literary market every year" (8). But this very selection mechanism implies that there are criteria and judgments of value according to which prizes allegedly validate literary texts for their aesthetic merit, when not on social and political grounds. Another function then is to establish hierarchies of value by instilling belief in the inherent merit of the literary works they legitimize. Finally, because they distinguish some books from others by promoting them and increasing their visibility in the marketplace, prizes also function as "an incredibly salable device," boosting book sales and even begetting other prizes (45). Literary awards can thus be situated at the intersection between the aesthetic and the commercial poles of the literary industries. Prizes consecrate books and sell them too.

In his wide-ranging *The Economy of Prestige: Prizes, Awards, and the Circulation of Cultural Value*, James English (2005) points to this ambivalence, contending that prizes operate at once as "tokens of esteem" (1) and as "*economic* transaction[s]" (5, original emphasis). As he explains, prizes "serve simultaneously as a means of recognizing an ostensibly higher, uniquely aesthetic form of value and as an arena in which such value often appears subject to the most businesslike system of production and exchange" (7). That is to say, prizes promote a view of literary works as both aesthetically singular and consumable. Yet, as English contends, they conflate not only symbolic and economic capital; they mediate between several other types of capital as well. Prizes are "the single best instrument for negotiating transactions between cultural and economic, cultural and social, or cultural and political capital—which is to say that they are our most effective institutional agents of *capital intraconversion*" (10, original emphasis).

The Porte Dorée literary prize conforms to this relational view of the political, economic, and literary fields insofar as it bridges different forms of capital and enacts several processes of conversion—namely it politicizes, legitimizes, and popularizes migrant literature in France. By selecting politically inflected novels, highlighting their stylistic contributions, and increasing their visibility in the marketplace, the prize mediates between three different conceptions of literary works: socially—and politically—engaged literature, "art for art's sake," and popular literature. These conceptions also correspond to competing notions of value: documentary, atemporal, and commercial. Furthermore, as a national prize, it advances an idea of French literature, operating in the present moment, that is attuned to current events, accessible to a mass readership, and thus reflective of the cultural tastes of an epoch. The study of the Porte Dorée prize illuminates the individual as well as institutional agents involved in the production of contemporary French literature. More than that, however, it highlights the ways in which the status of the authors and their prizewinning texts is determined collectively by various agents of the literary, political, and economic fields.

The Porte Dorée distinguishes itself from the plethora of French literary prizes in several ways. A hybrid award of sorts, it at once discovers new talents, consecrates already established writers, and incorporates lay readers into the nomination process. In addition to singling out authors and texts, it rewards a timely literary genre—the literature of exile and immigration—and thus fills a gap in the French literary prize system. Besides creating an archive of contemporary migrant novels, the prize vigorously promotes the books and their publishing houses and seeks to redress the balance between major and minor authors as well as large and small presses. What is more, as a readers' choice award, it allows new agents—such as young readers—to enter the game of literary consecration, thereby democratizing literary judgment and taste. The following section examines each of these value-making processes to explain what this prize reveals about broader cultural trends in which it participates.

CONSECRATING MIGRANT LITERATURE

The Porte Dorée intervenes unlike any other literary prize before it in the dynamics of French cultural memory. Although it may seem a belated addition to the French prize system, given the proliferation of literary prizes since the beginning of the twentieth century and the large corpus of French-language migrant texts, the Porte Dorée justifies its necessity in two crucial ways. First, it posits immigration as a constitutive part of France's national fabric. The prize presents itself as an extension of the immigration museum's permanent exhibit *Repères* (Landmarks), which showcases migratory flows to France from 1820 to the present. Even though it rewards contemporary literature, the prize adopts a diachronic approach that stresses the deep historical roots of immigration in the nation-state. Indeed most of the laureates portray contemporary France in light of past epochs and distant lands, thus broadening conceptions of French history and identity. Second, the Porte Dorée invites a reconsideration of contemporary French literature through the lens of immigration. Envisioned as a supplement to the museum's 2009 anthology *Nouvelles Odyssées: 50 auteurs racontent l'immigration* (New odysseys: 50 authors narrate immigration), the prize champions the vital role literature plays in representing the phenomenon of immigration in ways that differ from political and media discourses. As Lesne (2011) states, "when literature evokes immigration, it does so in infinitely more intelligent, delicate, and subtle ways than journalists or politicians do" (para. 2). Lesne and jury members stress the singular aesthetic forms through which each of the laureates approaches immigration, thus lending support to Bourdieu's (1993) idea that belief in the value of a work of art rests on "the (collective) belief which knows and acknowledges it as a work of art" (35). If belief in the aesthetic value of fictional texts rests on the endorsement of literary institutions, the Porte Dorée prize serves as a clear example of the impact such institutions can have on the literary field.

The Porte Dorée instills belief in its power to reward aesthetic value through the laudatory rhetoric of its book reviews and promotional materials, as well as through a carefully orchestrated selection process that overplays the fierce literary competition among prize entrants. For example, Julien Delmaire, the president of the jury that elected Prudhomme's *Les Grands* for the 2015 prize edition, legitimated the novel's aesthetic value by stating that "[t]his novel is anything but a trendy cultural product[;] it's a work of art that deserves long-term consecration."[6] As a prize for the best book of the year, chosen from a selection of novels published every editorial year, it creates hierarchies of value within the migrant literature category itself. Each year French publishing houses submit between forty and sixty novels about immigration to a reading committee composed of members of the Musée national de l'histoire de l'immigration and lay readers: historians, teachers, librarians, and the like. This committee then selects eight to ten novels, and from that group the jury chooses a winner. The laureate and other nominees attend the award ceremony, held in June, to discuss, promote, and sign their books in the Palais de la Porte Dorée. While the award follows the traditional mechanism and stages of prize consecration, it also seeks to change the rules of the game by introducing new agents of legitimation and attempting to redress the balance between agents traditionally privileged and agents less so.

Unlike more prestigious French prizes whose juries are fixed and homogeneous, the Porte Dorée's jury rotates. It consists of an eclectic blend of professional and lay readers: writers, literary critics, journalists, booksellers, politicians, members of the museum and its sponsoring organization, as well as fifteen- and sixteen-year-old high school students, who read the nominations under the guidance of their teachers. The prize administrators take pains to make the election process democratic by giving an equal voice to diverse—and presumably disinterested—agents of the literary, journalistic, editorial, political, educational, and economic fields. The composition of the jury underscores the entrance of new agents in the field of struggles for literary legitimation, such as prize sponsors and lay readers. The museum's sponsoring organization, Fondation EDF, offers a prize of €4,000 to allow laureates to pursue new writing projects. In exchange for patronage, however, the organization has a say in the selection of the winner, which points out the extent to which literary and financial transactions are imbricated.

Much as they try to include common readers in the deliberations, the prize administrators clearly draw on the jury members' prominent intellectual status to reinforce the symbolic capital of the prize. The biographical information and published works of the jury members are prominently displayed in all online promotional documents. So far the jury has mostly consisted of recognizable public figures: the politician Jacques Toubon (former minister of culture and of justice and president of the board of directors of the immigration history museum from 2007 to 2014); the writers Nathacha Appanah, Mehdi Charef, Alain Mabanckou, Eduardo Manet, and Léonora Miano; the historians Arlette Farge and Pap Ndiaye; and the linguist Henriette Walter, among others. The jury is furthermore headed by the previous year's laureate, who writes a laudatory review of the current year's winner. Thus goes the circular logic of literary consecration, whereby a consecrated author acquires the power to consecrate others in turn, through interviews, institutional promotion, and endorsements of successors.

However, the inclusion of young readers on the prize jury undeniably reflects a broader cultural trend: the rise of lay readers as legitimating agents and producers of value in the contemporary literary field. In its attempt to cultivate young readers—instructing them through reading, turning them into loyal customers—the Porte Dorée shares the educational goals of other readers' choice awards, such as the Prix Goncourt des lycéens and the Prix des Lectrices de *Elle*. Yet the prize's clout extends beyond young audiences to include any average reader interested in contemporary literature. Significantly the first awarding of the prize, to Alice Zeniter's *Jusque dans nos bras*, coincided with the second edition of the cultural festival known as Paris en toutes lettres (June 9–13, 2010), whose aim was to promote reading, writing, and general access to culture.[7] It was in this context that Zeniter's novel, with its timely topic and accessible style, was able to find new readers.

The organizers' *cafés littéraires*, held in the museum's multimedia library throughout the year, are another aspect of the program to capture lay readers. The cafés are meet-the-author events hosted by Élisabeth Lesne and occasionally by the high school jury members. These events mark a shift in the status of contemporary authors, whose public presence and direct contact with readers are increasingly expected and necessary for promoting their works. The literary cafés also foster a sense of competition among the selected books as commodities to be promoted, chosen, and consumed by reader-customers according to a supply-and-demand logic. The texts sanctioned by the Porte Dorée represent cultural products that are constructed and promoted collectively with a view to their accruing both economic and symbolic capital. As marketing strategy, the literary cafés effectively blur the line between promotion and consecration.

Unlike other prizes, the Porte Dorée promotes not only the laureate but all nominated authors and works, on both its website and through the above-mentioned literary cafés. Its online materials make a corpus of contemporary migrant texts available to the public. These promotional documents include the laureate's biography, his or her novel's encomiums, the jury's composition and its members' biographies, synopses of the other nominees' novels, as well as links to previous years' winners and audio interviews with the laureates. By marketing the winner in this fashion, the prize encourages comparative and collective readings under the category of the "literature of exile and immigration." Put differently, it invites similar readings of texts that, without the Porte Dorée prize, might not otherwise be considered novels of the immigration genre. For example, Prudhomme's *Les Grands* recounts the story of Super Mama Djombo, a band of musicians famous in Guinea-Bissau in the 1970s, and deals with immigration to France only indirectly and intermittently, and Ferrier's generically hybrid novel *Sympathie pour le fantôme*, while narrating the protagonist's immigration experience, touches on a host of themes, making it difficult to categorize. Had they not been grouped around the same theme and marketed together, the two novels could easily be read under a host of other umbrella categories, such as francophone or postmodern.

One drawback for the prizewinners then is the risk and concomitant expectations of being typecast as authors who write novels exclusively about immigration. Literary labels have the power to reduce the complex meanings of fictional texts. *Le Monde* dubbed Énard an authority on the Arab Spring and an advocate for an "Arab humanism."[8] By publishing his novel in Gallimard's Continents noirs series, Lopes was tied to African and African diasporic writing, a classification that dates to his publishing *Le Pleurer-rire* (1982) with Présence Africaine. The prizewinners are well aware of the simultaneously enabling and limiting effects of such awards. Zeniter, for instance, defends the singularity and thematic diversity of her literary trajectory. Her subsequent novels *Sombre dimanche* (2013) and *Juste avant l'oubli* (2015) do not tackle immigration but Hungarian communism and a failed love relationship, respectively. Yet in reading *Jusque dans nos bras*, a novel about an interethnic marriage, many reviewers stressed Zeniter's ethnically mixed identity, unwittingly turning her into a spokesperson for ethnic or immigrant topics. Aware of this danger, the author states, "I don't want to be labeled as a representative ethnic writer. I don't want to write books about the great cultural gap all my life. [...] But this book addresses questions of immigration and exile, and the fact that people give me credit for this topic even though I make a mockery of my characters, is something that touches me."[9] By invalidating the commonly fostered connection between authors' biographies and their fictional texts, Zeniter reminds us that immigration as a literary topic often interpellates authors, irrespective of their ethnic origin or citizenship status. The prize signals a shift in the way migrant literature is being conceptualized and produced in the twenty-first century. It presents migrant literature as a category defined by theme rather than biography, all the while constructed by marketing agents and cultural institutions. Nonmigrant writers are nevertheless still often saddled with the expectations traditionally related to the genre. Prizes in general, and the Porte Dorée in particular, continue to function as branding devices even in the case of authors who identify ethnically as French.

In some cases, however, authorial biography and migrant texts do match. Bui's (2016) *Le Silence de mon père* recounts her Vietnamese parents' difficult assimilation in France. The author-narrator starts by investigating her father's silence and her family's secrets but soon realizes that her parents' story implicates her in unforeseen ways. She comes to regard her identity as poised between two cultures, even though, up until then, she has asserted her Frenchness by denying her Vietnamese roots. Writing is a key tool that allows Bui the narrator to embrace her adoptive culture by saying "I"—which her parents consider "a French thing," as Vietnamese culture advocates the effacement of individuality (67). Through writing she also realizes the extent to which successful assimilation in France comes at the cost of suppressing one's cultural roots. More than a simple portrait of Bui's father, *Le Silence de mon père* helps the author come to terms with her long-repressed immigrant background and understand her place in France as a mixed-race author. It is in this sense of "recognition" (or "knowing herself again") and "reconciliation" (to her ethnic origin), that Bui welcomes the award and believes her novel is a good fit.[10] Asked about the ambivalent nature of a prize that promotes migrant literary works on the one hand and categorizes them rigidly on the other, Bui defended the necessity of the genre. Whereas in her life and writing she tried to "construct a fictive identity as a pureblood French woman," her belated discovery of migrant literature was a "revelation," for she recognized herself in the characters' experiences. For readers like Bui, whose parents failed to transmit their native culture, migrant texts provide much-needed models of hybrid identity. In valorizing the migrant genre, the Porte Dorée inscribes Doan Bui into what she regards as a "family of books and authors in which [she] recognizes herself."[11] The Porte Dorée highlights hybridity as a productive literary technique for interrogating French models of national belonging and promotes a lucrative genre in the French-language literary marketplace that French authors have embraced.

The Porte Dorée has showcased migrant authorship, and in contrast to other French literary awards it has collapsed the boundary between major and minor authors. Some laureates are well established writers with major prizes (Lopes, Énard, and Prudhomme), others are emerging novelists (Zeniter, Delmaire, and Djavadi), while others have a writing career in related fields (Bui). In cases such as Bui's the organizers reinforce the literary authority of newly discovered writers by mentioning their previous works in the promotional materials. Doan Bui, we learn, is a journalist who specializes in immigration, the coauthor of *Ils sont devenus français* (2010)—a journalistic investigation of famous French people of immigrant background—and the author of a prizewinning 2013 article about clandestine migrants attempting to reach Europe, "Les fantômes du fleuve." Overall the Porte Dorée prize aims both to recognize proven winners and to discover and encourage new talents. In the latter case it serves to upend the myth of "the great writer" and "the literary masterpiece" that still haunts the French cultural imaginary (Ducas 2013, 10). Yet seemingly arbitrary choices of idiosyncratic books can result. The election of Delmaire's debut novel *Georgia* for the 2014 prize illustrates the "contingencies of value"—in Barbara Herrnstein Smith's (1988) words—inherent in the process of literary judgment. The novel, which recounts the tragic story of an illegal Senegalese immigrant whom French authorities attempt to expel from France, attracted mixed reviews in the French press. Lukewarm critics cited its excessively lyrical and elaborate style, which contrasts sharply with the social marginalization and dark political issues the text explores. In this view Delmaire poured his talent as a renowned slam poet into the novel to unfortunate results. It appears the jury overlooked such criticism in light of *Georgia*'s political content. The novel conforms to the prize jury's interest in texts that showcase marginal subjects (such as clandestine immigrants and refugees) who are increasingly visible in contemporary societies. In his acceptance speech Delmaire himself reinforces the idea that the Porte Dorée is a political award that "is not afraid of being subjective and politically engaged."[12] These political criteria distinguish it from other French literary prizes that purport to reward solely aesthetic value.

The Porte Dorée's ideological agenda extends to the editorial field as well. The prize attempts to redress the imbalance not only between major and minor authors but also between large and small publishing houses. Smaller publishers usually stand fewer chances of winning the prestigious literary awards (the Goncourt, Femina, Renaudot, Médicis, Interallié, and the Prix de l'Académie française) in France's fall prize competition, on which Gallimard, Grasset, and Le Seuil seem to hold a monopoly. However, the Porte Dorée offers all nominees a chance to win by creating publicity around novels from presses both big and small. While titles that have already won major literary prizes certainly bring prestige to the Porte Dorée, they are sometimes excluded from the competition in order to allow unknown books a chance at critical and commercial success. As Lesne explains, three acclaimed novels, which should have competed on account of their immigrant themes—Marie NDiaye's *Trois femmes puissantes* (Gallimard in 2009, Prix Goncourt), Dany Laferrière's *L'Énigme du retour* (Grasset in 2009, Prix Médicis), and Jean-Michel Guenassia's *Le Club des incorrigibles optimistes* (Albin Michel in 2009, Prix Goncourt des lycéens)—were deliberately left out "to showcase less known titles that we hope will have many readers" (Lesne 2010). In this way the prize has attempted to promote minor players in the editorial and literary fields and to draw attention to an intermediary marketplace consisting of small and independent presses.

Democratic intentions notwithstanding, the Porte Dorée laureates have so far published primarily with renowned publishing houses (Actes Sud, Albin Michel, Gallimard, and Grasset)—with the exception of Négar Djavadi's *Désorientale*, published by Liana Levi. The reign of top presses among winners shows the continuation of hierarchies in the editorial world. It furthermore shows that top presses are a means by which the Porte Dorée accrues symbolic capital. Indeed the prestige of Gallimard's Continents noirs and L'Infini series, which published Lopes's and Ferrier's novels, increases that of the prize. Equally important publishers (Le Seuil, Stock, Flammarion, and Plon) have also figured prominently. That being said, the majority of entries, if not winners, appeared under the banner of lesser known presses such as L'Aube, La Fosse aux ours,

Galaade, L'Iconoclaste, Le Rouergue, Le Nouvel Attila, Léo Scheer, L'Olivier, Non-Lieu, Perrin, Sabine Wespieser, Vents d'ailleurs, Verticales, Zoé, and Zulma. Overall the decision of the Porte Dorée to support less recognized presses underscores Ducas's (2013) argument that today's competition among publishers has replaced literary rivalries among authors that flourished in the nineteenth century (12). Consecration is now increasingly predicated on promotion (12). A novel's nomination for the Porte Dorée brings a windfall of publicity and increased book sales to authors as well as their editors. For example, Énard's *Rue des voleurs* was first released in a print run of sixty thousand copies, then translated into multiple languages (Arabic, Catalan, Dutch, German, Spanish, Italian, and English), and now appears also in an audio version.[13] Énard's case shows how prizes can increase a book's literary and commercial value, leading to translations, reissues in paperback (in the Babel series from Actes Sud, 2014), the attention of book clubs (France Loisirs), and even more prizes (2012 Liste Goncourt/Choix de l'Orient).[14]

If the Porte Dorée serves as a barometer of contemporary tastes, what kind of literature does it promote? The Porte Dorée rewards primarily literary fiction and, in particular, novels—a genre that holds a hegemonic place among literary genres. Sanctioning an already consecrated and commercially viable form, the prize does not have any impact on existing aesthetic hierarchies. Instead it targets an accessible mass readership eager for fictional texts that address present-day concerns. Taken as a whole, the novels endorsed by the Porte Dorée rethink Frenchness at the start of the twenty-first century as something hybrid, multilingual, and polyphonic. These themes are not new, especially in light of postcolonial histories of immigration to the French metropole. Yet they are ever present in French media as well as in the French literary and political imaginary. The country's long-standing and still unresolved question is how to reconcile a liberal attitude to foreigners and cultural diversity on the one hand and the republican model of assimilating difference on the other. This tension between liberal cosmopolitanism and narrow identity models has reached new heights in today's French climate of right-wing nationalism, anti-immigrant and anti-Muslim sentiment, and fear of global terror.

The novels selected by the Porte Dorée respond to a political climate in which narrow identity questions and defensive models of national identity prevail. Despite their societal critiques and pro-immigration stance, they are critically and commercially successful because the migrant subjects they portray are fictional rather than real-life immigrants and do not pose any threats to the nation-state or challenge the status quo. The three novels examined below provide a counterpoint to conservative ideologies through the issues of historical legacy, memory, and borders. In so doing they propose an ethics of recognition of francophone, migrant, and non-European subjects and histories and of their belonging to the French and European nation-states. This recognition is limited paradoxically by the Porte Dorée itself. The national ideology of the Musée national de l'histoire de l'immigration, and the modes of literary consumption that the Porte Dorée encourages, severely limit the novels' politically transformative aims. The prize robs them of their political potential by subordinating their message to desired, expected, and commercially viable notions of nationhood.

THE ETHICS OF RECOGNITION: ZENITER, FERRIER, AND ÉNARD

Alice Zeniter's *Jusque dans nos bras* (2010; published in English as *Take This Man* in 2011) may strike some as a curious choice to inaugurate the Porte Dorée. The novelist was young and little known, and her novel took a light and humorous approach to immigration. Zeniter's work drew sharp contrast with the serious optics—the French Resistance in World War II, an African child-soldier's harsh life in France, immigrants' difficult return to their home country—adopted by the competition's more established writers, such as Antoine Audouard, Alain Blottière, and Vanessa Schneider. Mohamed Kacimi, the jury president, praised Zeniter's novel for "its nerve and audacity" and its being "very contemporary in inspiration as well as style and subject matter."[15] He added that the jury's choice was also motivated by the novel's uplifting idealism, optimism, and sense of justice. It was a largely symbolic choice, then, that rewarded a novel engaged with immediate political realities but in a comic tone that softened its critical edge.

Take This Man tackles an underportrayed topic in contemporary French literature: a *mariage blanc*—a marriage for nationality papers—between Alice and her childhood friend Mad, who would otherwise be expelled to Mali. Zeniter anchors her autofictional story of friendship in a political climate unfavorable to immigrants.[16] The story unfolds amid the rise of the right-wing Front National, the implementation of harsher immigration laws, and massive expulsions of illegal immigrants. In particular the novel responds directly to Jean-Marie Le Pen's securing second place in the first round of the presidential elections of April 21, 2002; the law of July 25, 2006, that sought to curb illegal immigration and restrict access to residence and citizenship; and Nicolas Sarkozy's election in May 2007, his founding of the Ministère de l'immigration, de l'intégration, de l'identité nationale et du codéveloppement (2007–10), and his launching of the debate on national identity in November 2010.

With such political landmarks as its backdrop, *Take This Man* offers an unsparing portrait of present-day France and advocates with urgency for the values of hospitality and responsibility toward foreigners. Yet, rather than press these values didactically, it adopts an informal and vernacular style marked by fast rhythms and the vocabulary of "millennials" (the generation born in the 1980s). As the heroine declares in a repetitious, mantralike fashion throughout the opening chapter, "[m]y generation is all about international terrorism and globalization, my generation doesn't dream about Hollywood but about London, Paris, Tokyo, and Singapore, my generation is all about traders who have to do without their twin towers" (11).

This mixture of social critique and engaging, accessible tone ostensibly accounted for the novel's appeal to the jury members. Yet the novel's success also likely derived from its adherence to the ideological mission of the Musée national de l'histoire de l'immigration and the Porte Dorée, which is to showcase immigration as inextricably linked to French history and national identity and to foster in the process a more tolerant attitude toward immigrants. The museum's own promotional texts confirm that "the mission of the Museum of the History of Immigration is to alter the current view of immigration through an approach that is at once cultural, educational, and civic. It gathers, protects, and showcases [. . .] the elements pertaining to the history of immigration in France."[17]

A fictional response to contemporary French and global politics, and a defense of immigrants' right to asylum, the novel met all criteria. Its very title, taken from "La Marseillaise," the national anthem of France, mocks French fears of "tall ferocious blacks coming *into our midst* [*jusque dans nos bras*] to marry our daughters and our consorts" (174; emphasis added). The novel questions the conservative notion of national identity through its ethnically mixed heroine, Alice, born of a French mother and Algerian father and raised in multicultural suburbs. For Zeniter the category of Frenchness is culturally constructed, and in her heroine's mind Frenchness should be a matter of personal choice rather than racial markers. The arbitrariness of French as a cultural category is clear in the main characters' identity aspirations. Alice downplays her Frenchness and exaggerates her Algerianness, while Mad claims to be more French than the French. Yet, despite Mad's French accent and education, he is marked as an outsider because of the color of his skin. The racism that Mad experiences, as do Alice and her Algerian-born father, together with her mother's reminder that the Declaration of the Rights of Man and of the Citizen protects those who wish to change nationality, prompt Alice to concede to the marriage for legal status. Saving her friend from deportation and taking his name "to create a two-headed *Super-Bougnoule* entity, ZeniterTraoré" (175) are her way of combatting "the Great History of Racism" (17) and hybridizing France. When watching a documentary about *harraga*—North African immigrants who attempt to enter Europe clandestinely but drown in the Mediterranean without "know[ing] the nationality of the water that gradually entered their lungs"—Alice is moved to declare that "[she] wished [she] could marry all of them" (87). Alice's wish to extend hospitality to clandestine immigrants is an act of bravura characteristic of a younger generation neither indifferent to immigration nor afraid to take a political stand. Through the reference to the human costs of Mediterranean migrations, however, the novel also seeks to shift what might appear as petty and self-centered debates about French national identity toward more urgent humanitarian crises.

On its face *Take This Man* is a parody of French discourses on national identity, an embrace of human rights, and an apology for immigration. The novel carries an unmistakably humanist message. In fact it is this very display of "good actions" and "good intentions" that *Le Nouvel Observateur* and *Le Monde* reviewers considered the novel's primary weakness.[18] The novel nevertheless attempts to exchange the current image of exclusionary France for that of France as *terre d'asile*—that is, a land of hospitality, a definition inscribed in both the French Constitution and the Declaration of the Rights of Man and of the Citizen of October 27, 1946—in order to remind readers of what models multicultural France should uphold in times of crisis. Zeniter approaches the question of national identity through an earlier conception of France as host to exiles and immigrants. In similar fashion Michaël Ferrier turns to the past to argue that present-day France should embrace openness and redefine itself in relation to its margins.

Like Zeniter's novel, Ferrier's autofictional *Sympathie pour le fantôme* (Sympathy for the ghost), published in 2010, continues the French debate on national identity and the praise of cultural hybridity, albeit from a geographical and temporal remove. The author-narrator, Michaël, is a literature professor at a Japanese university, which organizes an international conference on French national identity. He also appears regularly on a television program whose aim is to present a nonstereotypical portrait of French history. He then writes an account of "French history revisited by three ghosts" by excavating three nineteenth-century figures from Île de la Réunion, a French territory in the Indian Ocean, and their yet unacknowledged contributions to French art, literature, and economy (233). The first "ghost" is Ambroise Vollard, an art dealer with infallible flair, who after moving to Paris from Réunion discovers painters little known at the time, such as Cézanne, Matisse, Picasso, and Van Gogh. The second is Baudelaire's muse, Jeanne Duval, who represents "an altogether forbidden memory" (171), she having been excised from French literary history "because she is beautiful, because she is female, because she is black" (173), and, when mentioned at all, was denigrated, eroticized, and exoticized. The third story features Edmond Albius, a twelve-year-old slave and burgeoning scientist from Réunion who succeeded in producing vanilla by artificially fertilizing the flower through union of its male and female organs. Because he was a slave, he received no mention in history books or credit for his discovery, which greatly enriched his owner, French colonial society in the Indian Ocean, and France in general through the global market for vanilla. Ferrier's three stories aim to correct exclusionary accounts of official history and cast French national identity as racially and culturally hybrid. All three figures outpaced their time, shaped their society's tastes, and influenced the marketplace, and all were targets of racism and elided from official accounts. In Ferrier's account they are French, despite geographic and racial difference, yet they are "specters that have made us but that we have forgotten," haunting French history (172).

Ferrier's project of ghosting and creolizing French history nonetheless does not innovate at the level of content. Recuperating lost voices through the figure of the ghost has long been a common trope in postcolonial and feminist scholarship.[19] Although the author-narrator conveys the salutary role of counterdiscourses on official history, he situates its impact less in the realm of resistance than in that of "*remembrance*" (45; original emphasis). The three biographies he reconstructs are readily accessible; they are not irrecoverable archival material. His project is to simply recommemorate these peripheral biographies for French memory: "They have been erased from History, these people, they have been relegated to ship holds, I must get them out of there. Ghosts, in a way . . . [d]iverse, incomplete, mutilated memories, devoured by forgetting . . . There are destinies to tell, faces to put on forgotten names. Words to find for neglected, erased heroes" (44). The act of telling erased histories and forgotten heroes has of course its ethical challenges for the writer. Speaking for the subaltern, as Gayatri Chakravorty Spivak (1994) cautions, is not simply a gesture of filling in historical and epistemological lacunae with missing subjects and occluded histories. The project of recovery can instead often reproduce the very representational schema that substitutes "subject effects" for the missing subjects themselves (66). Ferrier's narrator attempts to solve the problem of discursive authority by emphasizing the spectral nature of the three figures. Ambroise Vollard, Jeanne Duval, and Edmond Albius are ghosts in the sense that they straddle the line between presence and absence, past and present, and authorized and alternative histories. As a ghost that "interrupts the presentness of the present," each of these figures reminds us that the present is incomplete, multiple, and hybrid (Weinstock 2004, 5). They are subjects of colonialism and slavery in the Indian Ocean who prompt reconsiderations of monolithic, pure, and positive narratives of the nation that view them as Other, rather than constitutive of French identity.

In the ethical task of fictionalizing "real" historical figures, the author-narrator searches for a specific representational strategy—a new generic form, a decentered point of view—making full and innovative use of the capacities of literary language to evoke absences. The narrator states that "the novel is a reminder," underscoring the genre's capacity to fill historical gaps and correct national amnesia through memorialistic practices (191). However, the reconstruction of memory requires a readjustment of the traditional lenses of writer and reader; linearity and chronology are no longer useful tools. Thus reconceived, the novel poses to the writer "problems of duration, movement, speed, repetition or stagnation, transformation," which require "a very precise and at the same time very mobile form—novel" (19). Embracing the idea of mobile narration, the author-narrator exuberantly casts himself as "an underwater narrator" who can pass above, under, and across any boundary or time periods, dazzling readers with his multilateral and transhistorical movements (239).[20] In this sense the ghost remains an apposite trope for interrogating monolithic conceptions (of identity, nation, origin), enlarging categories, and rethinking historical trajectories. For the author-narrator, following ghosts means shifting his focus from the center to the periphery and acknowledging that the margins constitute the center. In *Sympathie pour le fantôme* the center and periphery, the past and present, the living and the spectral are mutually informed.

Ferrier's project celebrates the peripheries, the polyphonies, and the mobilities that have always been constitutive of history, literature, and identity. The narrator delivers telltale metadiscursive clues to spell out his designs—"France, then, this is the topic" (46)—or when he repeatedly defines the new genre he is writing—"a novel in fragments and by repetitions [. . .] a book *in motion*, Tokyo subway style" (119, original emphasis) or "migrant, itinerant" writing (221). Indeed by switching between locales and time periods (Tokyo, Paris, Bordeaux, Saint-Malo, Réunion, and Maurice Islands; 1999, 1968, and 1829), the narrator creates the impression of constant motion, in terms of content as well as style (the novel is a mixture of genres: autofiction, biography, essay, and academic novel). Ferrier explodes conventional narratives—the official narrative of the French nation among them—that rely on a single location and a narrow time period. He accommodates in the process a multiplicity of contrasting perspectives in writing and reading practices. The narrator writes from Tokyo, far from the French homeland and the Île de la Réunion he writes about. The Japan of his account moreover appears far from homogeneous. Its capital is a place of diasporic encounters and intense debate on issues of national identity and immigration. His attempt to accurately "represent" French culture to a Japanese public foregrounds decentered perspectives and global histories marked by flows of people, artifacts, and commodities.[21] Ferrier's novel is hardly a stable narrative of the French nation.

In 2011, the year of Ferrier's Porte Dorée win, the Musée national de l'histoire de l'immigration and the Porte Dorée jury seemed to have no difficulty selecting a laureate from the eight novels that featured immigrant themes.[22] As Mustapha Harzoune (2011), a literary critic and member of the prize's selection committee, remarked, Sympathie pour le fantôme's "eulogy of hybridity in history and identities" comes along at the right time in a political context riven with debates about national identity (para. 6). A novel valorizing hybridity also likely had great appeal to the jury president, Eduardo Manet—himself a migrant writer of Cuban origin, with a global biography similar to Ferrier's—and to the thirty-five high school jury members, many of whom had immigrant backgrounds themselves.[23] Speculative considerations aside, Ferrier's novel effectively shows how official history has systematically marginalized peripheral figures. It offers new perspective on political debates about Frenchness by exploring the intersections of immigration and haunting, as well as casting the figure of the francophone migrant as a specter of the French.

Mathias Énard's Rue des voleurs (2012; published in translation as Street of Thieves in 2014)—the 2013 Porte Dorée winner—also takes up the idea of spectrality but does so in the context of the Arab Spring in 2011, the rise of Islamic fundamentalism, clandestine Mediterranean crossings, and the European economic crisis. Using these events as backdrop, the novel recounts the story of Lakhdar, a twenty-year-old Moroccan from Tangier who immigrates to Spain, propelled by both personal and political circumstances. Lakhdar stumbles, with Candidelike naïveté, from one misadventure to another on his voyage of perdition that takes him from Tangier to Barcelona, via Algeciras. Told in first-person retrospective narrative, the novel takes the form of a confession, as Lakhdar reflects on the past few years of his life from prison while awaiting trial for murder. Énard makes Lakhdar's story a violent thriller with dark characters such as thieves, drug dealers, prostitutes, and terrorists. By emphasizing the underemployed and lowbrow, Énard departs from the more traditional forms of migrant literature—the autobiographical, autofictional, and testimonial—that the other prize contenders employed.[24]

Street of Thieves offers a fresh approach to migrant literature in terms of both form and content. Its innovation led to two additional literary prizes: the Prix du Roman-News (2013), a media award for a francophone literary text on current events, and the Prix Liste Goncourt/Le Choix de l'Orient (2012), which served to validate further the novel's timeliness.[25] The Porte Dorée and French critics in general also lauded the novel's potential appeal to a wide readership despite, or perhaps because of, its inflammatory political themes. As Alice Zeniter declares, "[t]o write a Sindbadian saga about the Arab Spring so soon after the events is a challenge. And I find the outcome very successful."[26] To her fellow jury member, Michaël Ferrier, the novel is "courageous by its subject matter, a burning topic that could have led to the worst banalities or, on the contrary, to the worst extremes."[27] *Lire* and *Le Point* critics consider *Street of Thieves* the successful novel of the Arab Spring, though the author distanced himself from such readings.[28] Énard states, "The book is at the crossroads of several events. For me, the 'Arab Spring' is not a topic, but it functions as a setting in fiction. [...] I chose a contemporary setting but I could have set the narrative in the 1940s or in the nineteenth century. This direct grip on the contemporary offers me the portrait of a world in full swing, a world in flame that seeks to rebuild itself. What interests me is not so much the world surrounding this narrator but what he will think of it. [. . .] How can one find one's place in this battlefield that the present-day world is?"[29] In contrast to most critics Abdejlil Lahjomri, in *L'Observateur du Maroc*, urges against reading *Street of Thieves* as the Arab Spring novel or as a novel that could be labeled what he calls "emergency literature" (*la littérature de l'urgence*). He instead regards it as a generational tale of lost and hopeless young Moroccans trapped in a liminal position: "these in-between young people: between here and elsewhere, tradition and modernity, faith and secularism."[30] In Lahjomri's reading the thrust of the novel is contemporary Moroccan society in the wake of recent political revolutions.

While it is true that politics play a secondary role in the novel, which focuses more on the protagonist's perception of recent events than on the events themselves, *Street of Thieves* is unmistakably a story about clandestine immigration to a Europe in economic and political crisis. Lakhdar's crossing of the Moroccan-Spanish border brings to the fore the ways in which political events on opposite sides of the Strait of Gibraltar echo each other. His journey also reveals the ways in which youths—be they Moroccan, Algerian, Tunisian, or Catalan—share the ideals of love and liberty. Through these issues linking North Africa and western Europe, Énard calls into question the idea of Europe as a promised land, of Morocco (and North Africa, more generally) as Europe's Other, and of physical borders as impermeable markers of difference rather than the sutures that unite North and South.

As illustration the novel features a protagonist in constant movement, one whose identity is decentered in name, geography, culture, ideology, and religion. The fact that Lakhdar is a rare name in Morocco but common in Algeria and that he hails from Tangier—a westernized port city geographically closer to Algeciras than to Casablanca and peripheral vis-à-vis the other Arab revolutions—places him in a marginal position within his native culture. Being apolitical, he is also out of sync with the tumult of the Arab world. He catches only the aftermath of the Tunisian revolution when traveling to Tunis and feels nothing for the revolutionary hero Sidi Bouzid and his radical act of self-immolation. Instead Lakhdar seeks escape in the less heroic world of cheap foreign thrillers; he devours French and

Spanish detective novels, works by foreign authors (Paul Bowles, William Burroughs, Ángel Vázquez) on Tangier, and Arabic-language literature (by Ibn Battuta and Mohamed Choukri, among others). Fluent in French, Arabic, Spanish, and later Catalan, he constructs his identity through the dialogue between East and West. He transcends Moroccan culture when reading French thrillers in Tangier, while his sense of Arabness awakens when teaching Arabic in Barcelona.

These languages and literatures are Lakhdar's refuge from the chaotic world and his escape from entrapment. One trap is religious fundamentalism. Despite working for Sheikh Nureddin's "Muslim Group for the Propagation of Koranic Thought" (18)—which, unbeknown to him, seeks to islamicize Morocco by violence—he comes to believe that this is a God-forsaken world in which he is left with "no certainty, none" (265). However, realizing that he cannot drift endlessly, he decides to "choose [his] camp" (249). He murders Bassam, his childhood friend indoctrinated by Sheikh Nureddin, so as to deliver him from agony and the dreaded task of launching a bombing attack in Barcelona. When testifying in court, Lakhdar does not deny his crime. He simply insists on not being viewed reductively:

I am not a murderer, I am more than that.
I am not a Moroccan, I am not a Frenchman, I'm not a Spaniard, I'm more than that.
I am not a Muslim, I am more than that.
Do what you will with me. (263)

He pleads for the court to recognize his multifaceted and complex identity, irreducible to the narrow categories of nationality, religion, and even political violence.

Part bildungsroman and part picaresque novel, *Street of Thieves* portrays Lakhdar's identity quest as one in which external circumstances propel him into a downward spiral ending in murder. Lakhdar is an unusual protagonist for the migrant literary genre. He does not fit the more common portrait of immigrants who desire to leave their native country in search of a European Eldorado. An immigrant *malgré lui*, Lakhdar leaves Morocco out of love for Judit, a Spanish student he met in Tangier, and for fear of the Islamic fundamentalism that endangers his life. Lakhdar's immigration to Europe is a dark odyssey of odd jobs and misadventures. He works as a bookseller for Sheikh Nureddin's Muslim Group, as a cheap laborer for an exploitative French press, as a ship boy on the *Ibn Battuta* ferry between Tangier and Algeciras, and as a mortician's assistant for Marcelo Cruz, who repatriates the bodies of the immigrants drowned in the Strait of Gibraltar. In the end Lakhdar flees to Barcelona and winds up on "Carrer Robadors [. . .]—street of whores, of drug addicts, drunkards, of dropouts of all kinds," suggesting the destiny of Arab immigrants is a life of criminal marginality (188).

Street of Thieves illuminates the status of Muslim immigrants in present-day Europe by comparing Lakhdar's travels to the fourteenth-century Moroccan traveler and national hero Ibn Battuta, who ventured widely for thirty years before returning to his home country. Battuta's travels and tales of captivity—the novel's major intertext—serve as an ironic counterpoint and reverse identity model to Lakhdar's border crossings. The latter realizes that "I was not Ibn Battuta" (119) because "[a]t no time, in his travels, does Ibn Battuta speak of a passport, or papers, or safe-conducts; he seems to travel as he pleases" (227). Without the medieval traveler's freedom of movement, Lakhdar encounters checkpoints demanding the identity papers he does not possess. When the *Ibn Battuta* ferry cannot leave Algeciras due to unpaid debts, Lakhdar finds himself in the paradoxical situation of being in Europe physically yet denied the right of entry. He states that without a passport, "I was suspended, I was living in the Strait" (134); "I could only look at Spain from behind the Customs fences, just as hundreds of guys in my situation were looking at the barbed wire around Ceuta or Melilla; the sole difference being that I was on the continent" (135).

Lakhdar's in-between position activates his historical consciousness of previous contacts between the two sides of the strait, namely "the expedition of Tariq ibn Ziyad, the conqueror of Spain, and of those Berbers who had defeated the Visigoths" (132). This memory complicates the line between inside and outside, belonging and nonbelonging, Spanish and Moroccan. Lakhdar suggests at the same time that the memory of the Moorish invasion feeds European stereotypes about Arabs. In mock-ironic tone he describes the ferry's approach to the Andalusian coast as a restaging of conquest that ignites Spanish fears of Muslim immigrants: "I was commanding my own army of trucks, of old Renaults and Mercedes; together we would take Granada, and the Guardia Civil of Algeciras port wasn't going to stop us. [. . .] [F]inally [. . .] my cars of emigrants would leave the belly of the *Ibn Battuta* in a glorious procession, headed for the Alhambra: Spain would become Moroccan again, something it should never have stopped being" (132). Here twenty-first-century Moroccan immigrants, the spectral doubles of eighth-century Moors, expose European fears of immigration. It is not the vision of medieval Iberia as Al-Andalus, where Christians, Jews, and Muslims cohabited peacefully. The cosmopolitan Al-Andalus recedes under the inhospitable reality of "Fortress Europe," as Lakhdar discovers the divisive, rather than connective, nature of borders, as well as the perils and human costs of border crossing.

The novel juxtaposes Spanish visions of Tariq's reconquest with the description of similar fears and xenophobic attitudes in France through the narrative of Mounir, a Tunisian immigrant who lived in Paris before settling in Barcelona. Mounir recounts his arrival in Paris, via Lampedusa, after the Tunisian revolution and describes a French capital of unemployment, poverty, racism, and "endless suburbs," whose descriptions recall Mathieu Kassovitz's *La Haine* (202). The violence, economic hardships, and anti-immigrant sentiment of France reappear in Barcelona, where protest, violence, and persecution reign. The destitution of illegal immigrants, the rise of right-wing parties, and the Okupas and Indignants social movements have pushed the city to the brink of explosion. Lakhdar muses, "Barcelona was different, [. . .] but you felt it was all at a tipping point, that it wouldn't take much for the whole country to fall into violence and hatred as well, that France would follow, then Germany, and all of Europe would catch fire like the Arab world" (203–4). Lakhdar's bleak vision of Europe as a series of interrelated cataclysms contradicts the external view of the continent as a land of prosperity, democracy, and human rights. In its state of crisis Europe is "just an illusion" and Spain, "an African country like the others" (214). The novel makes visible transnational communities of migrant subjects bound together by a sense of shared vulnerability. At the same time, it unsettles the boundary between migrants and citizens, Europeans and non-Europeans, as all are confronted by a world on the verge of collapse. Through apocalyptic imagery and rhetoric Énard uncovers the thin line between self and other, and the inextricable ties that bind the histories, politics, and economic destinies of peoples on both sides of the border. *Street of Thieves* lends itself to political readings through an aesthetic of connectivity.

The three fictional texts discussed here address the current anti-immigration climate in France and Europe at large. Zeniter's, Ferrier's, and Énard's novels invite a rethinking of identity categories through the notions of shared nationality, shared memory, and shared histories. Each challenges French nationalism and the republican tradition of assimilation by proposing hospitality and humanitarianism as optics though which to apprehend national history and identity. Zeniter's narrator responds empathetically to the plight of clandestine immigrants to provoke a similar response in the reader. Ferrier's narrator likewise has "sympathy" for the ghosts he resurrects, vibrating, like a musical chord, in tune with another chord that is being struck at the same time—a musical phenomenon known as "ghost" (13). In turn Énard's novel suggests that policed borders conceal the historical reality of migrant flows and cultural hybridity and that humanitarian attitudes may lead to less tragic outcomes. While articulating social critiques, these texts also entertain and conform to the tastes and expectations of mass audiences. In other words these texts are "consumable" through an ethics of recognition.

Lopes's *Une enfant de Poto-Poto* and Prudhomme's *Les Grands* underscore for their part the hybrid postcolonial cultures of the Republic of the Congo and the Republic of Guinea-Bissau in the wake of the French and Portuguese empires, while Bui's *Le Silence de mon père* emphasizes the hybrid identities of France's ethnic minorities. Being French-language novels sprinkled with Congolese, Portuguese-based Creole, and Vietnamese terms, these works no doubt attracted the favor of the Porte Dorée jury members and their interest in fictional representations of a racially and linguistically diverse France. This recognition of diversity, we will see, is what the Musée national de l'histoire de l'immigration both fears and upholds.

THE PORTE DORÉE: MARKER OF OPENNESS
OR TOOL OF HEGEMONY?

In assessing the impact of the Porte Dorée prize on the production of contemporary French-language migrant literature, one should not overlook the fact that it operates under the auspices of the Musée national de l'histoire de l'immigration. A state-sponsored project launched in the early 1990s but finalized only in 2007, the museum aims to inscribe immigration in the French patrimony through the notion of a shared (French and immigrant) memory. It nevertheless faces the challenge of reconciling the idea of a multicultural France with the republican and secular model of French identity. It must also ask how it can celebrate diverse immigrant cultures without ghettoizing them according to the logic of multicultural discourse. The museum's permanent exhibit *Repères*, for one, has attracted strong criticisms. Anouk Cohen (2007) contends that, by presenting immigration in chronological and thematic clusters, the exhibit homogenizes what are otherwise diverse immigrant motivations and trajectories (404). The museum's notion of shared memory subsumes individual immigrant experiences and obscures in the process colonial migrations and contemporary European ones. Maryse Fauvel (2014) views the institution's conflation of colonial and European migrations to France as an illustration of universalism, which obscures immigrants' diverse choices and trajectories (27). For her the museum, which in appearance celebrates immigrant subjects, dominates and controls them by representing them only partially (21).

Although European migrations were proportionally higher than colonial migrations, the history of immigration in France remains largely associated with the country's colonial enterprise (Cohen 2007, 402). The museum building itself reflects France's ambivalent colonialism. A palimpsestic space, the Palais de la Porte Dorée contains residual traces of France's imperial past. Built in 1931 for the Colonial Exhibition, it housed the Musée des Colonies et de la France extérieure two years later. Its subsequent incarnations equally glorified French colonial history. Called the Musée de la France d'Outre-mer in 1935, it became the Musée des Arts africains et océaniens in 1960, the Musée national des Arts d'Afrique et d'Océanie from 1990 to 2003, and in 2007 the Cité nationale de l'histoire de l'immigration (later known as the Musée national de l'histoire de l'immigration). Its different stages undergird the idea that "the building remains the symbol of the colonized/immigrant dyad" (Monjaret and Roustan 2012, 33). In France immigration thus necessarily recalls the specter of colonization.

The museum's cultural legitimation project inevitably evokes France's history of discrimination against colonized and immigrant subjects. How then does the Porte Dorée reconcile the tension between the literary and the political? How does it legitimate the literary value of migrant texts without reducing them to instruments of sociopolitical messaging? The prize accomplishes both. The Porte Dorée celebrates the thematic and formal diversity of contemporary novels of immigration. Many of the prizewinning novels draw on the boundary between the colonial past and the multicultural present, resurrecting forgotten or silenced histories. They also expand the category of "colonized/immigrant" in light of new demographic realities such as the presence of clandestine immigrants and asylum seekers on the French territory. However, the prize also gathers texts under the same general category, producing a homogenizing effect not unlike that of the permanent exhibit of its museum-sponsor. In keeping with the patrimonial practices of the Musée national de l'histoire de l'immigration, the Porte Dorée seeks to define the contours of an emerging corpus of migrant novels within French literature. The Porte Dorée posits immigration as a legitimate category in the ever-evolving landscape of contemporary French literature.

These novels put forth a globalized conception of French literature through transnational themes and authorial background. Reading transnational French-language literature through the lens of a national prize creates a paradox, however. What unites these novels, beyond the theme of migration, is that they are written in French. Awarding a national literary prize to French as well as francophone authors on the one hand shows the capacity of the French literary establishment to embrace immigrant literary and linguistic influences. Indeed the authors' biographies attest to the cachet of cosmopolitan and global profiles for national prizes: Zeniter lives in France but wrote her debut novel from Hungary; Lopes is a diasporic Congolese writer; Prudhomme has lived in several African countries; Delmaire, Bui, and Djavadi represent French minorities; while Ferrier and Énard reside in Japan and Spain, respectively. The award proves on the other hand that institutionally sanctioned and aesthetically validated forms of contemporary literature emanate from the main center of the French-language publishing world. The authors are ethnically diverse and highly mobile, yet their novels are without exception published by French presses. The Porte Dorée is clearly an accrediting vehicle of the French publishing industry. It selects works that expand the notion of French literature in keeping with the context of globalization, yet in its vision the French literary establishment occupies a key place in this globalized context.

Even though the ethnic and geographical backgrounds of authors are no longer defining traits of contemporary French literature, language remains closely tied to French national identity. The Porte Dorée reactivates the myth of the universality of the French language in several ways. First, its transnational focus shows the global relevance of French in the present moment. Second, it stresses the ways in which foreign languages (such as Prudhomme's Portuguese Creole, Gauz's Ivorian Nouchi, Valérie Zenatti's Hebrew, or Maryam Madjidi's Persian) can enrich French. The discourse of linguistic enrichment contributes to the foundational myth of the French language as a welcoming host (Porra 2011, 168). Third, it underpins the conception of French as the language of human rights, which has its roots in the eighteenth century. A universalist rhetoric prevails in the novels' promotion by prize organizers and jury members and in their reception outside the Hexagon. Similar ideas attach to the Prix Liste Goncourt/Choix de l'Orient, which went in 2012 to Énard's *Street of Thieves*. That prize, like the Porte Dorée, aims to promote contemporary French literature abroad in an era when French literature is said to be losing prestige. Organized in Beirut during the twentieth anniversary of the Salon du livre, the prize was awarded to Énard's novel by several juries composed of francophone Middle Eastern students. Understandably they chose a novel that was "very relevant to the region," and the novel's political content also spoke to their conception of French as "a language of resistance."[31] The Liste

Goncourt complements the Porte Dorée insofar as it celebrates works from outside of France, while at the same time increasing the visibility and legitimacy of contemporary French literature.

The Porte Dorée contributes to the organization of the French literary field. It creates an archive of contemporary migrant novels reflective of current political contexts that are relevant to a contemporary readership. It also forges new literary tastes for topics such as politics and clandestinity. Through intense promotion it transforms migrant narratives into a market product. In this sense the award mediates tensions between the literary (by championing migrant mobility and cultural, ethnic, and linguistic hybridity), the political (by legitimating a particular representation of French history aligned with the vision of France of the Musée national de l'histoire de l'immigration), and the economic (by grouping texts under the same rubric for marketing purposes). But most important, the Porte Dorée seeks to reconfigure the process of literary consecration by blurring the boundaries between major and minor authors, large and small presses, and professional and lay readers. In doing so the Porte Dorée underscores the imbrication of different types of capital (literary, economic, political) and different types of players (individual and institutional), which collectively determine value in the literary marketplace. By retrieving institutionally marginal literary texts, it promotes a conception of French literature that is popular rather than elitist and that reflects the growing tastes of general readers in issues of diversity, heterogeneity, and hybridity. The Porte Dorée aims to draw the contours of Frenchness and French literature at the dawn of the twenty-first century. In lockstep with the aim of the Musée national de l'histoire de l'immigration to reestablish France's self-understanding as a host to immigrant subjects, the Porte Dorée reconceptualizes French literature as a host to French-language migrant texts. In celebrating works that harness the rhetoric of cultural enrichment of the French language and its *rayonnement* (global spread and prestige), the prize conveys the ideology of French universalism. The Porte Dorée literary prize functions as both a sign of openness to cultural and linguistic diversity and an instrument of French hegemony. The Académie française, to which we will now turn, plays a similar function.

4

CANONIZATION

Dany Laferrière at the
Académie française

The election of Dany Laferrière to the Académie française on December 12, 2013, crowned the prolific oeuvre of one of the most celebrated French-language authors. Born in Haiti, Laferrière escaped Jean-Claude Duvalier's dictatorship by fleeing in 1976 to Montréal, where he first garnered literary acclaim through his writings on incendiary topics and his nonchalant style. Since the publication of his debut novel, provocatively titled *Comment faire l'amour avec un Nègre sans se fatiguer* (1985; published in translation in 1987 as *How to Make Love to a Negro without Getting Tired*), his career has bloomed spectacularly. Laferrière's literary trajectory can be divided into three stages. In a first phase he emerged as a new Québécois author, publishing his novels in Montréal and acquiring a devoted readership within Québec. Subsequently his work was translated into foreign languages and found legitimation from literary critics and the media throughout North

America and Europe. More recently his novels have achieved consecration through national and international literary prizes, as well as inclusion in anthologies and curricula in Québec and Haiti. These different phases highlight Laferrière's trajectory from a nationally known writer to one of global acclaim. His joining the Académie française constitutes the latest stage in his struggle for literary prestige. What does this French recognition represent for Laferrière, who sets his works in Québec, Haiti, and the United States, considers French a colonial language, and critiques the term *francophonie*? How does his global background fit within a national institution that safeguards the French language and equates it with national identity? How should we read his fictional works now, in light of his induction into France's most prestigious cultural institution?

Taking into account both Laferrière's transnational positioning and his oeuvre as a whole helps us to understand the factors that led to his election to the Académie française. At every stage of his literary career Laferrière has carefully articulated an antitaxonomical aesthetics, refusing to be read through the lens of nationality, race, or language. He has positioned himself as an unclassifiable author who moves fluidly between the local and the global, the francophone and the French, the periphery and the center. Laferrière joined the Académie française on his own terms: not as a Haitian, Québécois, or francophone author, as the media coverage of the event suggested, but rather, as he put it, as a transnational author simultaneously connected to several locales and irreducible to fixed subject positions.

Yet the Académie française represents a very specific and highly symbolic center, which contrasts with Laferrière's desired transcendence of national categories. Founded by Cardinal Richelieu in 1635 during the reign of King Louis XIII, its main function has been to define the French language by systematizing its grammar and consecrating its usage. In keeping with the critic François de Malherbe's purist doctrine, the académie has sought from its beginnings to render the French language pure and eloquent, as an official standard for all. But the académie has also served as an important source of cultural patronage, awarding about sixty prizes every year. Among the most recognized are prizes that aim to promote the French language: Prix de l'Universalité de la langue française/Prix Rivarol (discontinued in 1970), Prix du Rayonnement de la langue et de la littérature française, Grand Prix de la Francophonie, Prix de la langue française, and Prix pour une oeuvre écrite en langue française par un étranger. The académie explicitly embraces an ideology of language defense and promotion. Aspiring authors, be they French-born or immigrant, know well that literary consecration is wholly predicated on writing in the national language.

However, the Académie française does not validate talent in the same way literary prizes do. Its value is primarily symbolic, in Bourdieu's sense of the word. As the "legitimizing institution *par excellence*," it has the power to confer symbolic capital on its members (Bourdieu 1993, 122). They are known as Immortals, a label derived from the motto instituted by Cardinal Richelieu—"To immortality"—which first alluded to the king's divine power and now refers to the French language. How specifically does the académie consecrate French-language intellectuals? It inserts them into the French cultural patrimony. By custom the newly elected members pay homage to the predecessor whose seat they take. Paying homage is a centuries-old ritual by which the inductees acknowledge the glorious French past that informs their present. Immigrant Immortals have deliberately mentioned the institution's prestigious history in their acceptance speech. Hector Bianciotti declared the académie the symbol of French "Culture" par excellence, while Assia Djebar summoned Diderot's "ghost" to guide her through the halls of the institution.[1] In turn Laferrière gave praise to Montesquieu and the late Bianciotti, whose "Seat 2" he assumed. Enjoying lifelong appointments, the *académiciens* institute rules about the French language in the spectral presence of the giants of French culture, arts, and sciences. It is not difficult therefore to understand why Laferrière would put forward his own candidacy and seek to inscribe his name and works in the *longue durée* of French culture.

Yet Laferrière does not attempt to smooth the contradiction between his transnational positioning and the national character of the académie. Laferrière's literary career has obeyed a carefully crafted strategy of distinction. Early on, in the late 1970s and 1980s, he began to persuade

Québécois publishers, critics, and media personalities of his works' literary value. Shortly thereafter he initiated an evolving relationship with France, eventually accepting the French language as a vehicle to reach global audiences. His admission to the académie now reveals that conservative French institutions have opened up to cultural diversity. Laferrière's marketing skills and shifting literary allegiances, as well as a propitious cultural context, have assured his "immortality."

These combined factors differentiate the author's case from the elections of other non-French-born members: Eugène Ionesco (1970), Léopold Sédar Senghor (1983), Hector Bianciotti (1996), François Cheng (2002), Assia Djebar (2005), Amin Maalouf (2011), Michael Edwards (2013), and Andreï Makine (2016). Laferrière's case is unique because it bypasses the election criteria the académie applied to the above-mentioned authors: French nationality, French location, and francophilia. Laferrière is neither a French citizen nor a resident of France. Unlike other foreign-born académiciens, he does not celebrate the myth of French universality. The election of a transnational author marks a new chapter in the history of the institution. This new chapter—what one might call Laferrière's "conquest" of the French literary establishment—has been prepared, to some extent, by his collaborations with Parisian presses (Belfond, Le Serpent à Plumes, and Grasset since 1989) and winning the 2009 Prix Médicis for *L'Énigme du retour*. The author is hardly unknown to the French literary establishment. In spite of his transnational self-positioning, Laferrière is acutely aware that France remains the coveted site of legitimation for contemporary French-language authors.

To assess fully the implications of Laferrière's election, it is helpful to consider his literary output. His writings offer clues on his art of the novel and expectations on how it should be read. The following analysis focuses on three novels from his prolific oeuvre that clearly illustrate his strategy of distinction and self-positioning in relation to the Québécois, Haitian, and French institutional fields. The novels under discussion are signposts that mark shifts in Laferrière's trajectory from exiled Haitian to Québécois, American, and eventually, French writer. At the same time they highlight the author's attempts to produce belief in the value of his own works, as he fashions himself as a transnational author who adamantly rejects national labels and who appeals to both academic and lay readers.

An institutional approach to Laferrière's career may at first glance seem at odds with a close reading of his works. However, what makes the combination of macro- and micro-approaches methodologically viable is the author's explicit use of the autofictional genre. Laferrière employs a narrative voice that comes unsettlingly close to an expression of his own life events, even as he insists that the author and narrator of his texts not be conflated. For one thing, he creates an authorial persona to deflect biographical readings and argues that "writing is artifice" (Laferrière 2013, 39). He views literature moreover as the space of freedom par excellence, insisting on authors' rights to their creative freedom under institutional constraints. His fictional texts nevertheless provide clear clues about his literary self-positionings. Laferrière's vision of literature and authorship is useful for explaining how such a flexible stance, alongside the author's transnational positioning, challenges the national ideology of the Académie française and pressures a conservative institution to redefine itself more flexibly in relation to alternative geographies and literary voices.

From the start of his career Laferrière cast himself as an emerging and original voice on the Québécois and global literary scenes. The author may now be well known to the francophone world, but it took several years for him to quit a factory job and launch a first novel, which appeared in 1985. His literary success owes much to timing and a rare talent for self-promotion. In the early 1980s the Canadian discourse of multiculturalism encouraged the celebration of difference, and accordingly Québécois literary institutions began to legitimize the works of migrant authors. The success of Régine Robin's novel *La Québécoite* (1983) and the growing readership of the literary magazine *Vice Versa*, which promoted the cultural worth of immigration, transculturalism, and multilingualism, contributed to the favor enjoyed by migrant literature. Exiled Haitian writers had also by that time already established cultural networks that enabled new Haitian authors to emerge in Québec. Despite these advances Laferrière nevertheless still faced the reality of racism and rigid conceptions about black writers. His literary strategy was consequently to distinguish himself through provocation.

Eschewing the traditional topics of Haitian-Québécois literature, as well as nostalgic and exotic portrayals of his native Haiti, Laferrière wrote instead about taboo subjects (interracial sex) and immigrants' difficult integration into a xenophobic Québec. Once he established himself as a Québécois author, however, he then felt free to reconnect thematically to Haitian culture. Literary consecration in other words later offered him the freedom to choose his topics and readjust his strategies.

From the 1980s to the present Laferrière has frequently shifted his literary positions, moving deftly between different national identifications and sometimes even rejecting them all. Yet his preoccupation with authorship and readership remains invariable. Savvy in the art of literary marketing and consecration, he continually circulates authorial images related to literary talent, value, and masterpiece. His novels suggest market consciousness insofar as they abound in characters who are agents of the literary field: writers, editors, readers, librarians, translators, and journalists. Through the *mise en abyme* of the production, marketing, and reception of works, the author stages what Bourdieu (1993) called "the field of cultural production" and attempts to clarify his own place in it. Laferrière's market awareness, far from being an exception, is indicative of a larger phenomenon in the contemporary literary field: the return of the author in debates about literature. In contrast to views that situate the author in an autonomous sphere (Bourdieu 1993), Laferrière's reflections posit the contemporary author as a self-conscious figure who actively participates in the promotion and circulation of his or her works. As Sarah Brouillette (2011) argues in *Postcolonial Writers in the Global Literary Marketplace*, authors "use their works both to theorize the literary field and to articulate self-criticism or self-defense" (viii). They create authorial personae that address implied readers to shape or correct the latter's hermeneutic practices. Postcolonial authors also self-reflexively represent their career experiences in their texts to preempt reductive readings of their works and loss of control over their literary identities (Brouillette 2011, 4–5). Laferrière adopts similar tactics. However, rather than display "anxiety about the political parameters of the literary marketplace," he instead instills belief in the value of his fictional texts by constructing and promoting their alleged value within these very texts (Brouillette 2011, 1). Laferrière thus regards the novel as a commodity endowed, through vigorous marketing, with literary value. The three novels analyzed below, published at different moments of Laferrière's career, illustrate the ways in which he constructs and promotes the idea of the exceptionally talented immigrant writer and that of his works as masterpieces.

LAFERRIÈRE CONQUERS QUÉBEC

Comment faire l'amour avec un Nègre sans se fatiguer, first published in English as *How to Make Love to a Negro without Getting Tired* in 1987, jolted critics by its treatment of eroticism and, in particular, interracial sex. It also shocked through its use of the derogative term "Negro," which recalled Aimé Césaire's political reappropriation of the word *nègre* in *Cahier d'un retour au pays natal* (1939; *Notebook of a Return to My Native Land*). Set in the mid-1970s and early 1980s, the novel recounts the daily experiences of two black immigrants, Vieux and Bouba, as they seduce McGill coeds, drink cheap wine, and listen to jazz in a squalid Montréal apartment. The text employs the stereotype of the sexually potent black man to expose racist attitudes among the Québécois. In this respect it exemplifies a tactic that Graham Huggan (2001) terms "strategic exoticism," whereby immigrant and ethnic minority authors critique the objectifying tendencies of dominant cultures and attempt to subvert power imbalances through tropes of the exotic (32).[2] Despite its politically limited force, Laferrière's exoticist aesthetic was nevertheless a way to compel Québécois readers to acknowledge the black immigrant writer and the ways in which exclusionary definitions of literature restrict immigrant authors' voice. Underneath the novel's sensationalism lies the story of an ambitious black writer who aspires to literary fame in North America. In mise en abyme style Vieux is writing a novel titled *Black Cruiser's Paradise*, which recounts the same events as Laferrière's *How to Make Love* (87). It is in fact the very novel we are reading. This metafictional quality invites us to read *How to Make Love* as a story both about a black author's struggle and about literary consecration in Québec in a broader sense.

Laferrière conceptualizes *How to Make Love* as a best seller; within the pages of his novel Vieux strives to write a best-selling novel. Laferrière's avatar, Vieux, resorts to textual and paratextual strategies to launch his book into the Québécois literary world. He plays with readers' horizon of expectations, saying he is writing "not really a novel—more like fantasies," and he exploits the commercial potential of eroticism, knowing that sexual fantasies carry shock value for North American readers (53). The reception of contemporary authors and texts, Vieux realizes, goes hand in hand with their promotion. That is why he creates and disseminates an image of himself as an exceptionally talented young writer who painstakingly types away at his manuscript. He even pins a note on his door that says "Do Not Disturb: Great Writer Writing Last Masterpiece" (138). He also claims that his precarious financial and social status in Québec does not allow him to produce "a so-so manuscript," thereby hinting that immigrant authors must work harder to be recognized (139). His success will derive as much from his labor as from his literary talents. At the end he announces the birth of a promising novel in search of benevolent readers: "My novel is a handsome hunk of hope. My only chance. *Take it*" (153).[3]

Truth be told, Vieux's *Black Cruiser's Paradise* is—as is, implicitly, Laferrière's *How to Make Love*—a short, plotless novel with a vernacular and accessible style—far from the paragon that the narrator claims it to be. *How to Make Love* attracted a few negative reviews in the Québécois and Canadian press, which cited these shortcomings. Critics pointed out that the slim and improvised form belied the image of the writer hard at work. They also faulted the novel's self-reflexive quest for literary success, which compromised any serious treatment of sexuality. This and an unraveled narrative structure at the end served to generate facile consumption by a mass readership eager for sensationalist diversion.[4] The Haitian critic Jean Jonassaint (1986) agreed that Laferrière's novel was no masterpiece, and he attributed its resounding success to VLB éditeur's publishing strategies in a Québécois market increasingly open to cultural difference (80).[5] Laferrière's writing "the novel of a winner" and "the fantasy of a successful book" attracted the sympathy of Québécois and Canadian audiences, who recognized these themes as typically

North American (80). The novel was favorably received in Québec as the story of the inner workings of a destitute but talented immigrant's literary consecration. Laferrière returned the racist gaze of the Québécois and anchored his text in Montréal rather than his native country.[6] In sum *How to Make Love* had novelty value. But more than that the novel boldly played a game with the cultural industry by staging its imaginary reception—a game that literary critics were eager to play.

The story of how Laferrière staged *How to Make Love*'s commercial and critical success shows how fictional works can act upon their context of reception and trigger critical and institutional recognition. One aspect of the author's strategy is to interpellate Québécois public figures by means of his narrative alter ego. Toward the end Vieux has a dream about his novel's warm reception. He sees it displayed in a Montréal bookstore, spots one of its readers, and chats with the bookseller, who informs him the novel is a big seller. Then his editor relates the critics' hearty acclaim, citing imaginary reviews in prominent Québécois newspapers by real critics, such as Gilles Marcotte and Jean-Éthier Blais, who calls Vieux "A New Genius" (144). (In an example of life imitating fiction Marcotte, prompted by Laferrière's ploy, later wrote a review of *How to Make Love*.) These reviews in turn lead Vieux to participate in a television interview with the journalist Denise Bombardier. (Bombardier also echoed the novel's fictional interview by inviting Laferrière to be a guest on her show.)

Intratextually Vieux's literary recognition occurs in a dream, suggesting that a black immigrant writer's consecration remains a fantasy, given the waking-world reality of the other's racist gaze (Thibeault 2011, 32). But at an extratextual level Laferrière did in fact obtain the literary visibility to which he so aspired. He not only secured an interview with Bombardier but also lobbied Québécois booksellers to display his novel in sidewalk-facing windows. The result? The novel sold five thousand copies in the first three weeks after its publication and rose to fourth place on best-seller lists (Laferrière 2010b, 170). But Laferrière's self-marketing as suffering author played an added role in his novel's success. Parodying the traditional rock-star poster, he circulated photos throughout Montréal of himself as a writer at work: sitting barefoot on a park bench next to his typewriter and a beer bottle. Rather than embracing the stereotype of the alcoholic black writer, he claimed a different heritage: "I was here not as a Negro but as a Beat writer. There is a lineage in American literature: Hemingway, Kerouac, Bukowski, Miller. Cool guys who drink" (Laferrière 2010b, 167–68). He presented himself above all as a North American author and asserted his value through literary affinities rather than national origin or immigrant status.

How to Make Love illustrates the process by which "marketing creates [myths] about identity and genealogy" (Squires 2009, 146). With this novel Laferrière positions himself as an author who participates in the Québécois literary sphere as an equal, not a cultural outsider. He moreover presents himself as a North American author (in the wider hemispheric sense of the term) who, contrary to expectations, chooses French over English or Creole. Yet Laferrière (2010b) is also "viscerally against *Francophonie*" (89)—for him a category that classifies authors based exclusively on their use of French, thereby restricting the complexity of authors' works. He also rejects the labels of "immigrant, ethnic, Caribbean, hybrid, postcolonial, or black writer" and challenges critics to view him as "a good writer [. . .] or a bad writer" (107). In clear opposition to identity politics, he insists that the category of "writer" is the only legitimate lens for interpreting his novels.

Since the publication of *How to Make Love*, Laferrière has continued to nourish, not without difficulty, the image of a prolific, talented, and universal author. His novels—set mostly in Haiti, but also in Québec and the United States—create the portrait of "a man in three pieces," connected to, or divided between, Port-au-Prince, Montréal, and Miami (Laferrière 2010b, 58). But by his own admission this tripartite affiliation puts limits on his aspirations for global renown. As he asserts, "I am too ambitious to belong to a single country. I am a global writer" (quoted in Thibeault 2011, 27). And who better to promote his international reception than the author himself? In *Cette grenade dans la main du jeune Nègre est-elle une arme ou un fruit?* (1993; published in translation in 1994 as *Why Must a Black Writer Write about Sex?*), he attributes *How to Make Love*'s global success to its provocative title. He enumerates the imaginary reactions of readers across the globe to show the ways in which his novel's title was applauded, critiqued, borrowed, censored, and even altered (Laferrière 1994b, 17–22). The frequent reference to his debut novel in subsequent works positions *How to Make Love* as the text that, in Laferrière's view, enabled his emergence and consecration as a global writer.

Despite Laferrière's unrelenting focus on his universality, critics continued to label him as "exotic." Aware of his reception in various literary fields, in essays and interviews he replies to those who misread his works and posits new labels to blur categories and confuse critics. In *Why Must a Black Writer Write about Sex?* Laferrière declares that "[he's] given up being a black writer" (192) and seeks "rest" (197), while in *Je suis fatigué* (I am tired), published in 2001, he threatens to stop writing because he is tired of being pigeonholed. In an about-face he writes in *J'écris comme je vis* (I write as I live) that his work is "an American auto-biography" in an effort to underscore his continental affiliation (2010b, 136). Amid this confusion of racial, national, continental, and linguistic labels, how should one go about reading Laferrière? *Je suis un écrivain japonais* (2008) tackles this question head-on.

THE NEGRO TURNS JAPANESE

Je suis un écrivain japonais (2008; released in translation as *I Am a Japanese Writer* in 2010) is Laferrière's most explicit critique of the market pressures placed on authors to produce works for consumption and of the institutions that determine their literary value. The novel argues at the same time for the fundamental place that authorial autonomy and imagination should occupy in literary production. The plot opens with a conversation between the narrator and his publisher that dramatizes the tension between commercial-institutional and authorial agendas. The publisher, envisioning huge sales, urges the narrator to write his book as fast as he can. But the narrator resists the demand for hyperproductivity; he has only a title for his manuscript ("I Am a Japanese Writer"), a contract ("ten thousand euros for five little words"), and little desire to write the book (Laferrière 2010a, 3). As in the case of *How to Make Love*, Laferrière uses the mise en abyme to expose the process of commercially driven writing, while simultaneously thwarting any attempt to derive meaning from his text.

The target of his critique is clear: the modes of critical interpretation and classification to which literary works have traditionally been subjected.

I Am a Japanese Writer is a collection of miscellaneous elements: the narrator's reflections on people, places, and the books he reads; scenes from a film he is making about a group of Japanese lesbians; and his interactions with two Japanese diplomats in Montréal. The plotless narrative is interspersed with the narrator's musings on the travels to northern Japan by Basho, a seventeenth-century Japanese poet. It is, as Laferrière calls it, "the inventory of my inner landscape provided by a vagabond poet"—a consciously rambling narrative that refuses to be neatly tied up (56). To critique the literary field and defend authorial autonomy, Laferrière wrote a work that, far from ignoring literary critics' expectations, makes them its subject matter. Critical paradigms and institutional practices have historically conditioned the novel's content and form. Laferrière's work shows the extent to which even counterreadings such as his can be subsumed to market imperatives and institutional constraints.

The novel enacts the globalization model of hypercommunication without content in order to interrogate it. This is evident in a series of ironies. One irony is the exuberant celebration of the narrator's novel in Québec and Japan before it is even written. Marketing makes books; form prevails over content. In Québec the title piques the interest of the Japanese consul, who offers to translate the book into Japanese. In Japan the narrator gains instant recognition, inserting himself, with the proposed title, into the country's intense, ongoing debates about national identity. Some potential readers embrace a foreign writer claiming to be Japanese as affirmation of Japan's cultural importance, while others fear that a black "Japanese" author might threaten Japan's cultural and literary integrity, especially if the novel were poorly received: "With that title, it's as if the writer had become [. . .] 'the Japanese writer *par excellence*'" (136). Seizing upon the hype, a well-known Japanese author produces a novel titled *I Am a Malagasy Writer*, thus aiding a trend against literary nationalisms (176). In yet another ironic twist the narrator's publisher advises that, as foreign presses begin to buy the rights, he should adapt the term "Japanese" to different market needs. The publisher suggests that, with a novel so "perfect for translation," they start with *I Am a Swedish Writer* and "do the same thing for every country that wants to publish it" (128). Japanese, as well as national identity more generally, functions here as an empty signifier that circulates globally to suit commercial logic.

In choosing for his title a term associated with an ethnically homogeneous culture, the narrator attempts to "neutralize" national identity and divert attention from cultural specificity (Mathis-Moser 2011, 79). The title is thus bait for literary critics and marketing agents, who rush to interpret and market his "new" identity. What they chase of course is not a novel but merely its simulacrum—a copy with no original, a book that does not exist beyond its eye-catching title. The narrator clarifies his anti-identitarian project to the many eager publishers and critics: "I am not a Japanese writer. I'm writing a book called 'I Am a Japanese Writer.' That doesn't make me a Japanese writer" (Laferrière 2010a, 74). His title's aim is, by his own admission, to deconstruct the traditional notions of literary identity: "[W]hat is a Japanese writer? Someone who lives and writes in Japan? Or someone who was born in Japan and writes in spite of it [. . .]? Or someone who was not born in Japan, who doesn't know the language, but who decided one fine day to become a Japanese writer? That's my situation" (8). These questions suggest that critical demands for authorial authenticity are futile in the face of the arbitrary geographical, ethnic, linguistic, or other criteria routinely employed to classify literary texts. The narrator's choice of a Japanese literary identity transcends identity politics. His Japan is "invented" (73), made up of cultural myths and clichés—for example, its being "a nation of smiling photographers" (119)—which he gleans from the French-language magazines of Québec. The narrator has never been to Japan nor is he interested in exploring Japanese culture in an unmediated way. Instead he derives his cultural knowledge of Japan not just from magazines but from the works of Basho, whom he calls a "vagabond poet" and reads on the subway (16). The narrator's own wandering through Montréal reinforces the idea of identity in constant motion, resistant to spatial location. "A moving target in a dazzling city," he evades all literary classifications (68).

The narrator struggles against labels through an entomological rhetoric reminiscent of Franz Kafka's "Metamorphosis." He complains that "[b]orn in the Caribbean, I automatically become a Caribbean writer. The bookstore, the library and the university rushed to *pin* that title on me" (12, emphasis added) ("*m'épingler*," in the etymological sense [Laferrière 2008, 27]), and he defends his creative freedom by stating, "Being a writer and a Caribbean doesn't necessarily make me a Caribbean writer" (2010a, 12). Similarly the Japanese diplomat who interviews him appears to him as "an entomologist slipping a black insect into a handsome lacquered case" (69), while the Japanese singer Midori photographs him "as if I were an object, or some insect" (134). The narrator responds defiantly to the exoticizing gaze of his hosts by declaring his wish to be, for them, "a cold, objective camera lens" (120). The novel's objective record of disparate thoughts and events, told from the narrator's ironic viewpoint, is the "cold lens" through which Laferrière interrogates literary classification.

Academic models for thinking about literature also come under attack. Laferrière's reference to "The Metamorphosis" alludes to the ways in which literary institutions transform writers into objects of study (or insects), de-individualizing (or de-humanizing) them in the process. In reaction to such reductive practices, Laferrière affirms, "I am me, this individual here."[7] The intertextual reference and the author's demand for recognition as a human, or individual, also recalls Kafka's position as an interstitial, unassimilated writer. As a Jew living in Prague and writing in German, as well as mediating between national and global literary spaces, Kafka registered the contradictions between ethnicity, territory, and language. Like Kafka, Laferrière probes the gaps between rigid categories and claims universal status without fully abandoning national literary spaces. Laferrière's literary vision draws on that of Jorge Luis Borges. In "The Argentine Writer and Tradition" Borges (1999) proposes a definition of Argentine literature that need not use Argentine themes and vernacular words or exclude foreign literary influences to be considered Argentine. For Borges local color does not equal authenticity. He claims instead that "we must believe that the universe is our birthright and try out every subject" (427). Similarly in *I Am a Japanese Writer* Laferrière (2010a) is no less Haitian or Québécois for choosing a Japanese subject matter. At one point the narrator states, "I'm not Borges" (176), but clearly this should be read against the grain. The novel stands against authenticity and does so in the shape of a labyrinthine, unclassifiable book of infinite interpretations. Borgesian in form, Japanese in content, and written in French, the novel also features a multinational cast of characters (Greek, Korean, Japanese, Haitian, Hungarian, Swiss), in defiance of clear national classifications.

The French translation of Basho's *The Narrow Road to the Interior* provides another intertextual commentary. *I Am a Japanese Writer*'s narrator is a vagabond reader who carries Basho's text with him at all times. Referencing the Japanese poet enables Laferrière to shift to a new subject position: the author as reader. In this way he reorients academic interpretations of texts away from the traditional lens of author location, nationality, and language toward the vantage points of readers and reading practices. Indeed the narrator promotes himself as a reader of world literature and an author whose literary influences are global. By citing his favorite writers from childhood—authors whose origin he ignored—he renders the question of authorial nationality moot:

> I don't understand all the attention paid to a writer's origins. Because, for me, Mishima was my neighbor. Very naturally, I repatriated the writers I read at the time. All of them: Flaubert, Goethe, Whitman, Shakespeare, Lope de Vega, Cervantes, Kipling, Senghor, Césaire, Roumain, Amado, Diderot—they all lived in my village. Otherwise, what were they doing in my room? Years later, when I became a writer and people asked me, "Are you a Haitian writer, a Caribbean writer or a French-language writer?" I answered without hesitation: I take on my reader's nationality. Which means that when a Japanese person reads me, I immediately become a Japanese writer. (14)

For the narrator, the space of the encounter between texts and readers belongs to "imagination and desire" (13). As such, it prevails over national identity or geographical location because it allows writers to be mobile and to "spen[d] their lives wandering the world and telling stories in all languages" (13). The narrator believes a writer's identity should dissolve in the act of reading, hence his dream of disappearing "in a line of Basho poetry" (107). At the end of the novel he tells his publisher, "I am no longer a writer" (179) and even "I am no longer" (139)—a final effort to erase his literary identity. He states that "[f]or literature to truly exist, books would have to be anonymous. No more ego, no more personal intervention" (170), even if in practice, it should be noted, the narrator seeks to "appropriate the story" (170) with a style and voice both "verbose" and "omnipresent" (Bernier 2008-9, 179-80).

The narrator's decision to let the text speak for itself accompanies his social decline. After his failure to produce the promised novel and his consequent slide into penury, his new indigent status is juxtaposed with a Haitian friend's professional success in Québec, recalling other Laferrière novels that end with the destitution of their immigrant protagonists. Left without a book contract, the narrator exchanges his flexible literary identity with "the scent of poverty" (139). Having previously rejected all labels, he now takes on a new one. The odor of Haitian culture permeates the narrator's evocation of Haitian poverty and homelessness. Although the novel promotes universality as a model preferable to that of cultural specificity, the narrator cannot escape his Haitian or Caribbean identity. Thus I Am a Japanese Writer at once rejects and retains national-cultural paradigms. Despite pretensions to be Japanese or even unclassifiable, it cannot avoid the imprint of the author's Haitian literary sensibility. Laferrière remains Haitian no matter what he does. His novel disproves the notion that an author can exchange one national identity for another at will, despite Laferrière's effort to make us believe it can. Laferrière's thematic return to Haiti in L'Énigme du retour (2009) fleshes out the questions already implicit in I Am a Japanese Writer: Is it possible to leave Haiti in the first place? And can one truly return?

THE CONSECRATED AUTHOR RETURNS

L'Énigme du retour, released in translation in 2011 as The Return, recounts the author-narrator Dany's travel back to Haiti after thirty-three years in North America. It opens with news of the death of his father, Windsor Laferrière, who had fled Haiti during François Duvalier's regime for exile in the United States. After the burial in New York, the narrator travels to Haiti to return his father's spirit to the patriarch's village. The voyage is thus a double return—of the father, by means of the son, whose first name, legally speaking, is also Windsor. The parallel journeys indicate the text's overriding preoccupation with filiation, heritage, and identity. But the notion of a stable Haitian identity that the narrator can recover becomes a chimera. Instead the novel interrogates the very possibility of exilic return.

The narrator Dany approaches his return ambivalently. He chooses to stay at a hotel—a nonplace—rather than at his mother's home, and from the hotel balcony he observes everyday life in Haiti, with its colorful people, their daily struggles, and the social gaps between rich and poor. His descriptions of present-day Haiti alternate with his memories of the Haiti of his childhood and adolescence. As he asserts,

> Images from the past
> constantly try to superimpose themselves on the present.
> I am navigating through two worlds. (137)

Dany straddles the divide between outsider and insider, observer and participant, the present and the past. The novel suggests this is not his first return. A panoply of well-known images from the past, which Laferrière amply documented in previous novels, intrudes into his present narration: his father's exile, his mother's loneliness, his growing up under dictatorship, and his own rushed departure for Québec. Indeed there are frequent allusions to scenes from Laferrière's earlier novels set in Haiti and Québec, in which the author returned physically to Haiti and mentioned his father's death.[8] Through intratextuality he creates a circular, self-enclosed, or spherical oeuvre that places different texts in dialogue, inviting comparative readings.[9] It is a novel about literary returns—the return of Dany Laferrière to previous novels and Haitian themes, as well as his return to Haiti as an author of critical acclaim.

As in *I Am a Japanese Writer*, the novel's intertexts reveal Laferrière's literary affiliations. Since the narrator's departure from Haiti as an adolescent, Aimé Césaire's prose poem *Notebook of a Return to My Native Land*, we are told, has remained by his side. The Martinican poet, hailed as the father of Negritude and founder of modern French Caribbean literature (Rosello 1995, 9), is his literary father. With a life story that parallels Windsor Laferrière's, Césaire helps the narrator mourn a father he did not know well. As the narrator states, "[i]n my dream, Césaire takes my father's place" (21). Contemporaries, both rose heroically against brutal political regimes, and both displayed an "all-powerful rage" against the abuses of power in their respective lands (41). The narrator duly recognizes, then casts off, his debts to his father figures. He leaves his father's unopened suitcase in a Manhattan bank, concluding that the weight of his father's past is not entirely his own, and he discharges a spiritual obligation to Césaire by giving his tattered copy of the *Notebook* to his nephew, Dany Charles, who aspires to become a writer and immigrate to North America. Césaire's *Notebook* reminds the narrator that his native island accompanies him everywhere, returning time and again through memory and writing. However, unlike the work of Césaire, the narrator's oeuvre is not politically engaged; his literary model is

> a man of serenity
> not some guy seething with anger. (57)

The two also differ on the use of French. Césaire believed in the revolutionary potential of language, "decoloniz[ing] language by inventing his own French," characterized by a hermetic style and linguistic erudition (Rosello 1995, 56). In contrast the author-narrator employs accessible language that aims to be transparent, not obscure, and to appeal to the greatest number of readers possible. While Césaire's text had a profound influence on the narrator's early years in exile, it is a legacy from which he eventually distances himself in order to assert his literary singularity.

The narrator-Laferrière may well insist on his distinctiveness, but in mediating between generations he cannot fully escape the impact of his father figures. Arboreal metaphors underscore the filiations that transcend his native Haiti. Césaire is "a charred tree trunk" due to his rage (41). His father Windsor is "the tree of which I am but a branch" (44). While "carved from the same tree" (46) as his father, and therefore culturally Haitian, the narrator wishes to leave the Haitian landscape behind:

I would like to lose
all awareness
of my being
to blend
into nature
and become a leaf,
a cloud
or the yellow of the rainbow. (208)

Generated by a father tree, the leaf also detaches from it and embarks on its own course. The narrator similarly acknowledges Césaire and Caribbean literature as formative but ultimately a relay or a node in a wider network of literary influences.

A poignant scene has the narrator retracing his father's footsteps. He walks the very path that took him from his native village to Port-au-Prince and abroad, thinking that his father

must have
looked into the sky at
that great life-size map and seen
all the hospitals, prisons, embassies,
feigned celebrations and lonely nights
that one day he would face.
[. . .] he must have seen my life too,
an extension of his
so similar to it. (219)

Father and son are defined by their journeys, with Haiti their point of departure. Ursula Mathis-Moser (2003) thus describes Dany Laferrière's literary trajectory, employing the concept of *la dérive* (drift), which to her implies "at once the act of drifting away, going with the stream, and the possibility of re-anchoring" (11).

The narrator of *The Return* re-anchors himself in Haiti after many years of drifting. But he seeks other forms of belonging beyond the literary ties to his country of origin. The constellations of his father's imagined vision raise the question of humankind's place in the universe and the narrator's place in a network of tangled trajectories. He explores the question of belonging at a subnational level as well, when recounting the episode of being viewed as a foreigner in his native Haiti. Speaking to a group of children in Creole, he is met with bemusement, despite the effort to display his Haitianness through language. The experience causes him to doubt language as a reliable criterion of identity in a country where first

> people try to find out
> if they're from the same city
> the same sex
> the same generation
> the same religion
> the same neighborhood as others. (147)

Identification with—and recognition of—his Haitianness occurs through universal human characteristics. Through scales both large and small, the narrator forges a networked consciousness that does not rely on nationality, ethnicity, or even language. His place in a community and the relationships that tie him to others depend on other factors. The author-narrator's recognition in Haiti ultimately comes through his literary achievement. Upon entering La Pléiade bookstore in Port-au-Prince, the narrator spots a reader perusing one of his books:

> I never imagined that one day I'd find myself at La Pléiade as a writer.
> As I move through this universe (the city, the people, the objects) that I've described so often, I don't feel like a writer, but more like a tree in its forest. I realize I didn't write those books to describe a landscape, but to continue being part of it. [. . .] The dictator threw me out the door of my own country. To return, I had to slip in through the window of the novel. (121)

Thus he describes his return to Haiti as an author. Having fled the country in his youth, he returns thirty-three years later a globally renowned writer, one whose literary output in exile is forever linked to his departure. His validation comes not only from his books' global circulation but also—and especially—from their reception in his native land. As the narrator of *I Am a Japanese Writer* might say, when a Haitian reader reads him, he becomes a Haitian writer. The trip home is a way to take stock of his trajectory. Indeed the novel teems with reflections on his literary career. He muses over his early years in Québec, typing on his old Remington 22, and his eventual recognition by the Québécois literary establishment; the impact of exile on his works; and the many authors, both Haitian and foreign, who shaped him in his youth. At first, to affirm his originality in Québec, he avoided Haitian topics. Here, though, he yields to Haitian tropes—namely hunger, "the subject of the great Haitian novel" (105)—and eagerly assumes his place in the Caribbean cultural landscape.

His books' popularity with Haitian readers brings his literary trajectory full circle. As the narrator puts it,

> This is not winter.
> This is not summer.
> This is not the North.
> This is not the South.
> Life is spherical now. (226)

The Return marks the end of Laferrière's "American autobiography," a cycle of interrelated novels centered on the Northern Hemisphere. And the celebrity of his oeuvre is suggested by its placement in La Pléiade, a bookstore whose name is synonymous with prestige in France. Éditions Gallimard's Bibliothèque de la Pléiade series publishes the complete works of canonical authors whose literary value is unimpeachable. Laferrière here nods to a French literary institution that determines the value of books. Fittingly *The Return* was published almost simultaneously by Éditions Boréal in Québec and Éditions Grasset in France, where it was expected to have a welcome reception among French readers.

The Return narrates the enigma of the author-narrator's arrival in literary terms. In fact its title's English translation omits the French title's crucial intertextual reference: V. S. Naipaul's *The Enigma of Arrival* (1987). Naipaul's novel tells the story of another Caribbean attempting to gain recognition away from his native island. Unlike Laferrière, however, Naipaul is inextricably linked to the postcolonial through his preoccupations with England's decline and the disabling effects of imperial rule on its former colonies. For Naipaul "arrival" connotes both postcolonial migrations to England and postcolonial authors' literary success in the metropole's center. At the heart of his novel also lies an enigma of origins. Naipaul is notorious for dismissing the Caribbean as a cultural space and for elevating India and England at its expense. Yet in his novel Naipaul's "arrival" at the center of English literature is ironically due to his drawing on Caribbean themes. Haiti similarly holds a prominent place in Laferrière's fictional works and has played no small part in his success.

The Return undoubtedly grounds Laferrière's oeuvre in the Caribbean. Its very title evokes the legacies of Césaire and Naipaul. As Gabrielle Parker (2013) states, "[t]he return to Césaire might prove a cultural acknowledgment of belonging" (85), while "yok[ing] together Naipaul and Césaire" in the title suggests that "Laferrière does anchor himself here in the islands" (86). More than that, however, the author's reclaiming Césaire also gestures to the French literary establishment. In light of this literary connection the narrator's bestowing of Césaire to his nephew is highly significant. The Martinican poet may be primarily associated with the French Caribbean, but his Paris education and choice to write in French, rather than Creole, link him culturally to France. Despite Césaire's ideological return to Africa through the Negritude movement, he continued to conceive Martinican identity as geographically part of France and culturally tied to the French language. What might Césaire's French connections, through his formative years in Paris and language choice, reveal to us about Laferrière's attitude toward France and the French language? Even if the author has so far avoided associations with France and their postcolonial implications, he nevertheless admits he "still ha[s] a score to settle" with Paris, which he wants to "integrate [...] in [his] mental universe," suggesting that in the long run, he seeks French literary consecration (Laferrière 2010b, 112).

The highest French recognition Laferrière has garnered is the 2009 Prix Médicis for *The Return*. The Médicis is traditionally given to French-language writers who do not yet enjoy the recognition their talent deserves.[10] It represents a curiously belated validation of the author, given he had been publishing with French presses to acclaim since the late 1980s. The award can be explained in part by the novel's original form. On the back cover Éditions Boréal and Grasset both touted the work as the mark of "a great writer" and "the novel of Dany Laferrière's maturity," respectively. *The Return* alternates between prose paragraphs and poetry that many critics interpreted as haiku. Besides being cued by the book jacket, critics expected this form due to Laferrière's previous use of haiku in *Éroshima* and because of the title *I Am a Japanese Writer*. Yet, as Patrick Coleman (2010) points out, if one runs the lines together, they form prose paragraphs of normal rhythm, which invites them to be seen as free verse and read as "slowed-down prose" (127). In response to critics' praise for the aesthetic value of his work, Laferrière insists on the contrary that he chose to mix poetry and prose to make the novel accessible to average readers. He moreover declares his intention to produce "average books" in which everything will be "the same."[11] One should read Laferrière's professed average talent not as modest self-assessment but as an aesthetic positioning that conveys his vision of literature as popular and universal. The goal, as he states it, is to reach the greatest number of lay readers. How then are we to read his election to the Académie française, an elitist institution that evokes ideas of timeless aesthetic value?

THE IMMORTALITY OF THE JAPANESE WRITER

Laferrière's induction into the Académie française is riddled with contradictions. For one, his location in the institutional field changes. His status shifts from that of a writer who critiques institutional labeling practices to that of agent for an institution charged with legislating on matters of French. Laferrière must now defend the language of the colonizer through a celebration of *francophonie*—the very label he contested as a signatory of the 2007 manifesto "Pour une 'littérature-monde' en français," which called for an end to the use of the term. How, then, is he to reconcile the académie's ideological mission of promoting francophone writing (through literary prizes, election of foreign members, and the elevation of French as universal) with an anti-identitarian aesthetics that undermines traditional categories of nation, ethnicity, and even language?

The media coverage of his induction exposed these contradictions, as well as the national lens through which the consecration of the migrant francophone author continues to be viewed when he or she is institutionally assimilated into the space of the French nation-state. Analysis of Haitian, Québécois, and French reporting on the event shows that major aspects of the discussions about Laferrière's election are related on the one hand to the uncertain status of the French language today and on the other hand to the ambivalent position of francophone authors in metropolitan centers marked increasingly by cultural and ethnic diversity. These connected issues of language and authorial positioning came to the fore through a commonplace binary of complicity and resistance that critics and journalists evoke time and again when discussing the consecration of transnational francophone authors by French national institutions. Is Laferrière a pawn who advances the académie's nationalist agenda or a pioneer who challenges it?[12] Does he need the académie to strengthen his literary status or does the académie need him to guarantee the immortality of the French language?[13]

Some suggest that by admitting francophone intellectuals the académie pursues a neocolonial agenda of language promotion to counteract the international ascendancy of English and native languages of former French colonies (e.g., Creole in Haiti). According to this view, to maintain the status of French as a global language the académie appropriated Laferrière, making him an instrument of French cultural diplomacy and an example of the French language's global spread. Others point out that, quite the opposite, Laferrière's induction represents a way to reform the institution from within; Laferrière holds the power to transform a fossilized institution by hybridizing the French language with Haitian Creole and Québécois French. In so doing he ostensibly compels the académie to welcome hybridity and correct its historical exclusions based on class, race, and gender.

Fittingly for his académie patrons, it mattered that Laferrière's oeuvre began in French rather than vernacular languages. The Romantic link between language and nation is difficult to break, even in an age of global migrations. Each of the three spatial entities with which Laferrière is associated discussed his victory in terms antithetical to his aesthetic positioning: national categories. Take, for example, his reception in Haiti. There Laferrière's election to the académie was celebrated as a national victory. The first Haitian to enter the Académie française, Laferrière would now be an ambassador of Haiti's culture—not its poverty or natural calamities—and testament to the académie's openness to cultural diversity.[14] Dissenting voices, however, criticized Laferrière for sanctioning French cultural values to the detriment of Haitian political causes. The writer Tontongi's response to the induction pulled in different directions. He viewed Laferrière as a Haitian writer—whereas the author is, in fact, diasporic—and saw the event as France's belated recognition of Haitian literature written in French. But Tontongi also suspected that the choice of a francophone writer was a political decision. For him it marked not the académie's embrace of *francophonie* but an effort to maintain Haiti's literary dependence on France by encouraging Haitians to write in French rather than Creole. He and the writer Lionnel Trouillot reproached Laferrière for failing to speak on behalf of Creole at a moment when the Haitian Creole Academy, created in 1987, was striving to counter French influence in Haiti.[15]

One could readily argue that Tontongi's accusation, tying literature to geography, is harsh and reductive. For his part Laferrière has always rejected the expectations that writers of former colonies produce *littérature engagée*. As he puts it, the writer's concern is not political but aesthetic: "[S]tyle. Or rather the absence of all style. No trace. So the reader can forget words and see things" (Laferrière 2010b, 53). He also adds, "I don't want to change the world, I want to change my world. Why does the task of having to change the world always fall to me, poor immigrant dying of solitude?" (142). Laferrière's vision of literature is both universal and practical: it enables authors from impoverished cultural spaces to transcend their locality. Laferrière's Haitian critics nonetheless raise a valid question: does consecration by the French center automatically depoliticize work originating from the peripheries?[16] Critics who argue in this vein narrowly position the author within a postcolonial history linking center and periphery. Yet they ignore the fact that Laferrière intentionally sidesteps the Haiti-France axis by championing an American aesthetics in his writing and positioning himself first and foremost as a writer of the American continent.

The media in Québec hailed Laferrière as the first Québécois and Canadian "Immortal." His recognition was in its view a victory for "minor" languages and literatures, in Deleuze and Guattari's (1986) sense. Echoing Québécois linguistic policy, which is fiercely protectionist, local critics called on Laferrière to defend the French language, the "bulwark for the Francophones of all continents," against the domination of anglophone Canada.[17] For them the Haitian-Québécois writer's election marked the opening of the académie to francophone countries and reinforced the image of Québec as a francophone province.

In France the media coverage of Laferrière's induction stressed his nationality and ethnicity. He was the académie's first Québécois, Canadian, and Haitian-Canadian member and its second black writer after Léopold Sédar Senghor.[18] As a "national" representative, Laferrière brought visibility to both his native and adoptive countries. In the words of Grégoire Leménager, it is not only Laferrière "but also Haiti and Québec that enter, for the first time, the Académie française."[19] But as a new académicien, he is ultimately enlisted in the cause of linguistic identity and preservation. As Bernard Pivot has pointed out, Laferrière was encouraged, against his will, to defend Creole against French in his youth in Haiti, French against English after arriving in Québec, and English against Spanish when living in Miami. In France he would be expected to do the same: "Wherever you may go, there is a suffering language. French from France suffers, too."[20] Laferrière's candidacy rested on his having written his entire oeuvre in French. His mere association with two linguistically embattled contexts— Haiti and Québec, where dominant and dominated languages vie for supremacy—made him the académie's spokesperson.

Predictably, given France's fetishistic attachment to its language, the French press underscored that Laferrière's election to the académie was not based on nationality but on his use of French. According to Pivot, the académie's choice of a candidate who is neither French nor resides in France proves that "the French language is the only nationality that counts."[21] This concept of nationality stands in contrast to past criteria of admission: French-language writer Jorge Semprún, for example, was discouraged from joining the institution because he was Spanish. Pivot's words echo those of the académie's permanent secretary, Hélène Carrère d'Encausse, who declared that "[l]anguage [. . .] is the nationality."[22] But Laferrière himself refuses linguistic allegiances and their battles in Haiti, Québec, and France. His works do not so much promote French as use it as a tool to reach global audiences, which would not be possible were he to publish in Creole.

Although Laferrière understates the ideological uses of a colonizer's language, one can regard his pragmatic approach to French as an attempt to counter the image of the postcolonial francophone writer historically connected to France. He diverges from other migrant writers elected to the académie who reiterated the myth of French as a universal language and their task of safeguarding its prestige through literature. François Cheng, for instance, mentions the rigor, genius, eloquence, and universality of the French language, that is, the allegedly intrinsic qualities used to construct the myth of French as a prestigious and global language. Cheng also admits his love for the language, which he made "his flesh and blood" and "the weapon or soul of [his] literary creation."[23] Assia Djebar identifies herself as a "French author" who considers French "almost a second skin."[24] Even if other languages inflect her French, she has made the French language "her own," thus underscoring its importance in her oeuvre.[25] In turn Amin Maalouf associates the spread and prestige of French in Lebanon not with colonialism but with François I's cultural diplomacy.[26] The British poet Michael Edwards, whose election is surprising given his nationality and the threat English is seen to pose to French, declares himself irresistibly attracted to the "organized beauty of the French language."[27] The latest "migrant" author to join the académie as of this writing is Andreï Makine, on March 3, 2016. He has declared his love for the French language and admiration for French literature throughout his literary works. In his acceptance speech he highlighted Russian intellectuals' admiration for French, which became "a second national language" during Tsar Peter the Great's reign and has been, ever since, a continuous source of literary inspiration.[28] In contrast Laferrière's conception of language moves away from questions of prestige, echoing Pascale Casanova's (2013) opinion that "[t]here is a dominant language if (and only if) speakers [. . .] *believe* in the dominant language's prestige," rather than in "the totally arbitrary nature of its domination" (380, original emphasis). Laferrière's pragmatic linguistic stance both demythologizes the French language and shifts attention from issues of colonial legacy to the purely literary.

In terms of race Laferrière's election was interpreted by some as the académie's openness to black writers and, to others, as an act of affirmative action; the election coincided with the Cameroonian author Léonora Miano's capture of the Prix Femina, the Senegalese sculptor Ousmane Sow's election to the Académie des Beaux-Arts, and the crowning of Flora Coquerel, who is French and Beninese, as Miss France. The Haitian writer Louis-Philippe Dalembert sums up the ambivalence surrounding Laferrière's election: "the election of a Black proposes a more tolerant image of the Hexagon" in a climate of mounting racism. However, Dalembert continues, the French institution still has a long way to go: "It will be even better when the Académie française will have not one, but four, five, six Blacks. When the election of a Black or an Arab, of a non-French francophone writer, will go completely unnoticed."[29] Dalembert formulates an ideal of inclusion without arbitrary categorizations, in contrast to the académie's rhetoric of inclusion that deliberately showcases its welcoming of gendered, national, ethnic, and religious difference.[30] Viewed in this context, Laferrière's election appears to be a political act of token multiculturalism. But can we reduce the académie's decision to cultural politics?

Election to the académie is a highly ritualized process. To fill a vacancy, candidates submit their application letter to the permanent secretary and may pay a visit, if invited, to each member of the académie. Candidates are elected by a majority of académiciens in secret voting. Upon election, new members pass through an elaborate series of performative acts, ceremonies, and speeches, both private and public. Prior to the public unveiling, an induction ceremony takes place behind closed doors. Surrounded by their sponsors (*parrains*), new members read a speech and in turn are addressed by a special committee of the académie. Inductees then take a reserved seat, are assigned a dictionary word, and receive the académie medal stamped with their name and the group's motto: To Immortality. Adorned in costume (green robe, bicorn hat, cape, and sword), the newly inducted delivers an encomium to his or her predecessor. An official reception follows under the cupola of the Institut de France in the presence of distinguished guests. The final step is a private audience with the president of the French Republic, who acts on the occasion in the office's capacity as protector of the académie.

All who achieve consecration require the intervention of a powerful sponsoring agent. In Laferrière's case the académicien Jean d'Ormesson—a key figure in Marguerite Yourcenar's election as the académie's first woman in 1980—urged him to submit a letter of candidacy. Then D'Ormesson, with assistance from Carrère d'Encausse, the permanent secretary, began the backroom process that culminated in Laferrière's election. Laferrière admits to his own participation in the "coup," as he calls it, securing favorable votes by writing to each of the thirty-seven members. As a result, "[t]he deal was sealed in a month!"[31] Facing five rivals in his competition for Seat 2, Laferrière won on his first attempt, with thirteen out of twenty-three votes.

According to Laferrière (2015) himself, he gained admission to "the most prestigious literary institution in the world" and did so on his own terms (35). Hardly passive, he returned the consecrating institution's empowering gaze, redefining the terms of his consecration through strategies that recall those already employed in his literary works. He framed his French consecration by (1) staging the reception of the election news in Haiti (a reminder of *How to Make Love*), (2) laying bare the constructedness of his académicien identity (as he did in *I Am a Japanese Writer*), and (3) stressing the Caribbean literary connections between himself and his predecessors (a central theme in *The Return*).

Laferrière's choice to await the election result in Port-au-Prince, rather than Montréal, Miami, or Paris, was a political statement. By his own admission he wanted "[t]o make a strong symbol out of my presence in my native country. To give the impression of being not a traveling writer, away from Haitians, but one of them."[32] Receiving the French distinction at a remove decentered France while elevating Haiti as an equally prominent locale in his literary geography. He furthermore declared that joining the French institution "[w]ins me a third country! I have a residence in Montréal, I hope to have one in France, and I plan to visit Haiti more often. It's the opposite of the slave triangle. People who come from the Third World are the most nomadic. They add identities. It's what protects them from anxieties about their identity."[33] France becomes the most recent layer of his palimpsestic identity through a rhetoric of annexation. By mentioning slavery in the Black Atlantic, Laferrière alludes to the French colonial expeditions that appropriated foreign lands. In a form of counterconquest Laferrière culturally incorporates Paris into his previous geographies rather than assimilates himself into the metropolis. His antiassimilationist stance reveals a special relation to not only his native country but also Québec; his election is a double victory, for Haiti and Québec. A Haitian origin, a literary birth in Québec, French consecration. Laferrière's writerly trajectory continually defies categorizations. Asked if he would reside in France for the académie's weekly meetings, Laferrière responded in tongue-in-cheek fashion: "I am not someone rooted, I travel a lot. When I'm in Haiti, I am a Québécois writer, when I'm in Québec, I am a Haitian writer. One should never take on the identity of the place in which one is located. One should be a moving target."[34] His symbolic location is transnational crossing. The Académie française is but the latest stop in his continuous movement.

Laferrière's two speeches, published as *Dany Laferrière à l'Académie française: Discours de réception* (Dany Laferrière at the Académie française: Acceptance speech) by Éditions du Boréal in 2015, show how the author situates himself in relation to several literary fields. In "Discours de l'épée" (Sword speech), delivered on May 26, 2015, at Paris's city hall, Laferrière pays homage to his formative years in Petit-Goâve and Port-au-Prince, while also reflecting on his prominent new place in the French cultural establishment. He endows his académicien identity with fairy-tale elements, crafted in ritualistic fashion out of pieces from different places. Rather than meekly accept the académie's recognition, he redirects it, through sartorial symbolism, toward Haiti and Québec, where his literary career began and quickly flourished. His "sword speech" revisits the three geographic spaces that shaped his literary identity: Haiti, Québec, and France. Its recollections of Port-au-Prince pay homage to his mother, who admired the académiciens' "fluid style" in contrast to traditional Haitian ornamentalism (Laferrière 2015, 17). Her advice to "write with simplicity" in the French style left a durable impression (17). His speech then turns to Petit-Goâve, his grandmother's village that inspired the content of many of his early and later works. Literary consecration is tied closely to the author's return to the site of his literary genesis.

It is no accident that Laferrière's académicien sword—traditionally a symbol of belonging to the royal household of the king of France—was made by the renowned Haitian sculptor Patrick Vilaire. "It's Haiti that has to arm me," explained Laferrière (2015), "not France" (22). Despite his apolitical positioning, Laferrière has always saluted Haiti as the first black republic to raise arms against the French colonizer. The sword from Port-au-Prince represents the memory of Haiti's bloody history and his solidarity with the Haitian people, who continue to live its political consequences. Its handle, traditionally engraved with symbols of the académicien's life and work, features the image of the voodoo god Legba, a patron of writers who appears in many of the author's works (23). Legba, and its capacity to mediate between life and death, the profane and the sacred, mortality and immortality, brings still another element of Haitian spirituality into the secular académie. Laferrière's consecration came with a decidedly Haitian stamp.

For his green robe Laferrière enlisted the renowned Québécois fashion designer Jean-Claude Poitras. He explained the decision thus: "I hoped for a designer in whom the Québécois would recognize themselves, because I wanted to associate this ceremony, so important to me, with these two societies that have shaped me equally. So that people know in Paris that I am a man in three pieces" (Laferrière 2015, 25). The speech pays homage to Montréal, his first site of literary consecration, and to the Québécois publishers who discovered and promoted him: Jacques Lanctôt of Lanctôt Éditeur and Pascal Assathiany of Éditions du Boréal. As he puts it, "though born in Haiti, it's in Québec that I was born as a writer" (26). While Laferrière also acknowledges the key role of French publishers in his early success—Pierre Belfond, Pierre Astier, and Charles Danzig of Éditions Belfond, Le Serpent à Plumes, and Éditions Grasset, respectively—he insists they do not overshadow the importance of his publishers in other sites: "[A]ll of my books published in France had been published first or simultaneously in Québec. Montréal is not in my eyes an intellectual branch of Paris, but a place of incubation" (28). However, Pascale Casanova (2007) famously termed Paris "the Greenwich meridian of literature," the place of modernity and the gold standard for all literary traditions (87). Laferrière counters the notion of Paris as the cultural center against which other sites measure their aesthetic distance. He tactically decenters France and dispels the image of Québécois culture as its provincial derivative. Instead he endows *la belle province* with anteriority and the power of literary consecration in its own right.

Two days later Laferrière delivered his second speech, "Discours de réception à l'Académie française" (Acceptance speech at the Académie française) in the presence of French president François Hollande and Québécois prime minister Philippe Couillard. As is the custom, Laferrière paid homage to his predecessor in Seat 2, Hector Bianciotti, the Argentine-born author who immigrated to France in 1961 and entered the académie in 1996. Laferrière's laudatory overview of Bianciotti's oeuvre underscored his ambition to master the French language, his classical French style, and Argentina's literary ties to France. He also drew parallels between Bianciotti's oeuvre and his own: both, in exile, tackled the themes of childhood, memory, and return. But equally important, they were both American and thus shared the "American destiny" of European colonization, slavery, and wars of independence (Laferrière 2015, 39). Laferrière continued with an excavation of American history closely attached to Seat 2. Evoking predecessor Alexandre Dumas Son, he stressed his Haitian roots and the last name of his grandfather, whose mother was a slave. Laferrière then cited Montesquieu's critique of slavery in the Americas, associating the philosopher, who also occupied the seat, with the American continent. Laferrière further remarked, "This chair is the seat of so many adventures linked to the Americas that I would not be surprised if one day it became the Académie's American Seat" (42). Yet he also acknowledged writers of the Negritude who created a path to induction for him and Bianciotti: the Martinican Aimé Césaire, Guyanese Léon-Gontran Damas, and Senegalese Léopold Sédar Senghor. Senghor's induction to the académie in 1983, stated Laferrière, "allowed us to pass smoothly from Negritude to Francophonie," adding, "[e]very time a writer born elsewhere enters this Cupola, a simple effort of the imagination can make us see the procession of protective shadows that accompanies him or her" (57). Before the authorities of France's most esteemed cultural institution, Laferrière took pains to trace a wider network of the historical and cultural connections that link France to other territories. Laferrière's claim is less of the French tradition than of a decentered, transnational literary lineage.

Laferrière's ritual of acceptance of the institutional recognition mirrors the intratextual strategies glimpsed in his novels, whose purpose is to conflate cultures, histories, and identities. His ambition "to make Québec and Haiti better known within the institution" succeeds insofar as he inserts a hybrid voice in the monolingual French literary field and demarcates himself from other legitimating agents (Laferrière 2015, 19). The author's election, his response to it, and its media coverage show that consecration today involves myriad players and contextual factors.

CONCLUSION

French Migrant Literature
in a Global Context

Economic globalization and large-scale migrations in the twenty-first century have profoundly altered the French literary field, forever changing the ways in which cultural agents produce, receive, and evaluate works. Migrant literature, defined here as fictional texts that narrate the experience of migration, is largely an outgrowth of the current era of intensified commodification. *The Migrant Canon* has traced the migrant genre from its origins in the multicultural vogue of the 1980s to its arrival in the mainstream of twenty-first-century French literature. Migration's place at the forefront of today's political debates and media coverage invites us to read migrant texts in a new light. This study has proposed that these texts occupy an intermediary position in the literary field through their engagement with different forms of value (aesthetic, economic, political, ethical), marketplace (elite, mass markets), and audience (national, global, lay, academic). Case studies of various agents (publishers, online reviewers, literary prizes, language academies) demonstrate that consecration occurs where the commercial strategies of publishers, the agendas of cultural institutions, the aesthetic visions of authors, and the intellectual and commercial demands of readers intersect. Migrant literature in the new millennium is at once a cultural artifact, a commodity, and a tool for political engagement. It has introduced new themes and pathways to canonization into the French literary field.

Bourdieu's framework of the literary field has little to say about the marketplace situated between the commercial and the cultural or about readers and their active role in the process of literary consecration. *The Migrant Canon* has attempted to expand this framework through attention to new forms of agency, ranging from lay to elite. Future studies of the contemporary French literary field could also fruitfully examine how book clubs construct the value of migrant texts, how readers' reports on manuscripts influence editorial decisions, the role of translators as cultural mediators, or the new popularity of literary festivals dedicated to contemporary literature, such as Les Correspondances de Manosque, in which authors of migrant fiction often participate.[1] As a mainstream genre, migrant literature provides a lens through which to examine changing mechanisms of literary consecration.

The novels considered address the migrant experience in both content (border crossing) and form (cultural and linguistic mixing). The result is a portrait of a globalized French literature. As Subha Xavier (2016) observes, migrant texts are "a symptom not of the end of the nation-state nor even its fragility but of its ongoing *cosmopolitanization*" (194, original emphasis). The new mechanisms of consecration explored in this study also connect migrant French literature to what Anna Guttman, Michel Hockx, and George Paizis (2006) have called "the global literary field" (xx). In their definition the global literary field—not to be confused with Pascale Casanova's (2007) "world republic of letters"—is "a community wherein local, if not necessarily national, tastes and identities interact, merge or conflict with a set of dominant literary forms and values that continue to be perceived as broadly 'Western' and that are linked with the

Euro-American intellectual establishment, or with multinational publishing giants, or with both" (Guttman et al. 2006, xx). Although this book has not focused on the global circulation of French migrant texts or the implications of publishing in France for other francophone regions, it recognizes the undeniable impact of the economic structures and institutions of the Global North.[2] The fact that the Maurician-born Ananda Devi and Nathacha Appanah, as well as the Chinese-born, Britain-based Wei-Wei, publish with French presses makes this influence evident.

Yet consecration by French agents does not end there. Expanding Guttman, Hockx, and Paizis's reflection, it is possible to envision the global literary field in terms of a network of consecrating agencies, wherein acts of legitimation performed in one place reverberate in another. Take, for instance, Mathias Énard's *Rue des voleurs* (2012)—published by Actes Sud and awarded the Prix littéraire de la Porte Dorée—which was soon validated in Lebanon through the Prix Liste Goncourt/Le Choix de l'Orient and translations into Arabic and other languages. Or consider French translations of migrant texts from other literatures, which also continue the genre's literary legitimation. For example, Liana Levi's and Éditions des Équateur's French translations of Fabrizio Gatti's *Bilal: Viaggiare, lavorare, morire da clandestini* (2008) and Emma-Jane Kirby's *The Optician of Lampedusa* (2016), respectively, link French literature to a booming, multilingual, and lucrative subgenre: narratives of clandestine migration. Consider also the globalized digital spaces of Amazon and other reading forums where French migrant texts are consumed, in original and translation, by multiply located readerships, both professional and popular. Another central player is the Académie française, which has expanded its national membership criteria to accommodate global authors such as Dany Laferrière. Study of the migrant genre, when focused on the interrelated axes of aesthetics, market forces, and institutional practices, illuminates the global dimensions of the French literary field.

But French migrant texts published in France continue to be shaped by the interests and practices of national institutions. *The Migrant Canon* argues for the relevance of local contexts to genre study. French institutions have historically protected and defended the national language, promoting foreign authors who have adopted it for their literary expression and extolled its qualities. The last two chapters highlighted the ongoing hegemonic tendencies displayed by the Musée national de l'histoire de l'immigration and the Académie française. Writing in French in a global moment is therefore not a neutral endeavor; French cultural institutions often embrace migrant literature for diplomatic purposes, that is, as a means to promote the French language and culture. The attribution of value to literary works is contingent upon local contexts as well as global forces and audiences.

Transnationalism, as a theoretical category, allows us to move flexibly between local and global forms of production, consecration, and circulation, illuminating what is left out when migrant texts are seen as only national or global, as if the terms were mutually exclusive. Paul Jay's (2010) *Global Matters: The Transnational Turn in Literary Studies* offers one conception of literary transnationalism that is particularly apposite for this study. Jay proposes to view transnational works as "both a product of and engaged with the forces of globalization" (6). In his analysis of globalized fiction produced by cosmopolitan, border-crossing authors Jay shows how global economic forces shape this fiction and how it, in turn, exposes the power imbalances inherent in histories of colonialism, nationalism, and globalization. The texts explored in *The Migrant Canon* similarly display awareness of hegemonic cultural centers and propose alternative identifications. Novels engage critically with the nation (e.g., works by Coulin, Énard, Ferrier, Redonnet, Zeniter), advocate transnational modes of belonging (Kundera, Lopes, Schmitt), and posit new terms— the subnational and the human (Laferrière) as well as noncommodified literary identities (Makine)—that complicate set categories.

Authors such as these show the diversity of today's French literary consecration. Indeed the notion of a globalized French literary field invites far more questions than can be answered here. Does critical attention to transnational identifications push authors and consecrating institutions to move beyond France's traditional politics of identity? Will such criticism spur the continuation of regional, hemispheric, and global concerns, from environmental migration to clandestine crossings to narratives of asylum? Might the attention to such themes now, in the wake of political and demographic upheaval, signal a more politically engaged role for contemporary authors, as active participants in the public sphere?

A few recent examples suggest this may be so. Consider the publication of Milan Kundera's works in the two-volume *Oeuvre* (2011), in Gallimard's Bibliothèque de la Pléiade series. The gilded edition contains French translations of his early texts in Czech, later essays and novels he wrote in French, and a preface by the critic François Ricard. Far from presenting a complete picture of its author's works, as Pléiade editions typically do, *Oeuvre* omits Kundera's early communist poems, plays, and articles written in Czech. Instead the author censors the political circumstances of his first works and includes only those he deems aesthetically mature. Kundera thus shapes the terms of his consecration. He erases his migrant trajectory and insists he be considered a "novelist" tout court (Ricard 2011, xii). It is a shift from authorial biography to the texts themselves that suggests an effort to surpass identity politics.

For other mainstream authors migration provides crucial context, if not the central theme. Sabri Louatah's four-volume *Les Sauvages* (2012-16) explores the ways the election of a Muslim president plunges France into chaos. Part detective novel and part family saga, *Les Sauvages* puts forth immigrant protagonists to better explore the place of Islam in contemporary French politics. Michel Houellebecq's *Soumission* (2015) narrates the election, in the near future, of a president belonging to a Muslim political party. In *Chanson douce* (2016) the reversal of traditional power roles between an immigrant, upper-class mother and her children's French, lower-class nanny allows Leïla Slimani to examine issues of class. Novels such as these, in which migration is a backdrop, point to the migrant genre's influence on books that are not explicitly or primarily about migration.

Novels about clandestine immigrants and asylum seekers signal yet another emerging subgenre.[3] In *À ce stade de la nuit* (2015) Maylis de Kerangal intervenes in media representations of clandestine immigration by historicizing Lampedusa, which she portrays as a literary and cinematic island, not merely a stop in the passage to Europe. With a more militant conception of authorial responsibility Marie Cosnay's nonfictional

Comment on expulse: Responsabilités en miettes (2011) and *Entre chagrin et néant: Audiences d'étrangers* (2011) individualize and humanize migrants who await deportation. Cosnay takes up migrants' legal rights to critique French immigration policies, as do numerous other authors. All sales revenue from the short-story collection *Bienvenue! 34 auteurs pour les réfugiés* (2015) has been directed to the United Nations Refugee Agency, placing the aesthetic aims of politically committed authors in critical dialogue with the economic logic of the literary marketplace.

Protean as genres are, migrant literature invites new questions and authorial stances in the current context of mass movements of people and humanitarian crises. In their responses to events in Europe, contemporary French authors have reasserted their legitimacy in the public sphere and interrogated the cultural, social, and political roles of literature. Texts such as those studied here further show the extent to which the migrant genre is part and parcel of the contemporary French canon. Migrant texts actively engage with their historical moment, and, as this book has tried to demonstrate, their features, effects, and institutional consecration are best understood at the juncture between the aesthetic, the political, and the economic. *The Migrant Canon* not only explores new mechanisms of consecration of migrant works; it also attempts to legitimate the genre.

NOTES

INTRODUCTION

1. Soon after its publication in Québec, *Ru* was awarded the 2010 Prix du Gouverneur général for fiction (the most prestigious Canadian literary prize), the 2010 Prix du grand public *La Presse* du Salon du livre de Montréal, and the 2011 Grand prix littéraire Archambault. Its 2010 French edition paved the way for the Grand prix RTL-*Lire* at the Salon du livre de Paris and for nominations for the Prix littéraire de la Porte Dorée, Prix Première, Prix Prince Pierre de Monaco, and Prix des cinq continents de la francophonie. In Canada the novel earned another series of accolades. Published by Random House Canada in the award-winning translator Sheila Fischman's English version, it was shortlisted for the 2012 Scotiabank Giller Prize and nominated for the Amazon.ca First Novel Award, and it won both the 2012 Governor General's Literary Award for Translation and the CBC's 2015 Canada Reads competition—a mass media and readers' choice award. Beyond France and Canada *Ru* also fared well, winning or being shortlisted for the Mondello Prize for Multiculturalism in Italy, the Asian Literary Prize, and the Francophone Ambassador's Literature Award in Denmark.

2. Louis-Bernard Robitaille, "Conte de fées pour Kim Thuy en France," *La Presse*, January 22, 2010, http://www.lapresse.ca/arts/livres/201001/22/01-941751-conte -de-fees-pour-kim-thuy-en-france.php.

3. The migrant genre can be extended to cinema as well. Recent films about migration include *Welcome* (dir. Philippe Lioret 2009), *Qu'ils reposent en révolte* (dir. Sylvain George 2010), *Le Havre* (dir. Aki Kaurismäki 2011), *Vol spécial* (dir. Fernand Melgar 2011), *La Cour de Babel* (dir. Julie Bertuccelli 2013), *L'Escale* (dir. Kaveh Bakhtiari 2013), *Les Messagers* (dir. Hélène Crouzillat and Laetitia Tura 2014), *Brûle la mer* (dir. Nathalie Nambot and Maki Berchache 2014), and *Bienvenue au Réfugistan* (dir. Anne Poiret 2016), among others. See also the monograph on "post-Beur" cinema by Higbee (2013).

4. See, for example, the 2016 novelistic responses to the terrorist attacks of January and November 2015 in France, such as Arnaud Cathrine's *À la place du cœur*, Christian Lejalé's *Paris, 13 novembre 2015*, Julien Suaudeau's *Ni le feu ni la foudre*, and Laurence Tardieu's *À la fin le silence* (issued in a twelve-thousand-copy print run and a finalist for the 2016 Prix Renaudot).

5. Marie-Christine Imbault, "Goncourt, Renaudot, Femina, Médicis, Académie . . . Noël en Ferrari," *Livres Hebdo*, October 16, 2013, http://www.livreshebdo.fr/article /goncourt-renaudot-femina-medicis-academie-noel-en-ferrari?xtmc=%22Goncourt +Renaudot+Femina+M%C3%A9dicis+Acad%C3%A9mie+No%C3%ABl+en +Ferrari%22&xtcr=1.

6. Catherine Andreucci et al., "Rentrée hiver 2013 (romans): Un grand souffle de fiction," *Livres Hebdo*, October 22, 2013, http://www.livreshebdo.fr/article/rentree -hiver-2013-romans-un-grand-souffle-de-fiction?xtmc=%22Rentr%C3%A9e+hiver +2013%22&xtcr=1.

7. Literary works about migration have emerged in other countries as well. For studies that analyze the status of migrant literature in Germany, Italy, Belgium, Switzerland, Sweden, Britain, and the United States see the work of Adelson (2005), Burns (2013), Lebrun, Collès, and Robinet (2007), Lindberg (2013), and Walkowitz (2006).

8. French literary criticism therefore continues to engage with migrant works, whereas Québécois critics have sounded the death knell of this category.

9. For multifaceted discussions of the manifesto "Pour une 'littérature-monde' en français" see the 2009 special issue of the *International Journal of Francophone Studies*, especially the articles by Lionnet, Sugnet, and Taban, as well as Hargreaves et al.'s (2010) *Transnational French Studies*.

10. Printed by Le Dilettante in a 2,222-copy print run for its August 2013 launch, *L'Extraordinaire voyage* was reprinted after its meteoric success, reaching 110,000 copies in print by September 2013 and selling 500,000 copies in France. A finalist for the 2013 Prix Renaudot, Renaudot des lycéens, Méditerranée des lycéens, Virilo, Salerno, and Eureggio awards, the novel won the 2014 Grand Prix Jules-Verne and the 2014 Prix Audiolib (for its audio version), awarded by a jury composed of editors, bloggers, and Internet users. It was also published in fifty countries and translated into thirty-nine languages (according to the author's website, www .romainpuertolas.com/fakir) and is being adapted to film by the Canadian director Ken Scott. Claude Combet, "Meilleures ventes: Le fakir dans l'armoire Ikea et . . . dans les meilleures ventes," *Livres Hebdo*, September 25, 2013, http://www .livreshebdo.fr/article/le-fakir-dans-larmoire-ikea-et-dans-les-meilleures-ventes.

11. Early studies focus on literary texts by second-generation Maghrebi (or "Beur"), African, and Caribbean authors in France (e.g., Laronde 1993; Hargreaves 1997; Cazenave 2003; and Albert 2005). Later studies go beyond thematic and stylistic analyses. Kathryn A. Kleppinger's (2016) *Branding the "Beur" Author: Minority*

Writing and the Media in France, 1983–2013, for instance, explores the mainstream media's promotion of Beur novels by drawing on Beur authors' television and radio interviews. Overall these studies draw attention to a decentered form of writing emerging at the center of French literature, which is in turn assigned a marginal place in the French canon. These books have all contributed important analyses of migrant authors' attempts to carve out a literary place in a France hostile to its postcolonial population.

12. By the turn of the twenty-first century, however, critics were stressing that the institutional co-optation of migrant texts had reached an impasse: the label "migrant writing," which no longer captured fully assimilated migrant authors, was obsolete, and the question of Québécois national identity had lost its urgency (Harel 2005, 14; Dupuis 2007, 137).

13. For example, Azouz Begag's *Le Gône du Chaâba* (1986) sold sixty thousand copies, but when his *L'Îlet-aux-vents* (1992) deviated from established banlieue themes, it sold only nine thousand copies and received little press coverage (Harzoune 2003).

14. Those French authors already mentioned are Adam, Condou, Coulin, de Kerangal, Gaudé, Janicot, Koening, Prudhomme, Redonnet, Schmitt, Schneider, Schultze, and Zalberg. French-born authors of foreign or mixed origin include Abécassis, Batista, Bui, Davrichewy, Delmaire, Ferrier, Guène, Kanor, Magoudi, Paulino-Neto, Pigani, Swiatly, Tranh Huy, Wagner, Weil, Zenatti, and Zeniter.

1. PRODUCTION

1. Claude Combet, "Meilleures ventes du 17 au 23 août 2015," *Livres Hebdo*, August 28, 2015, http://www.livreshebdo.fr/article/meilleures-ventes-du-17-au-23-aout -2015?xtmc=meilleures+ventes+du+17+au+23+ao%c3%BBt+2015&xtcr=1; "Anna Gavalda et *Billie* en tête," *Livres Hebdo*, October 9, 2013, http://www.livreshebdo .fr/article/anna-gavalda-et-billie-en-tete?xtmc=%22Anna+Gavalda+et+Billie+en +t%C3%AAte%22&xtcr=1.

2. Claude Combet, "Meilleures ventes: Le fakir dans l'armoire Ikea et . . . dans les meilleures ventes," *Livres Hebdo*, September 25, 2013, http://www.livreshebdo.fr /article/le-fakir-dans-larmoire-ikea-et-dans-les-meilleures-ventes; Fanny Taillandier, "Donner voix," *Livres Hebdo*, November 22, 2013, http://www.livreshebdo.fr /article/donner-voix?xtmc=carole+zalberg+feu+pour+feu&xtcr=4; Olivier Mony, "Daddy cool," *Livres Hebdo*, June 1, 2012, http://www.livreshebdo.fr/article/daddy -cool; Olivier Mony, "Quand on est deux amis," *Livres Hebdo*, November 13, 2015, http://www.livreshebdo.fr/article/quand-est-deux-amis.

3. Claude Combet, "Meilleures ventes du 3 au 9 novembre 2014," *Livres Hebdo*, November 14, 2014, http://www.livreshebdo.fr/article/meilleures-ventes-du-3 -au-9-novembre-2014.

4. The novel was an astounding success: it appeared for nineteen weeks in 2009 and 2010 on *Livres Hebdo*'s Top 50 list of best-selling novels, and for forty-two weeks in 2011 and twelve weeks in 2012 on its Top 20 list of best sellers.

5. Claude Combet et al., "Meilleures ventes 2011: Les bons sentiments," *Livres Hebdo*, January 27, 2012, http://www.livreshebdo.fr/article/meilleures-ventes-2011-les -bons-sentiments.

6. Successful migrant novels issued in paperback include Alcoba's *Le Bleu des abeilles* (Gallimard/Folio), Diome's *Le Ventre de l'Atlantique* (Anne Carrière/Le Livre de Poche), Coulin's *Samba pour la France* (Le Seuil/Points), Gaudé's *Eldorado* (Actes Sud/Babel), Gauz's *Debout-payé* (Le Nouvel Attila/Le Livre de Poche), Montaza-mi's *Le Meilleur des Jours* (Sabine Wespieser/Points), Schmitt's *Ulysse from Bagdad* (Albin Michel/Le Livre de Poche), Sinha's *Assommons les pauvres!* (L'Olivier/Points), Tajadod's *Elle joue* (Albin Michel/Le Livre de Poche), and Zenatti's *Jacob, Jacob* (L'Olivier/Points), among others.

7. In addition to the competition for paperback editions among the above-mentioned presses (Gallimard, Anne Carrière, etc.), there is competition among presses spe-cializing in paperbacks, such as Pocket, Folio, Babel, 10/18, Points, and J'ai lu. *Livres Hebdo* occasionally ranks the latter group, which underscores the hierarchical nature of the French publishing industry. In 2011, for instance, *Livres Hebdo* ranked Le Livre de Poche as the best-selling publishing house for paperbacks, whereas in 2015 it was Pocket that had the most titles on *Livres Hebdo*'s list of best-selling paperbacks. Combet et al., "Meilleures ventes 2011"; Claude Combet, "Meilleures ventes 2015: La potion magique," *Livres Hebdo*, January 22, 2016, http://www.livreshebdo.fr /article/meilleures-ventes-2015-la-potion-magique#308437.

8. Take, for instance, Alexandre Seurat's debut novel *La Maladroite* (2015), which was the only book Sylvie Gracia decided to publish in 2015 in Le Rouergue's La brune series. In preparation for launching the book in August 2015 Gracia began talking to booksellers in March; they read the novel's page proofs and contributed to its success by word-of-mouth selling. As a result *La Maladroite*, with an initial print run of six thousand copies, was reprinted three more times that year, for a total run of twenty-five thousand copies, sixteen thousand of which had sold by October 2015. Claude Combet, "Meilleures ventes du 5 au 11 octobre 2015," *Livres Hebdo*, October 16, 2015, http://www.livreshebdo.fr/article/meilleures-ventes-du -5-au-11-octobre-2015#296304.

9. "Sylvie Gracia: 'Cela reste artisanal,'" *Livres Hebdo*, December 14, 2012, http:// www.livreshebdo.fr/article/sylvie-gracia-cela-reste-artisanal?xtmc=%22Sylvie +Gracia%22&xtcr=2.

10. "Sophie de Sivry," *L'Iconoclaste*, accessed June 6, 2016, http://www.editions -iconoclaste.fr/spip.php?article50 (site discontinued).

11. Hakim Abderrezak (2009) identifies "illiterature"—a term conflating "illegal" and "literature"—as a new subgenre in Moroccan literature produced since the 1990s and centered on narratives about illegal immigration from Morocco to southern Europe across the Mediterranean Sea (461).

12. *Eldorado*'s popularity can be measured by its presence on best-seller lists. The paperback edition occupied thirteenth place on *Livres Hebdo*'s weekly list of best-selling novels for September 21–27, 2015. It was on this list for another three weeks in 2016.

13. Marine Landrot, "*Samba pour la France*," *Télérama*, September 18, 2013, http://www .telerama.fr/livres/delphine-coulin-samba-pour-la-france,65648.php; Fabienne Dumontet, "*Samba pour la France*, de Delphine Coulin: Ubu et les sans-papiers," *Le Monde*, January 6, 2011, http://www.lemonde.fr/livres/article/2011/01/06/samba -pour-la-france-de-delphine-coulin_1461633_3260.html.

14. "Collection Continents Noirs," June 12, 2016, Gallimard, http://www.gallimard.fr /Divers/Plus-sur-la-collection/Continents-noirs/(sourcenode)/116076.

15. "Henri Lopes lauréat du prix littéraire de la Porte Dorée 2012," June 6, 2012, Musée national de l'histoire de l'immigration, http://www.histoire-immigration.fr/art-et -culture/le-prix-litteraire-de-la-porte-doree/henri-lopes-laureat-du-prix-litteraire -de-la.

16. Tahar Bekri, review of *Une enfant de Poto-Poto*, by Henri Lopes, *Africultures*, February 27, 2012, http://www.africultures.com/php/?nav=article&no=10622.

17. Marine Durand et al., "Débat: Comment va la littérature française?," *Livres Hebdo*, May 13, 2016, http://www.livreshebdo.fr/article/comment-va-la-litterature -francaise?xtmc=%22Comment+va+la+litt%C3%A9rature+fran%C3%A7aise +%22&xtcr=1.

18. Aurélie Pasquelin, "En septembre, c'est aussi la rentrée des livres," *La Nouvelle République*, September 6, 2014, http://www.lanouvellerepublique.fr/Indre-et-Loire /Communes/Langeais/n/Contenus/Articles/2014/09/06/En-septembre-c-est -aussi-la-rentree-des-livres-2035875.

19. Lucie Delaporte, "*Debout-payé*, Gauz ou l'épopée du vigile," *Mediapart*, September 21, 2014, https://www.mediapart.fr/journal/france/210914/debout-paye-gauz-ou -lepopee-du-vigile; "*Debout-payé*, Gauz," *Lecture/Écriture* (blog), accessed September 17, 2014, http://lecture-ecriture.com/10233-Debout-pay%C3%A9--Gauz.

20. For novels by migrant authors that adopt Montesquieu's perspective see Andreï Makine's *Le Testament français* (1995), Ya Ding's *Le Jeu de l'eau et du feu* (1995), Chahdortt Djavann's *Comment peut-on être français?* (2006), and Maryam Madjidi's *Marx et la poupée* (2017).

21. Jean Birnbaum, "Solidarité vigile," *Le Monde*, September 4, 2014, http://www .lemonde.fr/livres/article/2014/09/04/solidarite-vigile_4481651_3260.html; Estelle

Lenartowich, "*Debout-payé*, paroles de vigile," *L'Express*, October 16, 2014, http://www.lexpress.fr/culture/livre/debout-paye-paroles-de-vigile_1611813.html.

22. Durand et al., "Débat: Comment va la littérature française?"

23. Birnbaum, "Solidarité vigile"; Marianne Payot, "Premiers romans: L'audace des débutants," *L'Express*, September 8, 2014, http://www.lexpress.fr/culture/livre/premiers-romans-l-audace-des-debutants_1572653.html.

24. Souen Léger, "Premiers romans: Anatomie d'un succès," *Livres Hebdo*, February 13, 2015, http://www.livreshebdo.fr/article/premiers-romans-anatomie-dun-succes?xtmc=%22Debout-pay%C3%A9%22&xtcr=48.

25. Gauz quoted in Marion Cocquet, "Noirs, donc vigiles: Les théorèmes de Gauz," *Le Point*, October 6, 2014, http://www.lepoint.fr/culture/noirs-donc-vigiles-les-theoremes-de-gauz-06-10-2014-1869705_3.php.

26. Marianne Payot, "Schmitt le bon Samaritain," *L'Express*, November 27, 2008, http://www.lexpress.fr/informations/schmitt-le-bon-samaritain_725752.html.

2. RECEPTION

1. For studies that emphasize the authority of lay readers as producers of literary meaning see works by Steiner (2008) and Hight et al. (2011). For the notion of a culture of participation see the compilation by Jenkins et al. (2016).

2. For a similar argument about postcolonial literature, its context of reception, narrative strategies, and appeal to heterogeneous publics see the monograph by Brouillette (2011).

3. For reviews that justify the number of stars the book received see postings by Critiques Libres reviewers Jules, January 8, 2004, http://www.critiqueslibres.com/i.php/vcrit/3734; and Saint Jean-Baptiste, November 9, 2003, http://www.critiqueslibres.com/i.php/vcrit/3734.

4. For details on the reception of Kundera and Makine in France see Porra's (2011) monograph (173–91).

5. For Kundera's *L'Ignorance* eighteen French-language reviews submitted between June 4, 2000, and November 8, 2016, to Amazon.fr and twenty reviews on Babelio from March 21, 2008, to January 4, 2017, were consulted. For *Ignorance* fifty English-language reviews on Amazon.com and thirty-three reviews on Amazon.ca between June 4, 2000, and November 8, 2016, were consulted. For Makine's *La Vie d'un homme inconnu* sixteen commentaries posted on Amazon.fr (February 24, 2009–April 22, 2016), twenty-five critiques on Babelio (June 18, 2009–January 4, 2017), eighteen reviews on Critiques Libres (March 3, 2009–November 6, 2016), and one commentary on Amazon.ca were consulted. For *The Life of an Unknown Man* twenty-nine English-language reviews posted on Amazon.com (November 14, 2010–December 5, 2016) were consulted. The latest review consulted for this study was dated February 1, 2017.

6. Kundera (2006) defines the provincialism of small nations as "the inability (or the refusal) to see one's own culture in the *large context*" (37, original emphasis). In *Ignorance* provincialism equals the Czechs' refusal to be interested in transnational matters.

7. filo, April 27, 2003, Amazon.fr, https://www.amazon.fr/Lignorance-Milan-Kundera /product-reviews/2070306100/ref=dpx_acr_txt?showViewpoints=1; A customer, October 30, 2002, Amazon.ca, https://www.amazon.ca/Ignorance-Novel-Milan -Kundera/product-reviews/0060002107/ref=dpx_acr_txt?showViewpoints=1.

8. For negative coverage of Kundera's French-language novels see Angelo Rinaldi, "Le bonheur est aux 'urgences,'" *L'Express*, January 15, 1998, http://www.lexpress .fr/culture/livre/l-identit_818701.html.

9. A. Peel, February 9, 2003, Amazon.com, https://www.amazon.com/Ignorance -Novel-Milan-Kundera/product-reviews/0060002107/ref=cm_cr_arp_d_viewopt _rvwer?ie=UTF8&reviewerType=all_reviews&pageNumber=1.

10. M. Benet, January 2, 2003, Amazon.ca, https://www.amazon.ca/Ignorance -Novel-Milan-Kundera/product-reviews/0060002107/ref=dpx_acr_txt ?showViewpoints=1.

11. Hadeel Altreikion, May 26, 2005, Amazon.com, https://www.amazon.com/Ignorance -Novel-Milan-Kundera/product-reviews/0060002107/ref=cm_cr_arp_d_viewopt _rvwer?ie=UTF8&reviewerType=all_reviews&pageNumber=1; Hana, October 19, 2014, Amazon.ca, https://www.amazon.ca/Ignorance-Novel-Milan-Kundera /product-reviews/0060002107/ref=dpx_acr_txt?showViewpoints=1; A. Peel, February 9, 2003; Rev Kurt, February 23, 2007, Amazon.com, https://www.amazon.com /Ignorance-Novel-Milan-Kundera/product-reviews/0060002107/ref=cm_cr_arp_d _viewopt_rvwer?ie=UTF8&reviewerType=all_reviews&pageNumber=1; Teresa Neeman, January 13, 2015, Amazon.com, https://www.amazon.com/Ignorance-Novel -Milan-Kundera/product-reviews/0060002107/ref=cm_cr_arp_d_viewopt_rvwer ?ie=UTF8&reviewerType=all_reviews&pageNumber=1. For additional readings of *Ignorance* as a migrant novel see the following reviews: A customer, June 4, 2003, Amazon.ca, https://www.amazon.ca/Ignorance-Novel-Milan-Kundera/product -reviews/0060002107/ref=dpx_acr_txt?showViewpoints=1; Bunee, October 8, 2009, Babelio, http://www.babelio.com/livres/Kundera-Lignorance/4806/critiques; Joy Bennett, October 22, 2003, Amazon.ca, https://www.amazon.ca/Ignorance-Novel -Milan-Kundera/product-reviews/0060002107/ref=dpx_acr_txt?showViewpoints =1; lDavidl, November 9, 2015, Babelio, http://www.babelio.com/livres/Kundera -Lignorance/4806/critiques; Max P., September 17, 2007, Amazon.fr, https://www .amazon.fr/Lignorance-Milan-Kundera/product-reviews/2070306100/ref=dpx _acr_txt?showViewpoints=1; nuitetoilee, February 23, 2014, Babelio, http://www .babelio.com/livres/Kundera-Lignorance/4806/critiques; Rouchka1344, September 2, 2010, Critiques Libres, http://www.critiqueslibres.com/i.php/vcrit/3734;

Soleada, June 11, 2008, Critiques Libres, http://www.critiqueslibres.com/i.php/vcrit/3734; Trevor Kettlewell, July 16, 2014, Amazon.com, https://www.amazon.com/Ignorance-Novel-Milan-Kundera/product-reviews/0060002107/ref=cm_cr_arp_d_viewopt_rvwer?ie=UTF8&reviewerType=all_reviews&pageNumber=1; Victor Cresskill, October 12, 2002, Amazon.ca, https://www.amazon.ca/Ignorance-Novel-Milan-Kundera/product-reviews/0060002107/ref=dpx_acr_txt?showViewpoints=1; and Un client, August 13, 2003, Amazon.fr, https://www.amazon.fr/Lignorance-Milan-Kundera/product-reviews/2070306100/ref=dpx_acr_txt?showViewpoints=1.

12. Syd Dithers, September 27, 2006, Amazon.com, https://www.amazon.com/Ignorance-Novel-Milan-Kundera/product-reviews/0060002107/ref=cm_cr_arp_d_viewopt_rvwer?ie=UTF8&reviewerType=all_reviews&pageNumber=1; lDavidl, November 9, 2015.

13. bibliovegevore, September 28, 2014, Babelio, http://www.babelio.com/livres/Kundera-Lignorance/4806/critiques; Loly Perez, September 1, 2013, Amazon.com, https://www.amazon.com/Ignorance-Novel-Milan-Kundera/product-reviews/0060002107/ref=cm_cr_arp_d_viewopt_rvwer?ie=UTF8&reviewerType=all_reviews&pageNumber=1; Soleada, June 11, 2008.

14. A customer, June 4, 2003.

15. A customer, November 10, 2003, Amazon.ca, https://www.amazon.ca/Ignorance-Novel-Milan-Kundera/product-reviews/0060002107/ref=dpx_acr_txt?showViewpoints=1. For readings of Kundera's oeuvre that foreground the author's biography see also Amazon Customer, June 2, 2016, Amazon.com, https://www.amazon.com/Ignorance-Novel-Milan-Kundera/product-reviews/0060002107/ref=cm_cr_arp_d_viewopt_rvwer?ie=UTF8&reviewerType=all_reviews&pageNumber=1; PuroShaggy, August 27, 2011, Amazon.com, https://www.amazon.com/Ignorance-Novel-Milan-Kundera/product-reviews/0060002107/ref=cm_cr_arp_d_viewopt_rvwer?ie=UTF8&reviewerType=all_reviews&pageNumber=1; Rouchka1344, September 2, 2010; Stewart, September 12, 2005, Amazon.com, https://www.amazon.com/Ignorance-Novel-Milan-Kundera/product-reviews/0060002107/ref=cm_cr_arp_d_viewopt_rvwer?ie=UTF8&reviewerType=all_reviews&pageNumber=1; and Trevor Kettlewell, July 16, 2014.

16. Kundera's (1988) theory and practice of the novel are riddled with contradictions. On the one hand he views the genre as "the realm of play and hypotheses," terms that suggest semantic complexity and openness to a multiplicity of meanings (78). As a space for literary experimentation par excellence, the novel is in this sense incompatible with totalitarian ideological frameworks that reduce works to a single truth (14). On the other hand Kundera makes great effort to control the reception of his works. For instance, he discourages biographical readings of his texts, revises subsequent editions, and closely supervises their translations. His

novels firmly guide readers through the use of omniscient narrators and an intrusive "'autobiographical' voice" that mocks, validates, or simply muses on characters and events (Frank 2008, 79). This attempt to impose aesthetic interpretations is at odds with his conception of the novel as open, ludic, and infinitely interpretable.

17. le dernier carré, October 4, 2014, Amazon.fr, https://www.amazon.fr/Lignorance-Milan-Kundera/product-reviews/2070306100/ref=dpx_acr_txt?showViewpoints =1; filo, April 27, 2003; Amazon Customer, October 21, 2002, Amazon.ca, https:// www.amazon.ca/Ignorance-Novel-Milan-Kundera/product-reviews/0060002107 /ref=dpx_acr_txt?showViewpoints=1.

18. Rouchka1344, September 2, 2010.

19. See, for example, Cosmoetica, October 9, 2008, Amazon.com, https://www.amazon .com/Ignorance-Novel-Milan-Kundera/product-reviews/0060002107/ref=cm _cr_arp_d_viewopt_rvwer?ie=UTF8&reviewerType=all_reviews&pageNumber=1; filo, April 27, 2003; S. Park, October 12, 2003, Amazon.ca, https://www.amazon.ca /Ignorance-Novel-Milan-Kundera/product-reviews/0060002107/ref=dpx_acr_txt ?showViewpoints=1.

20. le dernier carré, October 4, 2014.

21. *The Joke* (1967), *The Book of Laughter and Forgetting* (1979), and *The Unbearable Lightness of Being* (1984) helped create Kundera's legend in France and, if only partially, facilitated his integration into French literary circles. They appeared at an ideologically favorable time for Kundera, when the echoes of the Prague Spring in France (from January to August 1968), known as "May 68" (when French leftists began to project their ideal of politically engaged literature onto the Eastern Bloc), and the international renown of Alexander Solzhenitsyn and other exiles made central and eastern European writers a veritable cause célèbre (Rizek 2001, 166). See also Bessière's (2003) explanation of Kundera's success in France in the political climate after 1968: "From 1968 onwards, the French socialist and communist parties were allies and produced a *programme commun de la gauche*" (common leftist agenda); after Kundera becomes a French citizen in 1981, the French political leaders promoted "[un] *socialisme à visage humain* [a socialism with a human face]" (3, original emphasis).

22. For the former group see bibliovegevore, September 28, 2014; cedratier, August 25, 2015, Babelio, http://www.babelio.com/livres/Kundera-Lignorance/4806 /critiques; lDavidl, November 9, 2015; Jules, January 8, 2004; nuitetoilee, February 23, 2014. For the latter group see Betty, June 29, 2011, Amazon.fr, https://www .amazon.fr/Lignorance-Milan-Kundera/product-reviews/2070306100/ref=dpx _acr_txt?showViewpoints=1; Dersy, July 2, 2003, Amazon.fr, https://www.amazon .fr/Lignorance-Milan-Kundera/product-reviews/2070306100/ref=dpx_acr_txt ?showViewpoints=1; Laurence-64, August 12, 2015, Babelio, http://www.babelio .com/livres/Kundera-Lignorance/4806/critiques; Loutre_des_Rivieres, August 30,

2012, Babelio, http://www.babelio.com/livres/Kundera-Lignorance/4806/critiques; Saule, February 6, 2008, Critiques Libres, http://www.critiqueslibres.com/i.php /vcrit/3734; and Teresa Neeman, January 13, 2015.

23. Stewart, September 12, 2005.

24. In *The Act of Reading: A Theory of Aesthetic Response* the German critic Wolfgang Iser postulates his theory of reading as an event that occurs in the interaction between text and reader. For Iser (1978) reading is "an activity that is guided by the text" (163). This guidance operates through structural devices such as blanks, which he defines as "an empty space" situated at the points where different textual segments are abruptly juxtaposed (197). These blanks, because they conceal possible connections between narrative perspectives, incite readers to fill them in with "projections" (198). For Iser it is the reader's constantly changing position during the act of reading that highlights the text's overall framework. Iser's discussion of how blanks structure the text-reader interaction seems more easily applicable to eighteenth-century novels, which constellate several character perspectives (of the hero, the minor characters, the fictitious reader, and the narrator, for instance), which they organize hierarchically, with the hero's perspective on top (204). Whatever the value of reader response theory for earlier periods, Iser's explanation of how blanks structure readers' responses is relevant to *Ignorance*, given its elliptical form, Kundera's avowed fascination with eighteenth-century authors, his use of an obtrusive narrator who intervenes in the plot (as in Sterne's and Fielding's novels), and the guiding function of the narrative voice.

25. M. A Netzley, January 19, 2003, Amazon.ca, https://www.amazon.ca/Ignorance -Novel-Milan-Kundera/product-reviews/0060002107/ref=dpx_acr_txt ?showViewpoints=1.

26. Erixtc, November 11, 2014, Amazon.fr, https://www.amazon.fr/Lignorance-Milan -Kundera/product-reviews/2070306100/ref=dpx_acr_txt?showViewpoints=1; Nadal, July 16, 2012, Amazon.com, https://www.amazon.com/Ignorance-Novel -Milan-Kundera/product-reviews/0060002107/ref=cm_cr_arp_d_viewopt_rvwer?ie =UTF8&reviewerType=all_reviews&sortBy=recent&pageNumber=1.

27. Trevor Kettlewell, July 16, 2014.

28. For details about Kundera's Eurocentric and elitist conception of the novel see his *L'Art du roman* (1986), *Les Testaments trahis* (1993), and *Le Rideau* (2005).

29. Victor Cresskill, October 12, 2002; A customer, October 30, 2002.

30. nadirland@hotmail.com, November 7, 2002, Amazon.ca. https://www.amazon.ca /Ignorance-Novel-Milan-Kundera/product-reviews/0060002107/ref=dpx_acr_txt ?showViewpoints=1.

31. A customer, November 10, 2002, Amazon.ca, https://www.amazon.ca/Ignorance -Novel-Milan-Kundera/product-reviews/0060002107/ref=dpx_acr_txt ?showViewpoints=1.

32. Neithan, August 2, 2005, Critiques Libres, http://www.critiqueslibres.com/i.php/vcrit/3734.

33. Dr Martin Price, May 25, 2004, Amazon.com, https://www.amazon.com/Ignorance-Novel-Milan-Kundera/product-reviews/0060002107/ref=cm_cr_arp_d_viewopt_rvwer?ie=UTF8&reviewerType=all_reviews&pageNumber=1; Teca75, October 8, 2014, Amazon.fr, https://www.amazon.fr/Lignorance-Milan-Kundera/product-reviews/2070306100/ref=dpx_acr_txt?showViewpoints=1; bibliovegevore, September 28, 2014.

34. Mauricio Soto, January 24, 2006, Amazon.com, https://www.amazon.com/Ignorance-Novel-Milan-Kundera/product-reviews/0060002107/ref=cm_cr_arp_d_viewopt_rvwer?ie=UTF8&reviewerType=all_reviews&pageNumber=1.

35. PuroShaggy, August 27, 2011.

36. Trey S., April 10, 2003, Amazon.ca, https://www.amazon.ca/Ignorance-Novel-Milan-Kundera/product-reviews/0060002107/ref=dpx_acr_txt?showViewpoints=1.

37. Stewart, September 12, 2005; A customer, November 10, 2003; Amazon Customer, June 27, 2016, Amazon.ca, https://www.amazon.ca/Ignorance-Novel-Milan-Kundera/product-reviews/0060002107/ref=cm_cr_arp_d_viewopt_srt?showViewpoints=1&sortBy=recent&pageNumber=1.

38. Mandarine, December 26, 2011, Critiques Libres, http://www.critiqueslibres.com/i.php/vcrit/19256.

39. Shan-Ze, October 3, 2015, Babelio, http://www.babelio.com/livres/Makine-La-vie-dun-homme-inconnu/112241/critiques.

40. Tistou, December 24, 2011, Critiques Libres, http://www.critiqueslibres.com/i.php/vcrit/19256; Madimado, November 25, 2010, Babelio, http://www.babelio.com/livres/Makine-La-vie-dun-homme-inconnu/112241/critiques; JeanPierreV, March 10, 2016, Babelio, http://www.babelio.com/livres/Makine-La-vie-dun-homme-inconnu/112241/critiques; Frunny, May 18, 2012, Critiques Libres, http://www.critiqueslibres.com/i.php/vcrit/19256.

41. Nathafi, October 1, 2014, Critiques Libres, http://www.critiqueslibres.com/i.php/vcrit/19256; Pucksimberg, December 29, 2011, Critiques Libres, http://www.critiqueslibres.com/i.php/vcrit/19256; CoupdeSoleil, March 19, 2012, Amazon.fr, https://www.amazon.fr/Vie-dun-homme-inconnu/product-reviews/2757816373/ref=cm_cr_arp_d_viewopt_srt?showViewpoints=1&sortBy=recent&pageNumber=1; Alma, June 8, 2009, Critiques Libres, http://www.critiqueslibres.com/i.php/vcrit/19256.

42. Alma, June 8, 2009.

43. soleil, January 4, 2017, Babelio, http://www.babelio.com/livres/Makine-La-vie-dun-homme-inconnu/112241/critiques.

44. Isad, June 3, 2012, Critiques Libres, http://www.critiqueslibres.com/i.php/vcrit/19256.

45. Florence94, August 15, 2012, Babelio, http://www.babelio.com/livres/Makine-La
-vie-dun-homme-inconnu/112241/critiques; Madimado, November 25, 2010.

46. Renod, January 27, 2015, Babelio, http://www.babelio.com/livres/Makine-La-vie
-dun-homme-inconnu/112241/critiques.

47. Marvic, December 4, 2011, Critiques Libres, http://www.critiqueslibres.com/i.php
/vcrit/19256; Pucksimberg, December 29, 2011; Frunny, May 18, 2012; Olivier de
Brizule, October 22, 2009, Amazon.fr, https://www.amazon.fr/Lignorance-Milan
-Kundera/product-reviews/2070306100/ref=dpx_acr_txt?showViewpoints=1.

48. Débézed, May 24, 2012, Critiques Libres, http://www.critiqueslibres.com/i.php
/vcrit/19256.

49. Donatien, January 21, 2010, Critiques Libres, http://www.critiqueslibres.com/i
.php/vcrit/19256; Débézed, May 24, 2012.

50. Elya, January 21, 2012, Critiques Libres, http://www.critiqueslibres.com/i.php/vcrit
/19256.

51. Elya, January 21, 2012; Donatien, January 21, 2010; migo, January 31, 2011, Babelio, http://www.babelio.com/livres/Makine-La-vie-dun-homme-inconnu/112241
/critiques.

52. Friederike Knabe, November 14, 2010, Amazon.ca, https://www.amazon.ca/Vie
-homme-inconnu-andre%c3%AF-Makine/product-reviews/2757816373/ref=dpx
_acr_txt?showViewpoints=1.

53. Patilou, July 30, 2010, Babelio, http://www.babelio.com/livres/Makine-La-vie
-dun-homme-inconnu/112241/critiques.

3. CONSECRATION

1. In the 1980s the Renaudot and the Goncourt went to Michel del Castillo, René
Depestre, and Tahar Ben Jelloun, and in the 1990s the Goncourt, the Goncourt
des lycéens, the Médicis, the Femina, the Interallié, and the Grand Prix du roman
de l'Académie française recognized numerous other immigrant authors (Patrick
Chamoiseau, Amin Maalouf, Andreï Makine, Eduardo Manet, Nancy Huston,
Vassilis Alexakis, Hector Bianciotti, François Cheng, and Calixthe Beyala) for
their contributions to French literature.

2. Their recognitions include the Goncourt (Jonathan Littell, Atiq Rahimi, Leïla
Slimani), the Goncourt des lycéens (Shan Sa, Léonora Miano, Gaël Faye), the
Médicis (Dany Laferrière), the Femina (Dai Sijie, Nancy Huston), the Renaudot
(Ahmadou Kourouma, Nina Bouraoui, Alain Mabanckou, Tierno Monénembo), as
well as four prizes awarded by the Académie française: the Grand Prix du Roman
(Jonathan Littell, Vassilis Alexakis, Boualem Sansal, Hédi Kaddour), the Grand
Prix de littérature (Milan Kundera), the Prix du Rayonnement de la langue et de la
littérature française (Brina Svit), and the Grand Prix de la Francophonie (François
Cheng, Boualem Sansal, Nahal Tajadod).

3. "Pour une 'littérature-monde' en français," *Le Monde*, March 15, 2007, http://www
.lemonde.fr/livres/article/2007/03/15/des-ecrivains-plaident-pour-un-romanen
-francais-ouvert-sur-le-monde_883572_3260.html.

4. The prize derives its name from the Palais de la Porte Dorée (the Palace of the Golden
Door), where the Musée national de l'histoire de l'immigration is located, and from
the lines of Emma Lazarus's poem inscribed on the base of the Statue of Liberty,
in which the Golden Door is the symbol of immigrants traveling toward America
(Lesne 2010, para. 2). The Prix littéraire de la Porte Dorée thus seeks to connect
two museums of immigration—the Musée national de l'histoire de l'immigration
and the Ellis Island Immigration Museum—to suggest that immigration is equally
valorized in France as constitutive of the nation-state as it is in the United States.
In doing so the prize attempts to counter the republican model of the nation based
on the denial of difference.

5. As this book goes to press, the latest Porte Dorée laureate is Négar Djavadi's *Désorientale* (2016).

6. "Sylvain Prudhomme, lauréat du Prix littéraire de la Porte Dorée 2015," June 3, 2015,
Musée national de l'histoire de l'immigration, http://www.histoire-immigration
.fr/art-et-culture/le-prix-litteraire-de-la-porte-doree/sylvain-prudhomme-laureat
-du-prix-litteraire-de.

7. "Remise du prix littéraire de la Porte Dorée, le 12 juin 2010 à 17 heures, à la Cité
nationale de l'histoire de l'immigration," 3, Musée national de l'histoire de l'immigration, accessed December 3, 2015, http://www.histoire-immigration.fr/sites
/default/files/musee-numerique/documents/ext_media_fichier_778_DP_prix
_19052010.pdf.

8. Catherine Simon, "Mathias Énard: 'L'identité est elle aussi en movement,'" *Le
Monde*, September 4, 2012, http://www.lemonde.fr/livres/article/2012/09/04
/mathias-enard-l-identite-est-elle-aussi-en-mouvement_1753055_3260.html.

9. Zeniter quoted in Falila Gbadamassi, "Alice Zeniter: 'On donne l'impression qu'il
y a des hordes d'immigrés qui rôdent tels des loups à nos frontières,'" *Afrik.com*,
June 13, 2010, http://www.afrik.com/article20049.html.

10. "Doan Bui, lauréate du prix littéraire de la Porte Dorée 2016 pour *Le Silence de
mon père*," June 8, 2016, Musée national de l'histoire de l'immigration, http://www
.histoire-immigration.fr/art-et-culture/le-prix-litteraire-de-la-porte-doree/doan
-bui-laureate-du-prix-litteraire-de-la-porte.

11. Mustapha Harzoune, "Doan Bui, *Le silence de mon père*: Entretien avec la lauréate
2016 du Prix littéraire de la Porte Dorée," June 8, 2016, Musée national de l'histoire
de l'immigration, http://www.histoire-immigration.fr/doan-bui-le-silence-de-mon
-pere-entretien-avec-la-laureate-2016-du-prix-litteraire-de-la-porte-doree.

12. "Julien Delmaire, lauréat du Prix littéraire de la Porte Dorée 2014," June 4, 2014,
Musée national de l'histoire de l'immigration, http://www.histoire-immigration

.fr/art-et-culture/le-prix-litteraire-de-la-porte-doree/julien-delmaire-laureat-du
-prix-litteraire-de-la.

13. Grégoire Leménager, "Mathias Énard: Bardamu 2012," *Le Nouvel Observateur*, November 22, 2012, http://bibliobs.nouvelobs.com/rentree-litteraire-2012/20121120 .OBS9997/mathias-enard-bardamu-2012.html.

14. Evidence of the popularity of Énard's fictional works can be found in his previous novels' many awards and translations into foreign languages. *La Perfection du tir* (2003) won the 2004 Prix des cinq continents de la francophonie; *Zone* (2008) received the 2008 Prix Décembre and the 2009 Prix du Livre Inter and has been translated into eight languages to date, while *Parle-leur de batailles, de rois et d'éléphants* (2010) earned the Prix Goncourt des lycéens and has so far been translated into more than twenty languages. Énard also won the 2015 Prix Goncourt for *Boussole*.

15. Kacimi quoted in "Alice Zeniter lauréate du Prix littéraire de la Porte Dorée 2010," June 12, 2010, Musée national de l'histoire de l'immigration, http://www.histoire -immigration.fr/art-et-culture/le-prix-litteraire-de-la-porte-doree/alice-zeniter -laureate-du-prix-litteraire-de-la.

16. Autofiction refers to the literary genre introduced by Serge Doubrovsky in his 1977 novel *Fils*, which blurs the boundaries between literature and life, author and narrator.

17. "Remise du prix littéraire de la Porte Dorée, le 12 juin 2010 à 17 heures," 2.

18. David Caviglioli, "La bluette d'Alice Zeniter," *Le Nouvel Observateur*, March 30, 2010, http://bibliobs.nouvelobs.com/romans/20100330.BIB5118/la-bluette-d-039 -alice-zeniter.html; Nils C. Ahl, "*Jusque dans nos bras* d'Alice Zeniter: Alerte aux bons sentiments," *Le Monde*, May 6, 2010, http://www.lemonde.fr/livres/article /2010/05/06/jusque-dans-nos-bras-d-alice-zeniter_1347322_3260.html.

19. See, for example, works by Gordon (1996), Sharpe (2003), Spivak (1994), and Weinstock (2004).

20. There is clearly as much self-celebration in this mobility as there is optimism about its transformative power, a view that perhaps is not entirely justified relative to a narrative that tones down unsavory phenomena such as slavery and colonialism (just as it seeks to recuperate three marginal figures) and that emphasizes positive themes such as hybridity and diversity.

21. I use the term "represent" in the two senses that Gayatri C. Spivak (1994) delineates in "Can the Subaltern Speak?": "representation as speaking for"—the author-narrator's Creole identity makes him a representative of the three figures from Réunion—and "re-presentation, as in art or philosophy" (70)—he offers an alternative portrait of contemporary French culture to Japanese audiences.

22. The other novels in the prize competition addressed equally timely themes: clandestine immigration (Salim Bachi's *Amours et aventures de Sindbad le Marin* and Fatou Diome's *Celles qui attendent*), the plight of asylum seekers (Delphine Coulin's

Samba pour la France), struggling youths from the banlieue (Saphia Azzeddine's *La Mecque-Phuket* and Aya Cissoko and Marie Desplechin's *Danbé*), Portuguese immigration to France (Brigitte Paulino-Neto's *Dès que tu meurs, appelle-moi*), and contemporary societal changes (Léonora Miano's *Blues pour Elise*).

23. Michaël Ferrier was born in France to a Creole family with roots in Mauritius and India, grew up in Africa and Réunion, studied in France, and now lives in Japan. He is a global writer; his fictional texts address and sometimes juxtapose French, Japanese, and Réunion cultures, challenging the boundaries of neat literary traditions. Besides *Sympathie pour le fantôme*, Ferrier has published *Kizu* (2004), *Tokyo, petits portraits de l'aube* (2005), and *Fukushima, récit d'un désastre* (2012).

24. These include Maryse Condé's *La Vie sans fards*, Amin Maalouf's *Les Désorientés*, Alain Mabanckou's *Lumières de Pointe-Noire*, Sylvie Weil's *Le Hareng et le Saxophone*, Katrina Kalda's *Arithmétique des dieux*, and Yassaman Montazami's *Le Meilleur des Jours*.

25. The goal of this student prize was to expose young Middle Eastern readers to contemporary literature and to engage them in literary debates. Several Goncourt academy members, present in Beirut during the twentieth anniversary of the Salon du livre, exchanged their views on the 2013 Goncourt prize selections with these students. The prize-winning novel was also translated into Arabic—a significant achievement for Énard, who is a professor of Arabic at the University of Barcelona and who has extensive knowledge of Middle Eastern and Mediterranean cultures, having spent considerable time in the region.

26. Zeniter quoted in "Mathias Énard lauréat du Prix littéraire de la Porte Dorée 2013," June 4, 2013, Musée national de l'histoire de l'immigration, http://www.histoire -immigration.fr/art-et-culture/le-prix-litteraire-de-la-porte-doree/mathias-enard -laureat-du-prix-litteraire-de-la.

27. Ferrier quoted in "Mathias Énard lauréat du Prix littéraire de la Porte Dorée 2013."

28. Hubert Artus, "Mathias Énard, entre Printemps arabe et crise économique," *Lire*, September 11, 2012, http://www.lexpress.fr/culture/livre/rue-des-voleurs_1158826 .html; Marine de Tilly, "La guerre de Mathias Énard," *Le Point*, July 28, 2012, http:// www.lepoint.fr/livres/la-guerre-de-mathias-enard-28-07-2012-1490394_37.php.

29. Énard quoted in Chloé Domat, "Il n'y a pas assez de liens entre les littératures européenne et arabe," *Le Nouvel Observateur*, November 11, 2012, http://bibliobs .nouvelobs.com/rentree-litteraire-2012/20121105.OBS8092/il-n-y-a-pas-assez -de-liens-entre-les-litteratures-europenne-et-arabe.html.

30. Abdejlil Lahjomri, "Voyage littéraire dans un 'printemps' arabe qui ne le fut pas," *L'Observateur du Maroc*, November 8, 2013, para. 2, http://lobservateurdumaroc .info/2013/11/08/voyage-litteraire-printemps-arabe-fut-pas.

31. Priscille Lafitte, "*Rue des voleurs*, de Mathias Énard, premier lauréat du Goncourt des étudiants de Beyrouth," *France 24*, November 13, 2012, http://www.france24

.com/fr/20121101-liban-rue-voleurs-mathias-enard-laureat-prix-etudiant-beyrouth
-goncourt-litterature-contemporaine-francophonie.

4. CANONIZATION

1. Hector Bianciotti, "Discours de réception de Hector Bianciotti," January 23, 1997, Académie française, http://www.academie-francaise.fr/discours-de-reception-de -hector-bianciotti; Assia Djebar, "Discours de réception, et réponse de Pierre-Jean Rémy," June 22, 2006, Académie française, http://www.academie-francaise.fr /discours-de-reception-et-reponse-de-pierre-jean-remy.

2. However, strategic exoticism is bound to fail because to denounce the stereotype is to simultaneously reinforce it. In other words, "it is not possible to cite it without unleashing its stereotypical power" (Rosello 1998, 38).

3. "Il est dodu comme un dogue, mon roman. Ma seule chance. VA" (Laferrière [1987] 2010, 163).

4. See works by Beaudoin (1986), Desîlets (1986), and Dumas (1986), as well as Gabrielle Poulin, "*Comment faire l'amour avec un Nègre sans se fatiguer*, de Dany Laferrière: Le roman d'un dandy noir," *Le Droit*, February 1, 1986, 30.

5. The novel was first published in 1985 by VLB éditeur, then reedited for release in 1989 by the same press, followed by publication in Paris in the same year with Éditions Belfond and J'ai lu in 1990. Translated into English in 1987, it was reedited for release in London in 1991 and then translated into Spanish in 1997. In 1989 it was adapted to film by Jacques Wilbrod Benoît and released in a third edition by Typo in 2002—a rare feat in Québécois publishing history.

6. See the piece by Boivin (2003), as well as France Simard, "'Comment faire l'amour avec un Nègre sans se fatiguer?' Un roman, plusieurs premières," *Le Droit*, January 11, 1986, 25.

7. Laferrière quoted in Ghila Sroka, "Dany Laferrière: *Chronique de la dérive douce*," *Île en île*, November 2, 2000, http://ile-en-ile.org/dany-laferriere-chronique-de -la-derive-douce.

8. In *Pays sans chapeau* (1996), the author-narrator returns to Haiti for the first time after his exile to Québec to commemorate his grandmother's death, and he briefly mentions his father's death at the end of the novel. As Anne Marie Miraglia (2011, 84) points out, *L'Énigme du retour* can also be read as a return to, and a rewriting of, his father's death, alluded to in *Pays sans chapeau*. Furthermore, since Laferrière's works resonate with one another, his Haitian novels—*L'Odeur du café* (1991), *Le Goût des jeunes filles* (1992), and *Le Charme des après-midi sans fin* (1997), among others—could also be viewed as returns to Haiti through memory. The presence of the Haitian landscape and recurring family members creates intratextual relationships. Small wonder that *Chronique de la dérive douce*, which recounts the author-narrator's birth as a writer in Québec, was described as "the enigma of

arrival" and a complement to *L'Énigme du retour*. Chantal Guy, "VLB et Laferrière, prise 2," *La Presse*, April 24, 2012, http://www.lapresse.ca/arts/livres/201204/24/01 -4518482-vlb-et-laferriere-prise-2.php. For a full account of *L'Énigme*'s intertextual and intratextual references, see the essay by Parker (2013, esp. 89–90n14).

9. In an interview with Morency and Thibeault (2011) Laferrière employs the term "spherical" to describe *The Return*: "I would say that the difference between this novel and my other books is that it's more multiform, more spherical. It allows one to rediscover a spherical universe, in the sense that it's not only the real country and the dream country, it's also the country of childhood, memory, in other words, a mystical country" (16). This term could be effectively applied to his whole oeuvre.

10. *The Return* was well received in both France and Québec. In France, besides winning the Prix Médicis, it was also named the best French novel of the year by *Lire* magazine, and it figured among the ten best French novels of 2009 selected by *Télérama* and *France Culture*. In Québec the novel won the 2009 Grand Prix du livre de Montréal, the Prix des libraires du Québec, and the 2010 Grand Prix littéraire international Metropolis bleu. *The Return* was also a finalist for the 2010 Prix du Gouverneur général and nominated for the 2010 Prix du Grand public La Presse–Salon du livre de Montréal. A commercial success as well, it sold fifteen thousand copies in France and twenty thousand in Québec. Alain Beuve-Méry, "Dany Laferrière, Prix Médicis pour *L'Énigme du retour*," *Le Monde*, May 11, 2009, http://www.lemonde.fr/livres/article/2009/11/05/dany-laferriere-prix-medicis -pour-l-enigme-du-retour_1263203_3260.html.

11. Nathalie Crom, "Dany Laferrière: 'Je ne suis pas obligé de crier ma créolité sur tous les toits,'" *Télérama*, June 11, 2011, http://www.telerama.fr/livre/dany-laferriere-je -ne-suis-pas-oblige-de-crier-ma-creolite-sur-tous-les-toits,69864.php.

12. Tontongi (Eddy Toussaint), "Haïti-Langue: Les implications malheureuses de l'élection de Dany Laferrière à l'Académie française," *AlterPresse*, February 6, 2014, http://www.alterpresse.org/spip.php?article15940#.Vxp4LZMriOo.

13. Clint Bruce, "Dialectic of Immortality: Situating the Election of Dany Laferrière to the Académie Française," *Postcolonialist*, February 12, 2014, http://postcolonialist .com/arts/dialectic-of-immortality-situating-the-election-of-dany-laferriere-to -the-academie-francaise.

14. The Haitian writer Frankétienne quoted in Chantal Guy, "Dany Laferrière devient un 'immortel,'" *La Presse*, December 13, 2013, http://www.lapresse.ca/arts/livres /201312/13/01-4720582-dany-laferriere-devient-un-immortel.php.

15. Tontongi, "Haïti-Langue"; Tontongi quoted in Ève Lévesque, "L'élection de Dany Laferrière à l'Académie française suscite la controverse," *Le Journal de Montréal*, January 23, 2014, http://www.journaldemontreal.com/2014/01/23/lelection-de -dany-laferriere-a-lacademie-francaise-suscite-la-controverse.

16. Critics cite the example of Léopold Sédar Senghor, whom the French celebrated for his francophilia and whose Negritude was consecrated and consumed in France as a literary fad rather than a resistance movement. Tontongi, "Haïti-Langue."

17. Danièle Simpson, president of the Union des écrivaines et écrivains québécois, quoted in Guy, "Dany Laferrière devient un 'immortel.'"

18. Grégoire Leménager, "Dany Laferrière, de Port-au-Prince à l'Académie française," *Le Nouvel Observateur*, December 12, 2013, http://bibliobs.nouvelobs.com/actualites /20131212.OBS9394/dany-laferriere-un-haitien-a-l-academie-francaise.html; Jean-Claude Raspiengeas, "Dany Laferrière: 'Immortel, il faut que tu fasses la vaisselle!'," *La Croix*, March 21, 2014, http://www.la-croix.com/Culture/Actualite /Dany-Laferriere-Immortel-il-faut-que-tu-fasses-la-vaisselle-!-2014-03-21-1123753; Muriel Steinmetz, "Dany Laferrière, un écrivain d'Haïti chez les immortels," *L'Humanité*, December 19, 2013, http://www.humanite.fr/culture/dany-laferriere-un -ecrivain-d-haiti-chez-les-immor-555643.

19. Leménager, "Dany Laferrière, de Port-au-Prince à l'Académie française."

20. Bernard Pivot, "Lettre à Dany le vert," *Le Journal du Dimanche*, December 23, 2013, http://www.lejdd.fr/Chroniques/Bernard-Pivot/Lettre-a-Dany-le-vert-la -chronique-de-Bernard-Pivot-645304.

21. Pivot, "Lettre à Dany le vert."

22. Carrère d'Encausse quoted in Vincent Destouches, "Académie française: Dany Laferrière, vu de France," *L'Actualité*, December 12, 2013, http://www.lactualite .com/societe/le-fouineur/academie-francaise-dany-laferriere-vu-de-france.

23. François Cheng, "Discours de réception de François Cheng," June 19, 2003, para. 1, 4, Académie française, http://www.academie-francaise.fr/discours-de-reception -de-francois-cheng.

24. Assia Djebar, "Discours de réception, et réponse de Pierre-Jean Rémy," June 22, 2006, para. 89, 111, Académie française, http://www.academie-francaise.fr/discours -de-reception-et-reponse-de-pierre-jean-remy.

25. Djebar, "Discours de réception, et réponse de Pierre-Jean Rémy," para. 93.

26. Amin Maalouf, "Discours de réception de Amin Maalouf," June 14, 2012, para. 5, Académie française, http://www.academie-francaise.fr/discours-de-reception-de -amin-maalouf.

27. Michael Edwards, "Discours de réception de M. Michael Edwards," May 22, 2014, para. 4, Académie française, http://www.academie-francaise.fr/discours -de-reception-de-m-michael-edwards.

28. Andreï Makine, "Discours de réception de M. Andreï Makine," December 15, 2016, para. 3, Académie française, http://www.academie-francaise.fr/discours -de-reception-de-m-andrei-makine.

29. Dalembert quoted in Grégoire Leménager, "Dany Laferrière, le géant vert," *Le Nouvel Observateur*, December 22, 2013, http://bibliobs.nouvelobs.com/actualites /20131220.OBS0380/dany-laferriere-le-geant-vert.html.

30. The official website of the Académie française states that Senghor entered as a francophone author and spokesperson for the "entire *Francophonie*." "L'histoire," para. 17, Académie française, http://www. academie-francaise.fr/linstitution/lhistoire. In the media Cheng is known as the first person of Asian origin, and Djebar, the first Muslim North African woman, to join the institution.

31. Laferrière quoted in Raspiengeas, "Dany Laferrière: 'Immortel, il faut que tu fasses la vaisselle!'"

32. Laferrière quoted in Raspiengeas, "Dany Laferrière: 'Immortel, il faut que tu fasses la vaisselle!'"

33. Laferrière quoted in Leménager, "Dany Laferrière, le géant vert."

34. Laferrière quoted in Guy, "Dany Laferrière devient un 'immortel.'"

CONCLUSION

1. For studies of book clubs see works by Radway (1997), Long (2003), and Driscoll (2014). For an examination of how readers' reports illustrate the reception of literary works and how translations mediate the value of French-language texts, see Bush's (2016) monograph. For an analysis of literary festivals as a new form of consecration, see the book by Driscoll (2014) and the article by Sapiro (2016).

2. See Veldwachter's (2012) work for a discussion of how French publishing groups are now a part of transnational networks that market and distribute francophone literature—especially works by authors from regions peripheral to the French publishing industry such as the French Caribbean—in the contexts of asymmetries of power.

3. Mazauric (2012) traces the figure of the clandestine migrant in contemporary narratives. Although she examines primarily works by African and African diasporic authors, her study suggests this corpus is an emerging subgenre of migrant literature.

REFERENCES

Abderrezak, Hakim. 2009. "Burning the Sea: Clandestine Migration across the Strait of Gibraltar in Francophone Moroccan 'Illiterature.'" *Contemporary French and Francophone Studies* 13 (4): 461–69.

Adelson, Leslie A. 2005. *The Turkish Turn in Contemporary German Literature: Toward a New Critical Grammar of Migration*. New York: Palgrave Macmillan.

Ahmad, Aijaz. 1992. *In Theory: Classes, Nations, Literatures*. London: Verso.

Albert, Christiane. 2005. *L'Immigration dans le roman francophone contemporain*. Paris: Karthala.

Barbizet-Namer, Laure, ed. 2009. *Nouvelles Odyssées: 50 auteurs racontent l'immigration*. Anvers: Deckers Snoeck.

Beaudoin, Réjean. 1986. "Les mouches du plafond." *Liberté* 165 (June): 126–31.

Bernier, Frédérique. 2008–9. "Le roman n'aura pas lieu." *Contre-jour: Cahiers littéraires* 17:177–81.

Bessière, Jean. 2003. "The Reception of Milan Kundera in France." *Kosmas: Czechoslovak and Central European Journal* 17 (1): 1–14.

Biron, Michel, François Dumont, and Élisabeth Nardout-Lafarge. 2007. *Histoire de la littérature québécoise*. Montréal: Boréal.

Boivin, Aurélien. 2003. "*Comment faire l'amour avec un Nègre sans se fatiguer* ou une dénonciation du racisme à travers la baise." *Québec français* 131:94–97.

Bonn, Charles. 1995. *Littératures des immigrations: Un espace littéraire émergent*. Paris: L'Harmattan.

Borges, Jorge Luis. 1999. "The Argentine Writer and Tradition." In *Jorge Luis Borges: Selected Non-Fictions*, edited by Eliot Weinberger, 420–27. Translated by Esther Allen, Suzanne Jill Levine, and Eliot Weinberger. New York: Penguin.

Bourdieu, Pierre. 1993. *The Field of Cultural Production: Essays on Art and Literature*. Edited and introduced by Randal Johnson. New York: Columbia University Press.

———. 1996. *The Rules of Art: Genesis and Structure of the Literary Field*. Translated by Susan Emanuel. Stanford: Stanford University Press.

Boym, Svetlana. 2001. *The Future of Nostalgia*. New York: Basic Books.

Brennan, Timothy. 1997. *At Home in the World: Cosmopolitanism Now*. Cambridge M A : Harvard University Press.

Brouillette, Sarah. 2011. *Postcolonial Writers in the Global Literary Marketplace*. New York: Palgrave Macmillan.

Bui, Doan. 2016. *Le Silence de mon père*. Paris: L'Iconoclaste.

Burns, Jennifer. 2013. *Migrant Imaginaries: Figures in Italian Migration Literature*. Oxford: Peter Lang.

Bush, Ruth. 2016. *Publishing Africa in French: Literary Institutions and Decolonization, 1945-1967*. Liverpool: Liverpool University Press.

Casanova, Pascale. 2007. *The World Republic of Letters*. Translated by M. B. DeBevoise. Cambridge M A : Harvard University Press.

———. 2013. "What Is a Dominant Language? Giacomo Leopardi: Theoretician of Linguistic Inequality." Translated by Marlon Jones. *New Literary History* 44 (3): 379-99.

Cazenave, Odile. 2003. *Afrique sur Seine: Une nouvelle génération de romanciers africains à Paris*. Paris: L'Harmattan.

Césaire, Aimé. 1995. *Notebook of a Return to My Native Land / Cahier d'un retour au pays natal*. Translated by Mireille Rosello with Annie Pritchard. Newcastle upon Tyne: Bloodaxe Books.

Chartier, Daniel. 2003. *Dictionnaire des écrivains émigrés au Québec 1800-1999*. Montréal: Nota Bene.

Cohen, Anouk. 2007. "Quelles histoires pour un musée de l'immigration à Paris!" *Ethnologie Française* 37 (3): 401-8.

Coleman, Patrick. 2010. "Shifting and Uncertain Ground: Dany Laferrière Looks at His Native Haiti from a New Angle." *Inroads* 27:124-29.

Coulin, Delphine. 2011. *Samba pour la France*. Paris: Éditions du Seuil.

Deleuze, Gilles, and Félix Guattari. 1986. *Kafka: Toward a Minor Literature*. Translated by Dana Polan. Minneapolis: University of Minnesota Press.

Delmaire, Julien. 2013. *Georgia*. Paris: Grasset.

Denis, Benoît. 2010. "La consécration: Quelques notes introductives." *COnTEXTES* 7.

Desîlets, Christian. 1986. "*Comment faire l'amour avec un Nègre sans se fatiguer.*" *Nuit blanche* 22 (February–April): 5.

Doubrovsky, Serge. 1977. *Fils*. Paris: Galilée.

Driscoll, Beth. 2014. *The New Literary Middlebrow: Tastemakers and Reading in the Twenty-First Century*. Basingstoke: Palgrave Macmillan.

Ducas, Sylvie. 2013. *La Littérature à quel(s) prix? Histoire des prix littéraires*. Paris: La Découverte.

Duffy, Helena. 2015. "On connaît la musique: La vie culturelle au temps du siège de Leningrad dans *La Vie d'un homme inconnu* d'Andreï Makine." *Lublin Studies in Modern Languages and Literature* 39 (1): 142-62.

Dumas, Pierre-Raymond. 1986. "Laferrière: Comment faire pour écrire nègre + fantasme + blanche?" *Conjonction: Bulletin de l'Institut français d'Haïti* 170-71 (July-December): 78-79.

Dumontet, Danielle. 2014. "La revue *Vice Versa* et le procès d'autonomisation des 'écritures migrantes.'" *Zeitschrift für Kanada-Studien* 34: 87-104.

Dupuis, Gilles. 2007. "Redessiner la cartographie des écritures migrantes." *Globe: Revue Internationale d'Études Québécoises* 10 (1): 137-46.

Énard, Mathias. 2012. *Rue des voleurs*. Arles: Actes Sud.

———. 2014. *Street of Thieves*. Translated by Charlotte Mandell. Rochester: Open Letter.

English, James F. 2005. *The Economy of Prestige: Prizes, Awards, and the Circulation of Cultural Value*. Cambridge MA: Harvard University Press.

Farah, Alain. 2011. "Un Japon de papier." *Voix et Images* 36 (2): 41-52.

Fauvel, Maryse. 2014. *Exposer l'"autre": Essai sur la Cité nationale de l'histoire de l'immigration et le Musée du quai Branly*. Paris: L'Harmattan.

Ferrier, Michaël. 2010. *Sympathie pour le fantôme*. Paris: Gallimard.

Frank, Søren. 2008. *Migration and Literature: Günter Grass, Milan Kundera, Salman Rushdie, and Jan Kjærstad*. New York: Palgrave Macmillan.

Frow, John. 1995. *Cultural Studies and Cultural Value*. Oxford: Clarendon Press.

Gaudé, Laurent. (2006) 2009. *Eldorado*. Paris: J'ai lu.

Gauz. 2014. *Debout-payé*. Paris: Le Nouvel Attila.

Genette, Gérard. 1997. *Paratexts: Thresholds of Interpretation*. Translated by Jane E. Lewin. Cambridge: Cambridge University Press.

Gordon, Avery. 1996. *Ghostly Matters: Haunting and the Sociological Imagination*. Chicago: University of Chicago Press.

Guillory, John. 2000. "The Ethical Practice of Modernity: The Example of Reading." In *The Turn to Ethics*, edited by Marjorie Garber, Beatrice Hanssen, and Rebecca Walkowitz, 29-46. New York: Routledge.

Guttman, Anna, Michel Hockx, and George Paizis, eds. 2006. *The Global Literary Field*. Newcastle upon Tyne: Cambridge Scholars Publishing.

Harel, Simon. 2005. *Les Passages obligés de l'écriture migrante*. Montréal: XYZ éditeur.

Hargreaves, Alec G. 1997. *Immigration and Identity in Beur Fiction: Voices from the North African Immigrant Community in France*. New York: Berg.

Hargreaves, Alec G., Charles Forsdick, and David Murphy, eds. 2010. *Transnational French Studies: Postcolonialism and Littérature-monde*. Liverpool: Liverpool University Press.

Harzoune, Mustapha. 2003. "Littérature: Les chausse-trapes de l'intégration." *Mots Pluriels* 23.

———. 2011. "Michaël Ferrier, *Sympathie pour le fantôme*." *Hommes et Migrations*, no. 1291.

Higbee, Will. 2013. *Post-Beur Cinema: North African Émigré and Maghrebi-French Filmmaking in France since 2000*. Edinburgh: Edinburgh University Press.

Hight, Craig, Ann Hardy, Carolyn Michelle, and Adrian Athique, eds. 2011. "Editors' Introduction: Approaching the Online Audience; New Practices, New

Thinking." *Participations: Journal of Audience and Reception Studies*, special section, 8 (2): 554–58.

Holmes, Diana. 2010. "The Comfortable Reader: Romantic Bestsellers and Critical Disdain." *French Cultural Studies* 21 (4): 287–96.

Huggan, Graham. 2001. *The Postcolonial Exotic: Marketing the Margins*. London: Routledge.

Iser, Wolfgang. 1978. *The Act of Reading: A Theory of Aesthetic Response*. Baltimore: Johns Hopkins University Press.

Jauss, Hans Robert. 1982. *Toward an Aesthetic of Reception*. Translated by Timothy Bahti. Minneapolis: University of Minnesota Press.

Jay, Paul. 2010. *Global Matters: The Transnational Turn in Literary Studies*. Ithaca: Cornell University Press.

Jenkins, Henry, Mizuko Ito, and danah boyd, eds. 2016. *Participatory Culture in a Networked Era: A Conversation on Youth, Learning, Commerce, and Politics*. Cambridge: Polity Press.

Jonassaint, Jean. 1986. "L'avenir du roman québécois serait-il métis? *À corps joie* de Alix Renaud; *Comment faire l'amour avec un Nègre sans se fatiguer* de Dany Laferrière." *Lettres Québécoises: La Revue de l'Actualité Littéraire* 41:79–80.

Kafka, Franz. (1915) 1972. *The Metamorphosis*. Translated by Stanley Corngold. New York: Bantam Books.

Kleppinger, Kathryn A. 2016. *Branding the "Beur" Author: Minority Writing and the Media in France, 1983-2013*. Liverpool: Liverpool University Press.

Kundera, Milan. (1979) 1980. *The Book of Laughter and Forgetting*. Translated by Michael Henry Heim. New York: Knopf.

——. (1967) 1982. *The Joke*. Translated by Michael Henry Heim. New York: Harper & Row.

——. 1984. *The Unbearable Lightness of Being*. Translated by Michael Henry Heim. New York: Harper & Row.

——. 1986. *L'Art du roman*. Paris: Gallimard.

——. 1988. *The Art of the Novel*. Translated by Linda Asher. New York: Grove Press.

——. 1993. *Les Testaments trahis*. Paris: Gallimard-Jeunesse.

——. 1995. *La Lenteur*. Paris: Gallimard.

——. 1995. *Testaments Betrayed: An Essay in Nine Parts*. New York: Harper Collins Publishers.

——. 1996. *Slowness*. Translated by Linda Asher. New York: HarperCollins.

——. 1998. *L'Identité*. Paris: Gallimard.

——. 1998. *Identity*. Translated by Linda Asher. New York: Harper Flamingo.

——. 2002. *Ignorance*. Translated by Linda Asher. New York: HarperCollins.

——. 2003. *L'Ignorance*. Paris: Gallimard.

——. 2005. *Le Rideau: Essai en sept parties*. Paris: Gallimard.

——. 2006. *The Curtain: An Essay in Seven Parts*. Translated by Linda Asher. New York: Harper Perennial.

Laferrière, Dany. (1985) 2010. *Comment faire l'amour avec un Nègre sans se fatiguer*. Montréal: Typo.

———. (1987) 2010. *How to Make Love to a Negro without Getting Tired*. Translated by David Homel. Vancouver: Douglas & McIntyre.

———. (1993) 2002. *Cette Grenade dans la main du jeune Nègre est-elle une arme ou un fruit?* Montréal: VLB éditeur.

———. 1994a. *Chronique de la dérive douce*. Montréal: VLB éditeur.

———. 1994b. *Why Must a Black Writer Write about Sex?* Translated by David Homel. Toronto: Coach House Press.

———. (2001) 2005. *Je suis fatigué*. Montréal: Typo.

———. 2008. *Je suis un écrivain japonais*. Montréal: Boréal.

———. 2010a. *I Am a Japanese Writer*. Translated by David Homel. Vancouver: Douglas & McIntyre.

———. 2010b. *J'écris comme je vis: Entretien avec Bernard Magnier*. Montréal: Boréal.

———. (2009) 2010c. *L'Énigme du retour*. Montréal: Boréal.

———. 2011. *The Return*. Translated by David Homel. Vancouver: Douglas & McIntyre.

———. 2013. *Journal d'un écrivain en pyjama*. Montréal: Mémoire d'encrier.

———. 2015. *Dany Laferrière à l'Académie française: Discours de réception*. Montréal: Boréal.

Laronde, Michel. 1993. *Autour du roman beur: Immigration et identité*. Paris: L'Harmattan.

Lebrun, Monique, Luc Collès, and Marie-Cécile Robinet, eds. 2007. *La Littérature migrante dans l'espace francophone: Belgique–France–Québec–Suisse*. Fernelmont: Éditions Modulaires Européennes.

Legendre, Bertrand, and Corinne Abensour. 2007. *Regards sur l'édition*. Vol. 1, *Les petits éditeurs: Situations et perspectives*. Paris: Ministère de la Culture et de la Communication.

Leontsini, Mary. 2005. "Internet et la construction du goût littéraire: Le cas de *critiquelibres.com*." *Sociologie de l'Art* 2:63–89.

Leontsini, Mary, and Jean-Marc Leveratto. 2006. "Online Reading Practices and Reading Pleasure in a Transnational Context: The Reception of Coetzee's *Disgrace* on Amazon Sites." In *The Global Literary Field*, edited by Anna Guttman, Michel Hockx, and George Paizis, 165–80. Newcastle upon Tyne: Cambridge Scholars Publishing.

Lesne, Élisabeth. 2010. "La Cité crée son prix." *Hommes et Migrations*, no. 1284.

———. 2011. "Le Prix littéraire de la Porte Dorée." *Hommes et Migrations*, no. 1292.

Lindberg, Svante, ed. 2013. *Le Roman migrant au Québec et en Scandinavie: Performativité, conflits signifiants et créolisation*. Frankfurt am Main: Peter Lang.

Lionnet, Françoise. 2009. "Universalisms and francophonies." *International Journal of Francophone Studies* 12 (2–3): 203–21.

Long, Elisabeth. 2003. *Book Clubs: Women and the Uses of Reading in Everyday Life*. Chicago: Chicago University Press.

Lopes, Henri. 2012. *Une enfant de Poto-Poto*. Paris: Gallimard.

Makine, Andreï. 1995. *Le Testament français*. Paris: Folio.

——. 1997. *Dreams of My Russian Summer*. Translated by Geoffrey Strachan. New York: Arcade Publishing.

——. 2009. *La Vie d'un homme inconnu*. Paris: Éditions du Seuil.

——. 2012. *The Life of an Unknown Man*. Translated by Geoffrey Strachan. Minneapolis: Graywolf Press.

Mathis-Moser, Ursula. 2003. *Dany Laferrière: La dérive américaine*. Montréal: VLB éditeur.

——. 2011. "Les Japonais à la conquête d'une littérature-monde." *Voix et Images* 36 (2): 69–79.

Mathis-Moser, Ursula, and Birgit Mertz-Baumgartner, eds. 2012. *Passages et ancrages en France: Dictionnaire des écrivains migrants de langue française (1981-2011)*. Paris: Honoré Champion.

Mazauric, Catherine. 2012. *Mobilités d'Afrique en Europe: Récits et figures de l'aventure*. Paris: Karthala.

Miletić, Tijana. 2008. *European Literary Immigration into the French Language: Readings of Gary, Kristof, Kundera, and Semprun*. Amsterdam: Rodopi.

Miller, Laura J. 2000. "The Best-Seller List as Marketing Tool and Historical Fiction." *Book History* 3:286–304.

Miraglia, Anne Marie. 2011. "Le retour à la terre et l'absence du père dans *Pays sans chapeau* et *L'Énigme du retour* de Dany Laferrière." *Voix et Images* 36 (2): 81–92.

Moisan, Clément, and Renate Hildebrand, eds. 2001. *Ces Étrangers du dedans: Une histoire de l'écriture migrante au Québec (1937-1997)*. Montréal: Nota Bene.

Monjaret, Anne, and Mélanie Roustan. 2012. "Digestion patrimoniale: Contestations autour d'un ancien musée des colonies à Paris." *Civilisations* 61 (1): 23–42.

Morency, Jean, and Jimmy Thibeault. 2011. "Entretien avec Dany Laferrière." *Voix et Images* 36 (2): 15–23.

Motte, Warren. 2008. *Fiction Now: The French Novel in the Twenty-First Century*. Champaign IL: Dalkey Archive Press.

Naipaul, V. S. 1987. *The Enigma of Arrival*. Harmondsworth: Viking.

Parker, Gabrielle. 2013. "'Returns to the Native Land': Dany Laferrière's Unresolved Dilemma." In *Dany Laferrière: Essays on His Works*, edited by Lee Skallerup Bessette, 72–93. Toronto: Guernica.

Pireddu, Nicoletta. 2015. "European Ulyssiads: Claudio Magris, Milan Kundera, Eric-Emmanuel Schmitt." *Comparative Literature* 67 (3): 267–86.

Porra, Véronique. 2008. "Et s'il n'y avait pas de 'méridien littéraire' . . . Pour une relecture de la relation centre-periphérie à la lumière des littératures migrantes en France et au Québec." In *Écriture migrante/Migrant Writing*, edited by Danielle Dumontet and Frank Zipfel, 49–68. Hildesheim: Olms.

——. 2011. *Langue française, langue d'adoption: Une littérature "invitée" entre création, stratégies et contraintes (1946-2000)*. Hildesheim: Georg Olms.

Pouly, Marie-Pierre. 2016. "Playing Both Sides of the Field: The Anatomy of a 'Quality' Bestseller." *Poetics* 59: 20–34.

Procter, James, and Bethan Benwell. 2015. *Reading across Worlds: Transnational Book Groups and the Reception of Difference.* London: Palgrave Macmillan.

Prudhomme, Sylvain. 2014. *Les Grands.* Paris: L'Arbalète/Gallimard.

Pruteanu, Simona E. 2013. *L'Écriture migrante en France et au Québec (1985–2006): Une analyse comparative.* München: Lincom Europa.

Radway, Janice A. 1997. *A Feeling for Books: Book-of-the-Month Club, Literary Taste, and Middle-Class Desire.* Chapel Hill: University of North Carolina Press.

Redonnet, Marie. 2005. *Diego.* Paris: Éditions de Minuit.

Ricard, François. 2003. "Le piège de l'émigration." Afterword to *L'Ignorance*, by Milan Kundera, 225–37. Paris: Gallimard.

——. 2011. Preface to *Oeuvre*, vol. 1, by Milan Kundera, 9–18. Paris: Gallimard.

Rizek, Martin. 2001. *Comment devient-on Kundera? Images de l'écrivain, écrivain de l'image.* Paris: L'Harmattan.

Rosello, Mireille. 1995. "Aimé Césaire and the *Notebook of a Return to My Native Land* in the 1990s." Introduction to *Aimé Césaire: Notebook of a Return to My Native Land/ Cahier d'un retour au pays natal*, by Aimé Césaire, 9–68. Translated by Mireille Rosello and Annie Pritchard. Newcastle upon Tyne: Bloodaxe Books.

——. 1998. *Declining the Stereotype: Ethnicity and Representation in French Cultures.* Hanover: University Press of New England.

Rouet, François. 2007. *Le Livre: Mutations d'une industrie culturelle.* Paris: La Documentation française.

Sapiro, Gisèle. 2016. "The Metamorphosis of Modes of Consecration in the Literary Field: Academies, Literary Prizes, Festivals." *Poetics* 59 (December): 5–19.

Schmitt, Éric-Emmanuel. (2008) 2016. *Ulysse from Bagdad: Nouvelle édition, avec le journal d'écriture; Journal d'avant, journal d'après.* Paris: Le Livre de Poche.

Sharpe, Jenny. 2003. *Ghosts of Slavery: A Literary Archeology of Black Women's Lives.* Minneapolis: University of Minnesota Press.

Sibony, Daniel. 1991. *Entre-deux: L'origine en partage.* Paris: Éditions du Seuil.

Smith, Barbara Herrnstein. 1988. *Contingencies of Value: Alternative Perspectives for Critical Theory.* Cambridge MA: Harvard University Press.

Spivak, Gayatri C. 1994. "Can the Subaltern Speak?" In *Colonial Discourse and Post-Colonial Theory: A Reader*, edited by Patrick Williams and Laura Chrisman, 66–111. New York: Columbia University Press.

——. 1999. *A Critique of Postcolonial Reason: Toward a History of the Vanishing Present.* Cambridge MA: Harvard University Press.

Squires, Claire. 2009. *Marketing Literature: The Making of Contemporary Writing in Britain.* London: Palgrave Macmillan.

Steiner, Ann. 2008. "Private Criticism in the Public Sphere: Personal Writing on Literature in Readers' Reviews on *Amazon*." *Particip@tions* 5 (2).

Sugnet, Charles. 2009. "Pour une littérature-monde en français: Manifeste retro?" *International Journal of Francophone Studies* 12 (2–3): 237–52.

Taban, Carla. 2009. "Idéologie, esthétique et littérature-monde en français." *International Journal of Francophone Studies* 12 (2–3): 223–36.

Tadié, Jean-Yves, and Blanche Cerquiglini. 2012. *Le Roman d'hier à aujourd'hui*. Paris: Gallimard.

Thibeault, Jimmy. 2011. "'Je suis un individu': Le projet d'individualité dans l'oeuvre romanesque de Dany Laferrière." *Voix et Images* 36 (2): 25–40.

Thomas, Dominic. 2014. "Fortress Europe: Identity, Race and Surveillance." *International Journal of Francophone Studies* 17 (3–4): 445–68.

Thúy, Kim. 2010. *Ru*. Paris: Liana Levi.

Todorov, Tzvetan. 1990. *Genres in Discourse*. Translated by Catherine Porter. Cambridge: Cambridge University Press.

Veldwachter, Nadège. 2012. *Littérature francophone et mondialisation*. Paris: Karthala.

Wachtel, Andrew Baruch. 2006. *Remaining Relevant after Communism: The Role of the Writer in Eastern Europe*. Chicago: University of Chicago Press.

Walkowitz, Rebecca L., ed. 2006. *Immigrant Fictions: Contemporary Literature in an Age of Globalization*. Madison: University of Wisconsin Press.

———. 2015. *Born Translated: The Contemporary Novel in an Age of World Literature*. New York: Columbia University Press.

Weinstock, Jeffrey A., ed. 2004. *Spectral America: Phantoms and the National Imagination*. Madison: University of Wisconsin Press.

Xavier, Subha. 2016. *The Migrant Text: Making and Marketing a Global French Literature*. Montreal: McGill-Queen's University Press.

Zeniter, Alice. 2010. *Jusque dans nos bras*. Paris: Albin Michel.

———. 2011. *Take This Man*. Translated by Alison Anderson. New York: Europa Editions.

INDEX

Académie française: and election process, 154–55; history and function
of, 128–29; and language promotion, 150, 152
agents (of the literary field): the
Académie française as, 129; Bourdieu on, 14, 15; further studies of,
162, 185n1; literary prizes as, 57,
99, 100; online readers as, 65–66;
prize sponsors and lay readers as,
103; "profane," 33; publishers as, 34
authors: agency of, 15, 76–77; corpus
of, 8, 9–10; cosmopolitan and
global, 124–25, 128, 136, 181n23;
elite, Kundera and Makine as,
89; francophone, 8, 49; French,
of migrant novels, 27–28, 169n14;
major and minor, 107; migrant,
reception of, 18–24; politically
engaged, 28, 47, 58–59, 63, 165–66;
postcolonial, 9; on "return of the
author" debate, 132

best-seller lists, 6, 10–11, 37; Debout-
payé and, 52–58
Bourdieu, Pierre, 14–16, 102, 162

Brouillette, Sarah, 132–33

canon, 4–5, 14, 16, 166
canonization, 3, 33. *See also* consecration; legitimation
capital, 15, 16; Bourdieu on, 14; *capital
intraconversion*, 100; cultural, 49;
political, symbolic, and commercial, 59; social, symbolic, and
commercial, 48; symbolic, 8, 14,
31, 34, 108, 126, 129; symbolic and
economic, 36, 104. *See also* value
Casanova, Pascale, 9, 154, 158
center and periphery, 8–10; Laferrière
on, 128, 151–52
*Comment faire l'amour avec un Nègre sans
se fatiguer* (Laferrière), 133–37, 182n5
commodity: Bourdieu on, 16, 17;
Laferrière on the novel as, 133;
L'Ignorance as a, 85–86; migrant
literature as, 3, 33, 41, 67, 94; Porte
Dorée novels as, 104
consecration: Bourdieu on, 14, 15;
changes in, 66, 69, 126; Denis on,
33; materiality of books and, 33–34;
mechanisms of, 8, 9, 10, 15, 94, 95,

consecration *(cont.)*
162; popular forms of, 57–58;
prizes and, 102, 103; promotion as,
104, 109. *See also* canonization;
legitimation
contemporary French literature, 5;
Prix littéraire de la Porte Dorée
and, 98, 101, 124; transnational
dimensions of, 124–25, 162

Debout-payé (Gauz), 52–58
Denis, Benoît, 33
Diego (Redonnet), 42, 43–45
Driscoll, Beth, 17
Ducas, Sylvie: on literary prizes,
57–58, 72, 99; on mass readers,
68; on online review forums, 69;
on paperbacks, 36; on publishers'
strategies, 38, 109

Eldorado (Gaudé), 42–43, 45–46, 171n12
English, James, 99–100
L'Énigme du retour (Laferrière), 142–
49, 182n8, 183n10

Frow, John 67

Genette, Gérard, 40–41, 62
genre: Squires on, 42; Todorov on, 41
Georgia (Delmaire), 107
Guttman, Hockx, and Paizis, 162–63

hegemony: cultural and linguistic, 99;
of metropolitan centers, 9; Prix
littéraire de la Porte Dorée as a
tool of, 123–26
Huggan, Graham, 9, 133

intertexts: The Enigma of Arrival
(V. S. Naipaul), 147–48; Lettres
persanes (Montesquieu), 54–55,
171n20; The Metamorphosis
(Kafka), 140; The Narrow Road to
the Interior (Basho), 138, 139, 141,
142; Notebook of a Return to My
Native Land (Césaire), 133, 143–45,
148; The Odyssey (Homer), 46, 47,
59–60, 62, 77–79, 85; The Travels
(Ibn Battuta), 120
Iser, Wolfgang, 83, 176n24

Jay, Paul, 164
Je suis un écrivain japonais (Laferrière),
137–42
Jusque dans nos bras (Zeniter), 110–13

Kundera, Milan: on aesthetic value,
79; authorial agency of, 76; as elite
author, 84–85; French reception of,
76, 175n21; novelistic theories of,
174n16; and oeuvre, 165

Laferrière, Dany: career trajectory of,
127–28, 129–30; literary strategies
of, 131–33; as transnational author,
128, 130, 131, 156, 159
Laferrière, Dany, election to
Académie française, 128, 130;
Laferrière's response to, 155–59;
media coverage of, 150–54; significance of Laferrière's writing in
French for, 150–53
La Vie d'un homme inconnu (Makine):
analysis of, 87–88, 89–90, 91–93;
online reviews of, 90–91, 93–94

legitimation, 4, 8; competing forms of, 15–16; online readers' criteria of, 94; transnational, 163. *See also* canonization; consecration

L'Ignorance (Kundera): analysis of, 77–79; online reviews of, 79–87

literary field, 3, 20; Bourdieu on, 14–15; global, 162–63, 164–65

literary prizes: awarded to migrant authors, 97–98, 178nn1–2; Ducas on, 99; English on, 99–100; functions of, 99; for migrant novels, 11–13; of online review forums, 71–72; Prix Liste Goncourt / Le Choix de l'Orient, 125–26, 181n25

Makine, Andreï: authorial agency of, 77; French reception of, 89

marketing strategies, 37–38, 40–42; through addition of writers' diaries, 58–63; through cover design and publicity campaign, 52–58; through online review forums, 66, 72–75; through paratexts, 42–48; of the Prix littéraire de la Porte Dorée, 104–5; through series, 48–52; by word of mouth, 170n8

marketplace: Bourdieu on, 16; global literary, 72–73; intermediary, of small and medium-sized presses, 34–35, 40; and literary taxonomies, 40–42, 75

migrant genre, 5–7; academic reception of, 18–21, 168nn11–12; comic books, 5; emerging subgenre, 42, 165–66; films, 167n3; as global, 20, 168n7; novels, 5–7; plays, 5;

poems, 5; testimonials, 5; translations, 13–14

migrant literature in France, 3, 7–10, 105; as a commodity, 3; intermediary position in the literary field, 3, 16–17, 161–62; as mainstream, 10–14; middlebrow practices of, 17; and the political field, 17–18

migrant literature in the 1980s and 1990s: in France, 22–24; in Québec, 21–22, 169n12

migrant literature in the 2000s: French authors of, 27–28, 169n14; themes of, 24–27

Motte, Warren, 44

le Musée national de l'histoire de l'immigration, 111–12, 123–24

online readers: book reviews of, 65, 67, 69–71, 72–73, 94–95; as consecrating agents, 65–67, 68–69, 75–76; definition of, 68; as juries of literary prizes, 71–72

online review forums, 66, 69, 72–73; Amazon, 73; Babelio, Critiques Libres, Lecteurs, and SensCritique, 74–76; and impact on the literary field, 75; and literary taxonomies, 74–75

paratext, 40–41, 42

Porra, Véronique, 7, 19, 24

"Pour une 'littérature-monde' en français" manifesto, 8, 98

Prix littéraire de la Porte Dorée, 98–99, 100–101, 179n4; *cafés littéraires* of, 104; consecrating mechanisms

Prix littéraire de la Porte Dorée *(cont.)*
of, 101–2, 126; jury of, 102–4;
marker of openness or tool of
hegemony, 123–26; marketing practices of, 104–6; novels endorsed
by, 109–10; online promotional
materials of, 104–5; and promotion
of minor authors, 107; and promotion of smaller presses, 108–9
publishing houses: Gallimard, 72;
L'Iconoclaste, 39; J'ai lu, 45; medium
and small, 34–35, 38, 40; of migrant
novels, 38; Minuit, 43; Le Nouvel
Attila, 53, 55; L'Olivier, 38–39; and
series for migrant literature, 39–40
publishing industry: changes in,
34–38; commercial logic of, 35–37;
infrastructure of, 7; Paris as a key
site, 7, 125, 158

readers: academic, 46, 52; as consecrating agents, 66, 75; elite
and common, male and female,
liberal, 17; lay, 66–67, 69, 74, 76,
102–3; mass, 10, 36, 38, 45, 47,
68, 109; national, 9; national and
global, 68; professional and lay,
56, 58, 84, 90, 131
la rentrée littéraire, 6, 75
Ru (Thúy), 1–2, 167n1
Rue des voleurs (Énard), 116–22; and
the Prix Liste Goncourt / Le Choix
de l'Orient, 125

Samba pour la France (Coulin), 42–43,
46–48

series: La brune, 38, 39; Cadre rouge,
46; Continents noirs, 48–49; *le livre
de poche*, 36; for migrant literature,
39–40; Raconter la vie, 39
Sibony, Daniel, 8
Le Silence de mon père (Bui), 106
Spivak, Gayatri C., 114, 180n21
Squires, Claire, 37, 42
Sympathie pour le fantôme (Ferrier),
113–16

Thomas, Dominic, 18
Todorov, Tzvetan, 41
transnationalism, 164

Ulysse from Bagdad (Schmitt), 58–63
Une enfant de Poto-Poto (Lopes), 48–52

value, 2; aesthetic, 33; aesthetic and
political, 44; aesthetic, political, ethical, of migrant novels,
17; Bourdieu on, 14; competing
notions of, 100; as constructed
by literary prizes, 99, 124; as
constructed by online readers, 66, 67, 82; as constructed
through marketing practices, 40,
43; hierarchies of, 102; political, symbolic, commercial, 59;
production of belief in, 14, 37, 99,
102, 132–33; "regimes of value,"
67; symbolic, 129; symbolic and
economic, 16, 36; timeless, 15.
See also capital

Xavier, Subha, 8, 20, 162

CPSIA information can be obtained
at www.ICGtesting.com
Printed in the USA
LVHW07*1718230218
567707LV00004B/50/P